THE CHURCH OFFICE HANDBOOK

THE
CHURCH OFFICE HANDBOOK

A Basic Guide to Keeping Order

CAROL R. SHEARN

MOREHOUSE-BARLOW
Wilton, CT

For
JOSEPH P. SHEARN
my husband
LAURA J. WATSON
RENEE S. MILLER
JOSEPH P. SHEARN JR.
RICHARD W. MILLER
MICHAEL R. SHEARN
KEVIN S. SHEARN
my children

Forms #4384-09, "Request for Church Letter"; #4384-08, "Letter of Recommendation"; and #4388-04, "Prospect Visitation and Assignment Report" are used by permission. These forms are available through the Baptist Book Store Mail Order Center, P.O. Box 24420, Nashville, TN 37202, or your local Baptist Book Store.

Morehouse Barlow Co., Inc.
78 Danbury Road
Wilton, Connecticut 06897

Library of Congress Cataloging-in-Publication Data

Shearn, Carol R.
  The church office handbook.

  Bibliography: p.
  1. Church management. I. Title.
BV652.S46   1986   254   86–18200
ISBN 0–8192–1391–8

Printed in the United States of America

10 9 8 7 6 5 4 3 2 1

Contents

Preface

"This church has no membership records. How am I supposed to prepare a directory? I don't even know who's a member and who isn't."—Church Secretary

"I wish I had taken business administration instead of psychology when I was in school. Now I don't know what to do in the office, and I'm having trouble finding a secretary who has worked in a *church office*. I'm hoping to find someone who will *show me* what to do."—Pastor of Mission Church

"When I took over as church treasurer, I found out the checkbook had never been reconciled. The books were so out of balance, we had to open a new checking account and start over."—Volunteer Worker

These are just a few of the frustrations and concerns shared by pastors, secretaries, and volunteers with whom I talked in preparation for this book.

Facing the challenge of efficiently maintaining church records daily, secretaries and volunteers have no real training for the specific tasks that are unique to the church office. And additionally, many pastors of small congregations or of newly formed mission churches are bewildered by church office record keeping.

The *Church Office Handbook: A Basic Guide to Keeping Order* is based on my interviews with pastors, secretaries, and volunteers of many denominations. It also reflects my personal experiences while working in four very different churches, ranging in size from the 100-member Central United Methodist Church in Fort Myers, Florida, to the 2,500-member McGregor Baptist Church in Fort Myers, where I now serve as office manager.

Church secretaries have to perform tasks that they never learned in the business world or in school. If there is only one secretary, and if the pastor is not familiar with record-keeping procedures, how will she or he learn the necessary skills?

If a pastor does not know what records have been kept by the previous secretary, he will have no idea how to train a new person. To quote one pastor: "I don't know enough about what secretaries need to be doing in the office. I know what basic records need to be kept up, but what else is there? I don't know what's in the files. I don't think that should be my responsibility."

Some pastors who have no secretaries must do their own office work, in addition to their ministerial work. Perhaps a pastor will be starting a church, and the budget does not yet allow for a secretary. As one pastor in a 65-year-old downtown Lutheran church said, "The limited size of the congregation simply could not support a full-time pastor *and* a secretary."

Volunteers in the church assume duties that have been passed on from person to person. Whether church clerk, counting committee member, membership secretary, or treasurer, there are usually no guidelines for carrying on the work of the office. With no guidelines to follow, and no record-keeping procedures to facilitate the flow of work between people, the volunteer worker is limited in his or her ability to perform effectively.

"You should write a book," said Doug, the pastor of Central United Methodist Church in Fort Myers, after I reorganized that church's bookkeeping system. "I never understood the books before, but now I do. Your system is so simple."

The Church Office Handbook has been written for you—church secretary, pastor, or volunteer worker—to give you a simple, systematic, basic record-keeping system.

Throughout the book I make no distinction as to who the reader is. This is deliberate, since results of a survey have shown that exactly who does what in the record-keeping process varies greatly from church to church.

In one 200-member church, the pastor "does it all." He pays the bills, prepares the Sunday bulletin, answers the telephone, mails the newsletter. In other churches, a secretary prepares the bulletin, but a volunteer is treasurer. Still other churches employ a financial secretary, and all typing is done by volunteers. You may be any of these persons—pastor, secretary, or volunteer. The work you do may involve membership records, finances, or any other aspect of church work.

Whoever you are, and whatever work you are doing, here is a comprehensive guide to church office record keeping. You can apply the ideas, copy the forms, adapt the procedures, and otherwise use the book to save time and energy in your service for your church.

A *record* is any form of recorded information. A telephone call recorded on a "While-You-Were-Out" pad is a record. So is the church newsletter or a piece of correspondence. The treasurer's report is a record of the church's finances.

What types of records should be kept in the church office? Although record keeping will vary from church to church, as specific needs vary, the basic records that should be kept include:

Membership
  Rolls
  Additions and Deletions
  Changes of Address, Telephone Number, Other Personal Data

Visitors
    Prospects
    Outreach
Financial
    Checkbook
    Chart of Accounts
    General Ledger
    Contributions
    Accounts Payable
    Payroll
    Financial Statements (Treasurer's Reports)
    Quarterly Tax Returns
    Purchasing
    Inventory
Files
    General
    Accounts Payable
Mailing Information
    Incoming
    Outgoing
    Postal Regulations
Historical Background of Church
Minutes of Meetings and Organizations
Telephone Numbers of Services, Schools, and Institutions
Committees and Chairpersons
Correspondence
Policy and Procedure Manuals

This book is written for small- to medium-sized churches, in which paid office staff is limited, although the principles and examples can be adapted for any size church. The book shows how to keep records; it is a guidebook that, if followed, will ensure that duties will be carried on uniformly from person to person.

A number of excellent books written for church secretaries delve into the spiritual motivation of and heart for the ministry. Similarly, church administration and pastoral duties are covered in many excellent books written especially for pastors. But in this book I have deliberately omitted the philosophical, motivational, and spiritual emphasis of the individual positions of the staff and have stripped away everything but the nitty-gritty of record keeping. In each church, staff and volunteers, somehow, have to do the office work. This book is for those people.

PART ONE

GETTING YOURSELF ORGANIZED

Monday morning, 8 A.M. Lucy C., secretary in a 500-member church in Tallahassee, has every good intention of getting right to work on a list of committee members' names and addresses that had been requested by the chairman of the deacons. But Lucy instead begins her day by sorting through notes, mail, and miscellaneous information that was dropped on her desk over the weekend. Included in the notes from church members are numerous requests to fulfill, a half-dozen address changes, a list of supplies for Sunday School, orders for the pastor's taped sermon, and a pile of postcards to be addressed, stamped, and mailed.

A drop-in visitor, seeing that the pastor is busy, says to Lucy, "Well, I'll just sit and visit with you for awhile." After discussing the highs and lows of the pastor's Sunday morning sermon, he reminds Lucy that it has been two years since the last membership directory was printed.

In addition, the president of the women's missionary organization telephones. "I forgot to tell you last week that I need. . . ." She spends the next twenty-five minutes explaining a flyer Lucy is to prepare, label, and mail *by the next day*. "I'll be right over to see you," she tells Lucy.

At 11 A.M. Lucy, frustrated, looks at the piles of papers on her desk and moans, "How can I possibly keep track of all this information and get all this work done when the phone rings constantly, people keep dropping in, and there is more work than I can possibly do?"

Establishing priorities is one of the most difficult tasks that you, as a church worker, have. You have many "bosses," each one with a "top priority" project. Because so many people make demands on your time, it is easy to blame others for your inability to complete tasks quickly and well. You can, however, gain control over the flow of work, and accomplish all that needs to be done, if you are organized in the following areas:

1. Personal time and idea management.
2. Effective communication with other members of the staff and lay leaders of the church.
3. Recruitment and development of volunteer staff.
4. Tools of the trade.

Part I deals with these aspects of developing record-keeping procedures.

1

Time and Idea Management

Time management is vital in the church office, since your time is never your own. Not only must you accomplish the necessary record-keeping tasks quickly and well, you must be available to minister to the emotional and spiritual needs of the congregation, often at a most inopportune time.

Your ability to manage time will determine how much you accomplish. Be aware of time. How much of it is used to do the tasks at hand? How much time goes to drop-in visitors, emergencies, telephone calls, and last-minute requests?

TIME STUDY

How can you become more aware of time? Conduct a personal time study for at least two weeks but, ideally, for a longer period. When I served at the Cypress Lake Baptist Church, I carried a time study over a three-month period, which was most helpful because it covered such occasional or seasonal tasks as bimonthly communion, choir enrollment, reception of new members, and vacation Bible school, all of which would have been missed in a two-week study.

First, make copies of the "Daily Time Study" form (Figure 1), one page for each day.

Begin each day with a new page on which you have written the day and the date.

Keep track of your time by noting everything that occurs during your workday (Figure 2). Round off the time in five-minute periods. For example, the secretary in this case noted that from 8:00 to 8:15, she sorted Saturday's mail. From 8:15 to 8:25 there were people in the office, taking up non-productive time. From 8:25 to 8:40, she ran off copies on the copying machine. Note that the form should be filled in as each

DAILY TIME STUDY		
Day_____		Date_____
Time		
From	To	Tasks/Phones/Interruptions, etc.
———	———	————————
———	———	————————
———	———	————————
———	———	————————
———	———	————————
———	———	————————
———	———	————————
———	———	————————
———	———	————————
———	———	————————
———	———	————————
———	———	————————
———	———	————————
———	———	————————
———	———	————————
———	———	————————
———	———	————————
———	———	————————
———	———	————————
———	———	————————
———	———	————————
———	———	————————
———	———	————————
———	———	————————
———	———	————————
———	———	————————

Figure 1

DAILY TIME STUDY		
Day _Monday_		Date _6/3/85_
Time		
From	To	Tasks/Phones/Interruptions, etc.
8:00	8:15	Sort mail from Saturday
8:15	8:25	PIO/NP
8:25	8:40	Making copies
8:40	8:50	Phone/P
8:40	8:50	Typing Correspondence
8:50	9:05	PIO/P
9:05	10:30	Prepare newsletter
10:30	10:40	Talk with salesperson
10:40	10:45	Phone
10:45	11:15	Directory updates
11:15	11:30	Stamp + mail postcards
11:30	12:00	Prepare newsletter
12:00	1:00	Lunch
1:00	1:10	PIO/NP
1:10	1:20	Phone/P
1:20	1:30	Open, read + sort mail
1:30	1:45	Phone/P
1:45	1:55	Typing youth list
1:55	2:15	Sort dinner reservations
2:15	2:40	Type dinner list
2:40	2:55	Send new members letters
2:55	3:00	Phone
3:00	3:15	PIO/NP
3:15	3:25	PIO/P
3:25	4:00	Prepare newsletter

Figure 2

change of task or interruption occurs. At the end of the day, you cannot possibly remember everything you have done or how long it took. You can only keep track accurately if you write down everything you actually do, as you do it. This is very important. Your memory as to all the little interruptions and minor accomplishments will never serve you accurately.

At the end of the predetermined period of your time study, tally your results. Make a column for each item on your daily sheet (Figure 3). Write down the minutes under the appropriate columns. Then add the time taken for each item on your tally sheet.

After tallying each item, complete the process as follows: For this example only, results of a one-day time study is shown in Figure 4.

1. Multiply days worked by hours per day to give you total hours worked. (Converting all times to minutes will simplify your equations.)
2. Add the time for each item on your tally sheet, and total. This figure should equal your total hours worked.
3. Divide the *total time for each task* by the total hours worked for the percentage of time alloted to each task or time waster activity. For example,

Preparing newsletter = 2 hours, 20 minutes = 140 minutes
$$140 \div 480 = 29 \text{ percent}$$

The results will surprise you. You will be able to see exactly how much time it takes

GETTING YOURSELF ORGANIZED

Open, read + sort mail	PIO/NP	Making copies	Phone/P	Corres.	PIO/P	Prepare newsletter
:15	:10	:15	:10	:10	:15	1:25
:10	:10		:05		:10	:30
:25	:15		:10		:25	:25
	:35		:15			1:80=
			:05			2:20
			:45			

Talk with salesperson	Directory updates	Mailouts	New Mbrs. letters	Lunch	Youth	Prepare dinner list
:10	:30	:15	:15	1:00	:10	:20
						:25
						:45

Figure 3

to perform necessary tasks; how much time is used in ministering to the real needs of the congregation; and how much time is actually wasted by barriers to effective time management, such as drop-in visitors, telephone calls, last-minute requests, and worst of all, your lack of priorities.

If you are not careful with your time, the pile of little things will mount, and you will find yourself swimming in miscellaneous paperwork, handling papers over and over again, reshuffling and resorting.

By analyzing the results of your time study, you will be better able to schedule and delegate work. For example, in Figure 6 in chapter 3, tasks compiled from a two-month time study are listed. This form, inserted in a Sunday bulletin, attracted several dedicated volunteers.

TIME AND IDEA MANAGEMENT

To improve the effectiveness of time and work, here is a system called "Time and Idea Management in a 3 × 5 Box." A flexible, revolving "to do" list, your 3 × 5 mini-file will be a constant reminder of things to do, telephone calls to make, or important dates to remember. A big advantage of this system, over lists or daily calendars, is that you don't waste precious time rewriting yesterday's uncompleted tasks on today's list; or worse yet, you won't lose track of items listed on yesterday's or last week's calendar page.

The system will keep you from being distracted by minor details. You will be able to assign information and requests to appropriate time slots in your work schedule, to direct interruptions, and to establish priorities and accomplish more during your workday.

To set up your system, you will need the following:

```
one day = 8 hours = 480 minutes


            Results of Time Study

Task                                Time    %
Copies                               15     3
Correspondence                       10     2
Dinner list                          45     10
Directory updates                    30     6
Lunch                       (1:00)   60     13
Mail, open, read + sort              25     5
Mailouts                             15     3
New members letters                  15     3
Newsletter, prepare        (2:20)   140     29
People in office, productive         25     5
People in office, non-produc.        35     7
Phone, productive                    45     10
Salesperson, talk with               10     2
Youth                                10     2
            Total task min. =       480    100
```

Note: For brevity, use abbreviations, i.e., PIO (people in office); P (productive); NP (non-productive). Ignore times of less than five minutes, i.e., one brief phone call or interruption would not be noted.

Figure 4

One 3 × 5 file box
One set of 3 × 5 January through December index cards
One set of 3 × 5 1 through 31 index cards
A large pack of loose 3 × 5 paper for notes
One paper holder

All the above items are available at your local office supply store. Another source of 3 × 5 paper is your paper stock supplier or an instant-print shop. Paper trimmings are usually saved, and if requested, will be cut to size and often given free of charge to you. Index cards can be used, but they are not free, and they also are bulkier than paper.

Arrange the notes in the file box, with the current month in front, followed by the current date. The card for the next month is after 31, followed by those cards from the start of the month to yesterday's date. At the back of the box are the remaining months of the year. For example, if you're beginning the system on October 15th, as shown, the 15 divider is directly behind the card for October. The remainder of the numbers for the month are behind the 15—16 through 31. The following month, November, is next, with the dividers 1 through 14 behind. Place future months to the rear of the box, as shown in Figure 5. The cards are rotated daily.

After the box is set up, use it to store your notes, ideas, requests, memory joggers, and whatever else you wish to remember on a particular date.

Remember you must use the box daily. Important memory joggers will be lost in the file if the box is not used regularly.

The first thing in the morning, go over the day's notes and arrange tasks in the order you want to do them. High priority items are first. An impromptu meeting by drop-in visitors congregating near your desk, however, might keep you from concentrating on your first task.

The system allows for flexibility and interruptions: Do a low-priority task. Keep busy, and shift a mentally demanding job to a quieter time. A few seconds of reorganizing cards takes less time than rewriting notes.

Schedule a time to catch up on your low-priority small tasks. Better yet, having a volunteer come in for a morning or an afternoon to get them out of the way will help you catch up with your work.

Keep loose 3 × 5 notes in the note holder on your desk, with pencils and pens nearby, so that persons coming into the office have easy access to them.

When you are not in the office, such as evenings or Sundays, a visitor who wants to leave you a note will have this paper to write on. "Order bread for communion" or "The

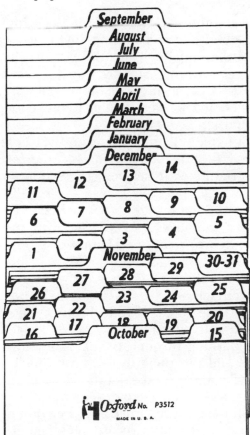

Figure 5

first-grade class needs crayons" or "Please call so-and-so" are brief notes that can be immediately filed in the box, to be taken care of later. Your church members will get used to using this system, and you are saved the time of rewriting their messages on a to-do list.

Another important feature of this system is that when someone comes into your office and wants to give you information, such as a change of address, you can hand them a piece of paper to write it down for you. (If it is more than a brief message, you will need larger paper, but I usually find that the small paper produces shorter, more concise notes.) Remember you want to save time. By having people write their own notes, you can keep on working. People will see that you are busy and will not stay around to chat. You also save time because you don't have to write the information yourself and you can quickly read and file the message or information in the appropriate place in your box.

The English humorist Cyril Northcote Parkinson wrote a satire on business practices. He stated, "Work expands to meet the time available for its completion." How true. How often do you, seeing that it is 30 minutes before quitting time, stretch a 15-minute job to the full half hour? Eliminate this negative force through the use of your time-management box.

Since developing Time Management in a 3 × 5 Box, I no longer waste blocks of time. Jobs in the 3 × 5 box that have no deadline, such as cleaning out a drawer, sorting and reorganizing one file pocket, or stamping booklets with the church's name and address, fit into little pockets of time that would otherwise be wasted. My file box has a pile of notes clipped together for mini-blocks of time. Thus I am able to keep on top of minor details and tasks.

One afternoon in May several years ago, a mother of a high-school senior came into the office and asked if the church was planning anything special for the graduates. It was already too late in the month to plan a dinner, so the pastor suggested a gift presentation to the graduates during Sunday worship service. We decided to order hardcover graduates' books from the local Christian bookstore, but their stock of books was already well picked over, and we were unable to buy enough of the same book. We had to make do with several kinds of books.

Immediately I wrote a note: "Remind pastor and youth leader to plan dinner and ceremony for graduates." I filed it under *April,* and the following April 1st, when I looked at that date, I was reminded to set the wheels in motion for special graduation events.

In our area, passes for the toll bridge to Sanibel Island are free to our ministers, but they must be renewed annually. I keep a note in my file, and each year on September 1st I am reminded to write the County Commissioner's Office and renew the passes.

Does a brilliant idea flash through your mind while you are busy preparing the bulletin? Write a note to yourself and file it. Too busy this week to think about it? And next week is the big business meeting and you will still be too busy? No problem. You'll be reminded of it if you file it in your box.

Ideas are like comets flashing through the sky—brilliant, but lasting only a short while. Capture your ideas and put them to work for you. When you get a good idea stop what you are doing, take a 3 × 5 note, jot the idea down, and file it. When you are feeling creative and seeking a new challenge in your work, study your ideas and develop them into projects that will benefit your work and the church.

Managing ideas is an effective tool of record keeping.

2

Establishing Effective Communication with Staff and Church Leaders

To manage records in and for the church successfully, it is necessary for all the key people to understand what record keeping means, why records must be kept, who is responsible for maintaining the records, and how communication flows logically through the office. This is accomplished through the coordination of tasks, staff meetings, and an understanding of the personal preferences of the staff and lay leaders.

COORDINATION OF TASKS

It is up to the church staff to coordinate the channels of information necessary to maintain accurate church records. For any particular record keeping, a line of communication, or "flow chart," should be set up. (See Chapter 6 for information on developing flow charts.)

In church work, when volunteers serve as officers or as leaders of the church while they also maintain their homes, families, and careers, there is very little time left for them to communicate with others. They are usually not at the church, except for services, which is why communication is poor. Therefore the office staff is responsible for communicating information to the leaders of the church, as well as seeking information by calling people and asking questions. Usually that responsibility will fall upon the secretary, as in the following example of one Baptist church.

This church has a certain way of receiving new members into the church: The person comes forward in church and completes a "decision card," giving such personal information as name, address, birthdate, and church previously attended. The membership process is as follows: (1) a deacon visits the prospective member's home; (2) the secretary enters data for the new member in the church records; and (3) the church clerk requests a letter of recommendation from the new member's old church. When this process is completed, the new member is invited to participate in a reception and banquet for all new members.

A problem existed with the system, in that the deacons, the secretary, the church clerk, and even the pastor did not understand what information was needed or why it was needed by the other people involved.

Sometimes a deacon, not being able to contact a new member, would keep the card at home, and at times lose track of it, sometimes for months. The secretary then did not have the new member's data to enter into her records, and the church clerk had no information, so she never sent a request for a letter of recommendation. No one who handled new member records was aware of the entire process involved in record keeping.

The solution lay with proper communication to each person by the office staff. The church secretary first conferred with the pastor, noting each step in the membership process as defined in the church constitution. She then contacted the chairman of the deacons, asking such questions as, "What do you do with the information? Where do you put the cards when you finish with them? At what point are you finished with your part of the process?" so that she knew exactly what the deacons did with the decision cards. She explained why it was necessary to receive the cards in the office by a certain time.

The secretary followed the same procedure with the church clerk, who explained the process of requesting letters of recommendation. After a number of telephone calls to the chairman and the clerk, clarifying points of possible misunderstanding, the secretary fully understood the full process, and wrote it down.

The chairman of the deacons was given copies of the full record-keeping process so that it could be explained at the next deacons' meeting. The church clerk felt comfortable in her understanding of the process and was assured by the secretary that the completed decision cards would be passed on to her in a timely manner.

Now on Mondays, the pastor gives the names of those who joined on Sunday to the secretary. When she recognizes names of new members who have not yet had cards turned in, she calls the chairman of the deacons and requests the cards. And because the deacons are more aware of the necessity of maintaining accurate records, they make an effort to meet with all new members on the day they join the church and turn in the signed decision cards usually by the following morning.

A process that was aggravating for all was thus resolved.

STAFF MEETINGS

For one church in Sarasota, Florida, brief weekly staff meetings provide information about upcoming events to the pastor, the minister of music, the secretary, the part-time custodian, and the volunteer leaders of youth, missions, trustees, and men's organization and for other involved groups.

An open invitation is extended to lay leaders to come to the staff meeting if they have, in their area of responsibility, any upcoming events that should be discussed or noted on the church calendar. Meetings are held at the same time every week, Tuesdays at 1 P.M.

The pastor keeps the meeting brief. Going through the calendar, up to at least one month in advance, each day's activities is noted. Programs are discussed, including what has to be done by the secretary, custodian, and any other person involved in preparing for events. Everyone knows what is happening. Record keeping is easy because notes are made about what will go into the bulletin or newsletter, dates and times are accurate, and necessary supplies are noted. There are no last-minute surprises.

In another church, the pastor didn't consider Mary, his secretary, "staff" and did not include her in staff meetings. Thus one Wednesday morning Joan, the chairperson of the publicity committee, phoned Mary. "Are the flyers ready for me to pick up?" she asked.

"You must be mistaken," replied Mary. "I don't have any flyers."

Joan explained that, in staff meeting, the pastor had told her that he wanted 10,000 flyers mailed to the entire community for the revival that was to take place the following week.

"Oh, I forgot to tell you," the pastor said, on being questioned by Mary. "I told Joan you'd have those flyers ready for her."

A task that could have been coordinated weeks in advance, with volunteers to type, print, fold, label, and sort, turned into a nightmare for Mary.

The failure to plan ahead is virtually eliminated in regular staff meetings where everyone concerned presents their upcoming programs, needs, and activities.

Staff meetings should include everyone involved in the record-keeping process. Of course the ministerial staff will conduct its own program-development meetings, which do not affect record keeping. Or if they do, information will be presented in the staff meeting the following week.

At the very least, pastor and office workers should spend ten minutes every morning going over the schedules for the day.

UNDERSTANDING PERSONAL PREFERENCES

How does a person want the telephone answered? Mail distributed? Callers received? Everyone is different. One pastor wants all his mail opened, with the junk mail thrown away, and he wants the telephone dialed for him. Another pastor does not want any mail opened, he likes his correspondence typed in block style, and he is irritated by telephone messages from salespersons.

The only way to have a harmonious working relationship is by open, honest communication. Ask questions. "Do you have a preference for your correspondence? Do you prefer that a person calls you back, or would you rather call him?" Or pastor, ask your secretary, "Do you have any ideas for making this job easier and better?"

Communication saves time because work does not have to be redone, records are handled the way the pastor and the church leaders want them to be, and you have a happier work environment.

If you cannot communicate in person, pick up the telephone and call, or write a brief note or postcard.

I find it effective, when I am unable to reach someone by telephone to clarify information, to mail a postcard, saying:

"Please call church office. I need to talk with you about

_____

Thank you."

I sign my name and rubber-stamp the church's name, address, and phone number underneath the thank you.

In almost every case, a person who is not at home to receive telephone calls during the day will respond to the postcard and call me.

3

Recruiting and Developing a Volunteer Staff

Although this chapter is directed toward pastors and secretaries, if you are a volunteer I believe it will help you gain some insight into your role as a valuable resource in serving in your church office.

I believe that churches, even with their limited resources for hiring additional staff, can accomplish all record-keeping procedures with the help of volunteers.

But how do you go about recruiting, training, and keeping volunteers?

RECRUITING VOLUNTEERS

First, determine what you want volunteers to do. If you have completed your time study (discussed in chapter 1), you will have a list of tasks that are done in the church office.

What work can a volunteer do? Special mailings, maintaining mail lists, filing, answering the telephone, printing, mimeographing, and typing are just a few examples.

When I served as office manager at Trinity United Methodist Church in Sarasota, Florida, I was the only paid staff person besides the pastor and the minister of music. However, much of the work of that 1,000-member church was accomplished through the help of a volunteer staff of twenty persons or more. Two men operated the offset press (and still do), taking turns and sharing the work. Six or eight men and women came in every Tuesday afternoon to stuff, label, sort, and count the newsletters to be mailed. Several women consistently gave a morning or an afternoon a week to help with typing, answer the telephone, or whatever else needed to be done. Someone was always ready to pitch in and help.

Place a notice in your bulletin or newsletter: "Volunteers Wanted for help in the church office." If you have room, include a form similar to the one shown in Figure 6, so you will have an idea of the interests and abilities of the volunteers.

A few people will call in and volunteer. Start with them. Ask questions. Find out their interests and especially their capabilities.

It is important to realize the wants and needs of your volunteer. And equally important, the volunteer should understand and be willing to accept his or her limitations.

Once a ninety-year-old woman called me several times, wanting to come to the office and help. Because I was busy when she arrived, I did not take the time to chat with her for awhile to find out a little bit about her. I made a big mistake in asking her to sort a large stack of papers, a task that required organizational skill and a good memory. After 15 minutes of explaining the work to her, I realized I had a problem, for she could not remember what I had said. I suggested that perhaps she would like to do something else, but she said no, she could do this task. Not wanting to hurt her feelings, I spent the rest of the morning working with her, neglecting important correspondence.

Edna K., age 75, who presently helps out in the McGregor Baptist Church Office, said, "I don't want a job with pressure. I couldn't handle it. But I love to come in and help." She puts labels on bulk mailings, maintains our mailing list, and helps with other jobs.

Volunteers should be offered satisfying roles that draw on their individual interests and abilities. But give your workers suitable tasks. Ask them their preference of the work to be done, and consider their backgrounds and education.

When you talk with your volunteers, you will find out who has had previous church office experience, who has been a bookkeeper, who doesn't mind filing. Communication is the key to effective volunteer help in the office.

Use the services of all persons who volunteer to work in the office. Although you may have one person who does a particular job well, there will probably be others who can do the same work. Avoid hard feelings by explaining that a back up person is necessary, and alternate work weekly or monthly. By doing this, you will not be left short-handed when someone goes on vacation, gets sick, moves away, or is otherwise unable to assist.

TRAINING VOLUNTEERS IS ESSENTIAL

Take as much time as necessary to train volunteers, assisting them to do the job as well as you can. Pass on "tricks of the trade," as you think of them. Provide volunteers with as much information as possible about the work, so they will feel confident and feel they are part of the team.

Present work to be done in a way that will not intimidate the worker. Don't throw everything at him or her and say, "Here it is."

Train the volunteers yourself. If you train a volunteer, who trains another volunteer, who then trains another volunteer, it is possible that things will be left out or that the work will be done in a way that is inconsistent with how you would like it done. Everyone does things just a little differently, and sees things in a slightly different way. By the time information is passed on to two or three other persons, it has a way of changing. I find that by training volunteers myself I have better control over the work that goes

```
NAME_____ Date_____

I am interested in:
___Mimeographing
    ___Sermon - weekly, by Wednesday
    ___Bulletin - Thursday afternoon or Friday morning
    ___Special Projects - as needed
    ___Singles Calendar and Newsletter - monthly
    ___Youth Calendar - monthly
    ___Youth Newsletter - monthly
___Computer
    ___Singles Mailing List - weekly updates
    ___Youth Mailing List - weekly updates, letters
    ___Wordprocessing
        ___New Members/New Christians/Music Dept. Letters - weekly
        ___Prospect Packets - weekly, usually Wednesday afternoon
        ___Misc. Letters
        ___Singles Newsletter - monthly
        ___Visitors' Letters - weekly, by Wednesday
___Directory Updates - done manually, weekly, by Wednesday
___Sending for New Members' Church Letters - monthly
___Bulk Mailouts
    ___Singles - monthly
    ___Challenge - monthly
    ___Youth - monthly
___Typing - miscellaneous as needed
___Anything that needs done.

How often would you like to work in the church office?
    ___weekly, full day
    ___weekly, one half day
    ___once a month, full day
    ___once a monce, half day
    ___more often, as needed
    ___other_____

What day(s) would be best for you?_____

Mornings or afternoons?_____

Are you available on short notice?    ___Yes    ___No

Comments:_____
_____
_____
_____
_____
_____
```

Figure 6

out of the office. Even though it initially takes more time, it is well worth the extra effort.

Tell a person all he or she needs to know about a job, and you will keep volunteers who feel needed, who are challenged, and who can carry on the work of the church record keeping.

KEEPING VOLUNTEERS

If you want to keep these fantastic volunteers, treat them well. Forget about the person of leisure who has nothing better to do than volunteer time. Today's adults are busy with their personal lives. They are looking for a challenge while at the same time serving God.

Be ready for volunteers when they arrive. Don't waste their time by making them wait an hour to be trained for a job, or worse yet, by not having the job ready for them to do. Very few people will complain that their time is being wasted. They will simply stop coming.

Our monthly newsletter is printed at a local shop. The printer knows that I have volunteers help to label and mail the newsletter and that he is expected to deliver the finished product on time. On a few occasions, he has called to say it would be late, so I could inform the volunteers. The workers appreciate not having to kill time waiting around the church office.

The condition of the work space for volunteers will tell them if they are valued as important resources in the church office. Is there adequate work space? Are supplies provided? Is the equipment in good working order?

You will not keep a volunteer if you stick him or her in a corner. One woman I know was recruited to type the monthly financial statement. The typewriter she was to use had been placed in a corner of an out-of-the-way workroom on a desk surrounded by old boxes and junk. To top it off, her chair was a high stool. Needless to say, she did not stick with the job for more than a few months. She did not feel like a member of the team, and it was a humiliating experience for her. Provide a pleasant work environment for volunteers if you want to keep them.

Affirm your workers. Express your appreciation. Drop them a note, saying what it is that you appreciate about them. Be specific. For example, instead of "Thanks for your help," you might say, "You did a great job getting the newsletter out on time yesterday. Thanks!"

Delegate work that is challenging and fun to those persons wanting to take on the responsibility. Free yourself to concentrate on developing special projects, studying problem areas, rearranging files, reorganizing, and completing tasks that would never be done with limited office staff.

Understand that volunteers give their time for their own enrichment as well as that of the church. Keep all conversation positive and uplifting. Do not discuss problems of the church, either with the volunteer or with other staff members in the presence of volunteers. Even if a volunteer initiates a conversation about problem areas, quickly steer him or her away from such negative conversation. It will drag you and your volunteer down quickly.

In one church, a very capable woman volunteered to come in and reconcile the checkbook and prepare the financial statement on a monthly basis. She cornered the minister of education about some difficulties the church was having, and he too willingly participated in a lengthy negative discussion about the troublesome problems. One month the woman did not show up, nor did she show up the second month. Finally the pastor approached her after church one Sunday and asked her what had happened.

She hastily answered, "I don't want to talk about it," and hurried on her way.

After six months had passed, the church secretary happened to see her in the supermarket. "We've missed you," the secretary said.

"Oh, I just had to get out of that office. Every time I went there, I got so depressed and nervous," answered the woman.

Volunteers are first of all church members. Although some problems may exist within any church at times, remember that the volunteers really do not want to hear about them, even if it seems that they do. Keep all conversation and communication in the church office positive, helpful, and uplifting. Communicate the love of Jesus at all times, and you will build a volunteer staff that is dedicated, eager to serve, and fun to work with.

4

Tools to Expedite Record Keeping

The proper use of the available tools will help you expedite record keeping. Develop your organizational ability by using two common tools you learned in school: the alphabet and the outline.

Further enhance your office procedures through an efficient use of equipment. Use the telephone as your ally in expediting record-keeping procedures. Obtain the proper basic equipment for your office.

THE ALPHABET

You might say, "Well, now . . . no kidding!"

Many tasks can be made more pleasant by putting items in alphabetical order before they are handled. It is amazing the number of church secretaries I've seen who have their files organized in no particular way, and they wonder why they are going crazy because they can never find anything.

Some financial secretaries try to post unsorted offering envelopes to a file of alphabetized records. It is time-consuming and hard on the eyes, and it is easy to make mistakes in going back and forth through the alphabet. It is much easier to put the envelopes in alphabetical order and make one pass right through the stack.

Our church has a fellowship supper each Wednesday, and the members fill out their reservation slips and place them in the offering plate on Sunday. These slips of paper have to be alphabetized and typed on a list each week. The person who used to do this task had a very cumbersome way of sorting, making a separate pile for each letter.

Here is a way of alphabetizing in a confined area. Although you will be resorting each document several times before you finish, you will find this method saves time, can be done in a small work area, and is less frustrating than trying to make twenty-six piles at once. The method breaks a big job into small bites that can be handled easily.

Don't try to alphabetize strictly right away. Begin by dividing into eight main groups, as shown in Figure 7. Sort first A–B–C, D–E–F, G–H–I, J–K–L, M–N–O, P–Q–R, S–T–U, and V–W–X–Y–Z.

In the second sort, take each pile and break it down by individual letters (A, B, C). Next, it is helpful with a large group of records to break down each letter even further, by vowels or blends. For example, Ab, Ag, Am, Ap, At or Ba, Be, Bi, Bo, Bu. Finally, put the alphabetized records face down, in order, as you work through the piles.

With practice you will zip through an alphabetizing procedure with the speed (almost) of a data processing sorter.

At one church I served in, I asked a volunteer to alphabetize a list of handwritten names that were to be typed. She didn't know where to begin. Now she certainly knew the alphabet, but she simply didn't know how to use it as a tool in organizing a list. The list, which was to be used to check off names at a banquet, would have been quite cumbersome and time-consuming to use if it were typed with the names out of order.

To alphabetize information on a page: Start with A, and glance up and down the page, number the first one you find as "1"; the next in order will be "2," no matter where it is on the page, and so on. After all names are numbered, use a ruler to guide you right through the numbered alphabet, listing all names in order.

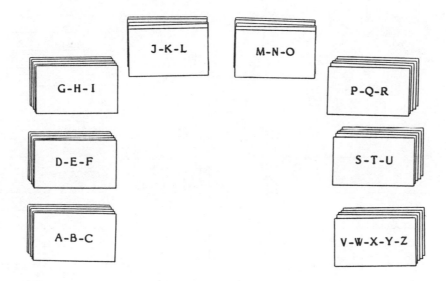

Figure 7

THE OUTLINE

Using an outline as a guide to prepare meeting agendas, sermon notes, reports, and other papers helps you organize your thoughts or material logically. I have used an outline format to set up general files, to prepare charts of bookkeeping accounts, to organize membership records, and even to compose an interest-survey form for the congregation. Here are two basic forms of outlines. The first example, in Figure 8, has only main headings and subheadings; the second example also includes sub-subheadings.

These basic outlines can be varied in many ways. You can use single or double spacing, capitals, and underlines. You can use numbers or roman numerals for major headings. For minor headings or subheadings that require more than one line, it is acceptable to block the second line beneath the first or to indent two to five spaces. A word-phrase style or a style of complete sentences may be better for a particular piece of work.

Whatever variations you prefer, here are some principles of good outlining:

1. Roman numerals are used for main headings only.
2. Roman numerals, usually aligned to the left, are aligned to the right for outlines, so that the period is in the same position for each numeral.
3. If Roman numerals are used for the main headings, subheadings will have capital letters or Arabic numbers.
4. No main heading or subheading stands alone. For every "1" there must be a "2"; for every "A," a "B"; for each "I," a "II." A single item will usually be better listed under another heading.

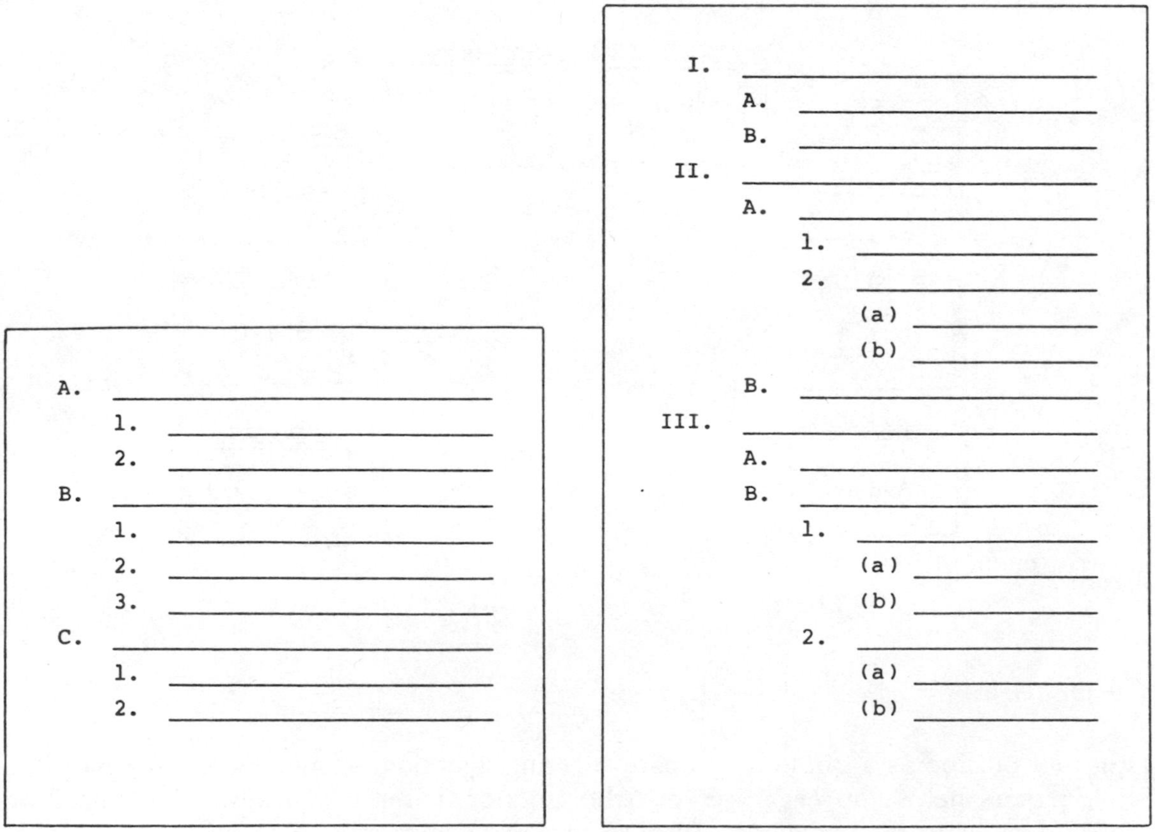

Figure 8

GETTING YOURSELF ORGANIZED

5. Headings and subheadings are written in parallel form, either by sentences or topics but never by both.
6. If the headings use numerals, the subheadings are letters. Sub-subheadings under letters are small numerals; under numerals, they are small letters.
7. Use small (*a*) and (*b*) under 1. and 2.; and under (a) and (b), use (1) and (2).

You may prefer a word or phrase outline, such as the one shown in Figure 9, which one pastor uses for his monthly business meeting, or you might prefer a complete sentence outline for preparing teaching notes or sermons. The pastor of McGregor

```
                BUSINESS MEETING
                OCTOBER 15, 19___


     1.    Opening prayer

     2.    Minutes of last month's meeting

     3.    Reports

           a.    Sunday School
           b.    Financial
           c.    Missions
                 (1)  Foreign
                 (2)  State
                 (3)  Local

     4.    Old Business

           a.    Parking lot
                 (1)  Cost of paving
                 (2)  Installation of handrails
                      in handicapped area
           b.    Fund-raising

     5.    New Business

           a.    Church-wide dinner
           b.    Christmas pageant
           c.    Other?

     6.    Adjournment

     7.    Closing Prayer
```

Figure 9

Baptist Church uses a detailed outline for the delivery of his weekly sermons. Using a steno book, he writes full sentences with the major headings, subheadings, and sub-subheadings clearly defined. He can then flip through the fully outlined sermon on Sunday mornings, confident that every point he wanted to cover is there. His delivery is logical, precise, and to the point. And the message is easy to type for printing.

THE TELEPHONE

Is it your enemy or is it a useful tool to help you accomplish your work?

Telephone calls eat up a good portion of the day in a church office. Here are some tips on how to save time and expedite work through the proper use of the telephone.

The telephone is your link with the members of the congregation, as well as with prospects, visitors, salespeople, and media people. What you say in a telephone conversation is important. Be tactful. Offer to help. Because you serve the needs of the congregation, it is very important to be pleasant and courteous to anyone who telephones. It is wise to assume that whoever is calling is important, and to answer the telephone accordingly. Always answer promptly. Let your caller know, "You are important. I am here to help you." If you are one of several persons who may answer the telephone, identify yourself by saying, "_____ _____ Church, Ann Smith." It isn't necessary to say "good morning" or "good afternoon" if the tone of your voice conveys that message.

Unfortunately calls can come at the most inopportune time. No matter how busy you are, put a smile on your face before you pick up that receiver. It is difficult to sound agitated when you are smiling. Avoid any implication that the call is an intrusion.

When taking a message, be sure to obtain all essential information. For example, if someone is sick or hospitalized, write down such details as the room number and who called in information, and include the action to be taken by the pastor or others.

Be sure to get the caller's telephone number. Often a caller will say, "He already has my number." Well, the pastor may already have the number, but it may be at home on his dresser or in his car. You should say to the caller, "May I have the number anyhow, so the pastor [or whoever] will not have to look it up."

When your caller identifies himself or herself, use that name in speaking with him or her. It not only compliments the caller, it also helps you remember that person's name.

Often callers do not want to give any information. In that case, say, "Will _____ know what you are calling about?" Sometimes out-of-town callers leave their names, but not their purpose in calling (intentionally). It is particularly frustrating to return a long-distance call only to find that it is to an office-supply salesperson. Find out the purpose of the call if at all possible.

If you suspect that the caller needs pastoral counseling, ask, "Are you calling in regard to a spiritual matter, or for counseling." Don't pry into private matters if you sense that the caller is troubled.

Many times I've heard an audible sigh of relief as a caller realizes that he does not have to give his story to anyone but the pastor.

Make your good-byes swift. Be courteous and listen to problems but don't initiate or extend conversations. Habitual callers will get the idea that you always have time to chat.

Use a plausible excuse to terminate conversations, such as, "I'd really like to talk with you more, but I'm hurrying to get the bulletin ready for the printer," or, "Excuse me, let me interrupt you. I'd like to connect you with [the pastor, secretary, minister of music], who can handle that problem for you" and so on. It is a waste of your time and the caller's time to have them explain a problem in detail, only to pass the call on to someone else. Be friendly but firm when passing the call on to someone else. Let the caller know that you are willing to listen but that someone else can solve the problem, so you are transferring the call.

Have telephones installed where they are needed. One church has the secretary's office on the first floor and her workroom on the second floor. The youth minister's office is also on the second floor. He had a telephone in his office, but if one line rang while he was on the other line, the secretary had to drop what she was doing and run downstairs to answer the telephone. This was dangerous, because in her haste she could have tripped and fallen. It also wasted both her and the caller's time.

Another problem was that when the ministers were out of the office and the secretary was operating an office machine, she could not even *hear* the telephone ring. Many times church members complained to the pastor, "Why doesn't someone answer the phone?" or "Is the office closed on Fridays?" (which was the day the secretary was usually alone in the building, upstairs printing the bulletin).

The installation of a telephone in the workroom solved a problem that had plagued the secretary for years. A loud bell sounded over the clamor of any office machine, and she heard all incoming calls.

Do not hesitate to ask a person to repeat a name or number, or spell out a name. Say "I'm sorry, but I'm having trouble hearing you."

It is particularly important to enunciate clearly when giving numbers and letters over the phone. If a caller cannot understand a spelling of a name, exaggerate your pronunciation. For example, I spell my last name, "Shearn," which is pronounced like the girl's name Sharon—very slowly, like this: SSS-H-EEE (pause) AAA (pause) RRR (pause) NNN. I do not give the person on the other end of the line the opportunity to misspell my name.

I learned this lesson a number of years ago when I had applied for the office manager's position at Trinity United Methodist Church. Having not yet moved into the area, I had told the pastor I would call him as soon as my family was settled in town, the following month. After unpacking I called the church office and spoke with the secretary, leaving my name and phone number. A week passed, and no call came from the pastor. Finally I worked up enough courage to call him back, thinking he had decided to hire someone else.

"Oh, was that you?" asked the pastor. "The spelling was so different from your name. I thought it was someone else calling about the job, and threw the message away. I had just about given up on you."

I learned then always to spell my name clearly and precisely.

OFFICE EQUIPMENT

Adequate office equipment should be a top priority for the church. Just as a custodian would not be expected to change a ceiling light bulb without a ladder or the kitchen committee would not be expected to serve a pancake breakfast without a stove, the church office worker should not be expected to perform the record-keeping duties of the church without the proper equipment. Because the work in the church office is not a visible justification of monies spent, many secretaries, pastors, and volunteers struggle with inadequate equipment that keeps them from expediting work and getting on with the more creative aspects of their positions.

I know of one couple who graciously contributed $5,000 to a mission church. "Use it any way you want," said the man, but he was incensed to find that the pastor "wasted the money on printing equipment."

"I thought they would use it for spreading the Gospel, not for toys for the office," he angrily stated. What he did not realize was that the pastor was freed to spend his time visiting his congregation, since he no longer had to waste time in the office cranking a manual duplicator to print bulletins and newsletters. The pastor also printed his sermons and distributed them to shut-ins, visitors, and hospitalized members. What better way to spread the Gospel?

Typewriter

The typewriter is the basic office machine. One mission pastor struggled along with his manual typewriter. "Why," I asked him, "when electric typewriters are so inexpensive, are you using a manual one?"

"How inexpensive are they? A used one for $200? I didn't know that." He had no knowledge of office equipment, and no one in his newly formed church gave a thought to what equipment he was using. He plugged away at the manual keyboard, using time that could have been spent serving the needs of the congregation.

You can cut your typing time in half by using an electric typewriter.

Besides the time saved, the quality of work produced by an electric typewriter is far better. Since electric typewriters are available in a great variety of styles, before choosing one for your office visit several office supply stores and acquaint yourself with the machines available. Consider these special features when selecting a typewriter:

1. Type style and size: Does the machine have 10, 12, and proportional spacing type sizes? (10 is Pica, or 10 characters to the inch. 12 is Elite, or 12 characters to the inch. Proportional spacing produces a type-set quality, with individual letters taking up different widths, for example *i* takes less space than *w*.) Are there a variety of type styles? Different styles and sizes of types? Different styles and sizes of type will enhance bulletins, newsletters, and special work. Lengthy work too large for one page of 10-pitch type will fit with ease when done with proportional spacing.
2. Line spacing: The usual line spacing on a typewriter is six lines to the inch. An important feature is the ability to adjust the platen for a half-line. This feature really helps, for example, if the bulletin is filled with information, and you have more lines than will fit on the page. By half-spacing between paragraphs, you can easily squeeze all necessary information on the page. Similarly when there is more space than needed, a space and a half between paragraphs will spread the print out and give a balanced look to the finished page.
3. Half-space key: This key moves the carriage one-half space. When correcting finished type, this key allows you to squeeze an extra letter into a corrected word, using the same space between two other words. Or if you need to delete a letter from a word, the half-space key allows you center that word between two others. The key also allows you to right-justify lines of type.

GETTING YOURSELF ORGANIZED

4. Platen (roller) width: The width of the platen varies. The wider the platen, the easier it is to work with stencils. There will be no need to cut them apart and then glue them back together, if you have a wide platen. Fourteen-inch paper will not fit on the commonly used 13-inch platen. Eliminate that frustration by selecting a typewriter with a wide enough platen.

To increase your typing speed, electronic typewriters have such features as memory storage, memory correction, and phrase recall.

Adding Machine-Calculator, With Printer

Throw away that antique adding machine you are using. In several small churches I visited, I was amazed to see old relics being used—large, heavy clunkers that could not be moved around, that took up desk space, and that had no printout. Printing calculators are cost-efficient, very inexpensive, and convenient.

The mechanics of your job should be simple, and an electronic calculator will simplify your work. An inexpensive printing calculator starts at about $40, a minor expense when it comes to the amount of time saved.

Copier

What can a copier do for you? How much time will it save? "Why should we buy a copier?" asks the pastor of a 400-member church. "We have an instant-print shop right up the street."

"Right up the street is two miles away," responds the secretary. "And let's face it, if volunteers in the church have to run to the print shop to get the work done, they just won't do it."

The time saved by the copier more than pays for it by producing quality work that can be done by anyone, no training required.

A copier can reproduce printed matter quickly and easily. It facilitates making address labels. And it eliminates messy carbons.

Workers in the church, such as Sunday School teachers, can make copies at times that are convenient for them, and the church secretary does not have to make copies for them.

Today when so many women who serve as teachers and leaders in the church work full-time and are also busy with their families, it is very difficult for them to have work ready ahead of time for the secretary to duplicate during the week. It is unreasonable to expect these volunteers to give up their time to make a special trip to the church to drop off work for the secretary to print out. Even with the volunteer help in my office, I appreciate that the Sunday School teachers, music leaders, and missions leaders can come in and, without my assistance, make copies.

Plain-paper copy machines have an advantage over coated-paper machines because they can accommodate many types of paper, such as colored paper and letterhead, and the copies will look almost like the original. Plain-paper copies also last longer than coated-paper copies.

Copiers vary greatly, from machines that print a same-size reproduction on one side of the paper only to complex duplicators that copy both sides at once, enlarge or reduce, sort, and collate. Somewhere in that range is a copier that will fit the needs and budget of your church.

Mimeograph and Stencil Maker

The mimeographing process is inexpensive (½ to 1½ cents per copy), easy to operate, and fast. The machine accommodates paper and card stock from 3 × 5 inches up to 8½ × 14 inches. One disadvantage is that it is difficult to use colored inks.

Typed stencils can be saved and reused; but they are messy. Also, you can't use clip art or drawings unless you use special instruments to draw them on the stencil or buy special mimeograph clip-art and use a special cement to apply them.

An electronic stencil maker will allow you to type copy on plain paper, and you can use clip-art, photographs, or other material. Even half-tone photographs can be used. The stencil maker reproduces the page electronically and the copies are true to the original.

The stencil and the original are placed on a cylinder, and as the machine scans the original, a stylus burns the stencil, exactly duplicating the original. An electronic stencil can produce over 5,000 copies.

Offset Press and Platemaker

Use an offset press if you want your finished work to look professional. A. B. Dick Company makes a very good table-top model that is used extensively in churches. The capabilities of this machine include bulletins, letterhead, newsletters, envelopes, flyers, postcards, brochures, and tickets.

A platemaker makes a copy of your original for reproduction on the press.

The cost might be difficult to justify for small churches. The amount of work produced per hour, the speed, and the quality of work eliminates the need to take work to outside printers, however. But for a very small church, it may be too large an expense.

It is also important to consider who is going to operate this equipment. Although the quality of copies produced on a mimeograph depends mostly on the stencil, the quality of work produced on an offset press depends on the platemaker, the press, and very importantly, the operator. Is a member of your staff going to learn how to operate the equipment?

In two churches in which I served, I trained volunteers to operate the printing equipment. Jim T. and Joe C., members at Trinity in Sarasota, took great pride in their work and maintained the equipment well. Barney M., at Cypress Lake Baptist Church in Fort Myers, was equally skilled in producing quality work and maintaining the equipment.

Even with a limited staff, producing quality work on an offset press can be done if you have willing volunteers and if you have first learned all there is to know about the machine.

Cleaning up the press must be done whenever the machine is used. But the process is fairly simple, once it is mastered, and takes little time. It is possible to clean the A. B. Dick tabletop model in minutes.

Folding Machine

This machine saves the most time of any piece of equipment in the church office. What takes two hours to fold by hand takes ten minutes by machine. Thus it is a waste of time to fold by hand; buy a folder and use the extra time for more important tasks. Many types of folders are available. Some even have perforating wheels on them, which are used to make tear-off forms such as tickets or visitors' cards, so that church visitors can tear off information to keep and drop a filled-out card in the offering plate on Sunday.

Be aware of the need for good equipment. When sales people call on you, keep an open mind and learn from them about new products. Go to a few product demonstrations. Ask a lot of questions. Choose the right equipment for your office and let the equipment work for you.

Computers

Although most small churches are not currently in the market to buy computers, many of them are thinking about it—looking around and trying to learn as much as possible about the use of computers in the church.

Since this is a topic of wide interest, I have covered it in Part VI, Using Computers in the Church Office.

PART TWO

KEEPING TRACK OF PEOPLE

Eighteen-year-old Melanie, an enthusiastic new Christian, joins a local church, by going forward in church during the invitation. People welcome her, and she feels at home. However, weeks go by before a deacon calls on her at her home.

"No one has been to see me but you," she exclaims. "I haven't received my offering envelopes, I haven't received a phone call or a letter, and no one even knows who I am." She informs him of her decision to join another church.

Personal recognition—a feeling of belonging to a church body—can affect a person's decision to join or to remain in a church. An oversight in recording Melanie's personal data in the church office kept her off the visitation and mailing lists and kept her from receiving her new member's packet of information.

Ann V., a recently widowed senior adult, calls her pastor in tears. "It has been four months since my husband passed away. I just received the newsletter, and it's still addressed to "Mr. & Mrs."

"I'm sorry," he exclaims. "Our church secretary is new, and we've been behind on updating our mailing list. We're trying to get caught up with our records."

"It's been rough these past few months," she replies. "Getting this newsletter today was the last straw for me."

Don and Barbara, a young couple with two children, visit a small church where the people seem very friendly. However, after several weeks no one has called on them. On their third visit, they complete a second visitor's card, and check the box marked, "Would like minister to call." Somehow the minister "misses" their card, and he does not visit or call them. They join another church.

Keeping accurate, up-to-date people records for highly mobile congregations is a large task, even for small churches. But it is a very important task and should have top priority in any church office.

People in the church expect to have their names spelled correctly. They expect to have their mail addressed correctly. Keep in mind that, although people are busy with their own lives, they expect their church to know if there have been changes in names, addresses, marital status, or other vital information.

If visitors and prospects do not feel that they are wanted, they will go elsewhere. For them to feel welcome and at home, they must be called and nurtured.

What kind of files do you need for people? Chapter 5 details basic files for people and tells how to maintain the information on these records.

Chapter 6 talks about membership records and provides methods for keeping track of incoming and outgoing members, as well as for changing personal data.

A system of recording visitors' and prospects' information will help pastors and church members keep track of these persons and give them the attention they need. Chapter 7 shows a way to record and keep track of visitors and prospects.

5

Files for People

The Rolodex, Individual Record Card, and the Family Record Card are three very basic files that will help you keep track of people in your church.

In addition, the Chronological Roll will provide a historical record of your membership.

ROLODEX

A Rolodex is a card file in which a separate card is used for each person or family. Many kinds are available, and personal preference will determine the one that is best for you. Several sizes of cards are available. The 2 × 4-inch size is convenient, because it provides enough space for basic information—name, address, and telephone number—yet it does not waste space.

A smaller size (1½ × 2¾) is difficult to work with, both when typing information on the card and when flipping through the cards. Another disadvantage of these small cards is that they are not available in colors and cannot be color-coded.

Whatever your personal preference, give each staff member a Rolodex, in which a card for each family can be filed alphabetically (see Figure 10).

Use different-colored cards to indicate a person's relationship to the church. The color-coding will give you quicker access to the cards in your file:

White: Members. Most cards will be white.
Blue: Nonmembers. List persons who attend the church, or who are otherwise associated with it but who have not joined.

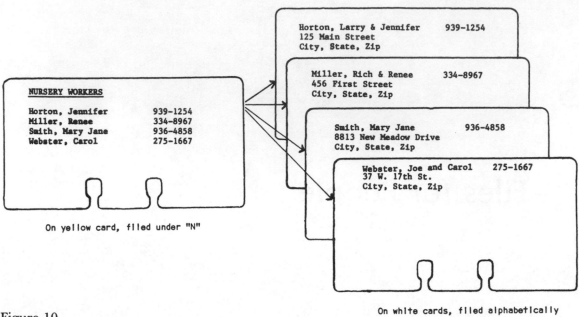

NURSERY WORKERS

Horton, Jennifer   939-1254
Miller, Renee   334-8967
Smith, Mary Jane   936-4858
Webster, Carol   275-1667

On yellow card, filed under "N"

Horton, Larry & Jennifer   939-1254
125 Main Street
City, State, Zip

Miller, Rich & Renee   334-8967
456 First Street
City, State, Zip

Smith, Mary Jane   936-4858
8813 New Meadow Drive
City, State, Zip

Webster, Joe and Carol   275-1667
37 W. 17th St.
City, State, Zip

On white cards, filed alphabetically

Figure 10

Pink: Churches, schools, institutions. List local numbers, as well as the church denomination's district or state offices.

Yellow: List services, suppliers, paid workers, emergency numbers. Include all members who serve as officers or in emergency capacities, such as deacons, trustees, secretary, nursery workers. Enter the persons' names and telephone numbers only. You or someone else might want to reach a deacon, or a nursery worker, but cannot remember whom to call. By listing persons under categories as well as individuals, anyone will be able to find the person. Church organization officers and committees should be listed on yellow cards (names and telephone numbers only). Also include fire, police, and ambulance and insurance companies, by category.

In the front of the Rolodex file, place a color-key card. This way, someone using the file while you are not in the office will be able to understand the color-coding and locate a necessary name quickly.

An up-to-date Rolodex, available at all times, serves the needs of the people in the congregation. For example, a choir member, after choir practice in the evening, might want to call those members who were not present. Your Rolodex will be available. Or a Sunday School teacher may want to sit at your desk after church on Sunday and make telephone calls or send postcards to absent members. Your file will be there to help the church worker accomplish his or her work quickly.

Remember that personal data are not recorded on the Rolodex file. All confidential information should be entered on individual record cards or family record cards, which are locked up at the end of each day.

In one church, three full file drawers contain individual file folders for each member of the church. In the folders are copies of baptism certificates, marriage licenses, and death notices. Yellowed newspaper clippings of the accomplishments of long-gone members are also filed. For the most part, though, the files are empty. A church just does not need that much information to justify a folder for each person. Valuable space and supplies are wasted.

Membership record cards, though, can provide important data. You might need no more than 3 × 5 index cards to record a family's name, address, and telephone number.

Donna G., the secretary of a 100-member church in a rural town in Indiana, says that "their name goes on a card, and I put it in the file. If they attend, they're members. If they don't attend, they aren't members, and I take the card out of the file." Most pastors and secretaries I talked with, however, want to maintain a more permanent, accurate membership file. Two types of records, an Individual Record Card and a Family Record Card, are basic forms that can be used to maintain membership records.

This Individual Record Card (Figure 11) provides detailed information on a member. In addition to a name, address, and telephone number, the names of the member's family, as well as the relationship of each immediate family member, are recorded. The names of other relatives should also be included. This is helpful for the future if a pastor or staff members leave a church. Thus, when family names are kept on each individual record card, new staff members can easily pick up family relationships. For example, Mary Smith might be Susie Miller's aunt. Or Henry Jones, an adult, might be the brother of Don King, also an adult.

It also helps when the files need to be revised. When you have lost track of inactive members, it is easy to contact a relative for their whereabouts.

When making address corrections on these cards, do not obliterate old addresses.

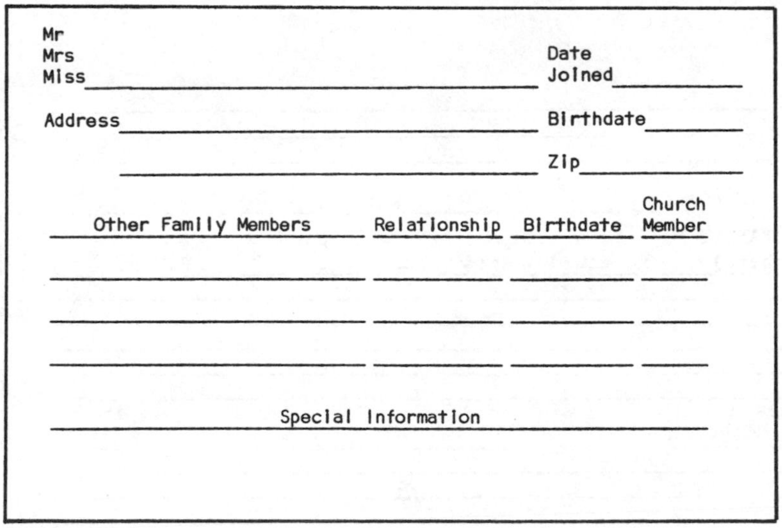
Mr
Mrs
Miss ______ Date Joined ______

Address ______ Birthdate ______

______ Zip ______

Other Family Members	Relationship	Birthdate	Church Member

Special Information

Figure 11

Cross out the old address with a ruled line, and add the new address below it. This provides a trail if you or someone else has to trace members in the future.

Individual Record Cards give flexibility in adding, deleting, or changing individuals' personal information.

Keep these cards in a 4 × 6 file, divided into three sections, Active Members, Inactive Members, and Nonresident Members. When it is time to make an annual report, it is simply a matter of counting the cards in each section to determine your congregation's status.

You may even want to keep a fourth section, Deleted Members. All cards of deleted members would be included here, with the reason for each deletion noted.

For those who prefer to have the information for an entire family on one card, Figure 12 shows a Family Record Card that has been used successfully by several churches.

The family name and address is typed at the top of the card. The blank lines are for changes of address. Spaces are provided for all family members who join the church. Under Separate Card, a "+" indicates that the family member shown has his or her own family record card. For instance, suppose a son gets married. A "+" is put by his name, and a new card is prepared for him and his new family.

Any family member with a separate address has a "+" on the family record card, and a new card is prepared for that family member.

When names of members are counted to determine the size of the actual membership, or at the end of the year for the annual report, any name with a "+" beside it would not be counted in the grand total.

The column Perm. Rec. is where a person's record number is placed. (See Chronological Membership Record, Figure 13.)

Pam S., the membership secretary for an 800-member Christian Church, says, "If I

Employment: Husband ____________ **Wife** ____________

PERSONS IN FAMILY (Church Members)	Date Received	Separate Card	Entered on Perm. Rec.	Pastor

PERSONS IN FAMILY (Not Church Members)	RELATIONSHIP	BIRTH DATE

Figure 12

CHRONOLOGICAL MEMBERSHIP RECORD

Membership Number	How Received	Prior Church or Date of Baptism	Date Received or Dismissed	Name	Birthdate	Current Status	How Dismissed	New Church or Comments	Dismissal Number

Figure 13

A = ___   I = ___   N = ___

receive a request for a letter from another church for one of our members, I look up that person's name in the alphabetical card file, find his record number, and then go right to the chronological roll and find his name immediately. It saves a lot of time."

You should put the names of immediate family members who do not join, such as a husband of a woman who joins or the parents of a child who joins, under Other Family Members. Similarly enter the names of children who live in the same household but who have not become members with their parents.

One disadvantage of using the family record card is that it does not provide much room for personal data. Another disadvantage is that it is not as easy to keep track of individual members.

Children move out of their parents' household, couples separate, a family member may die, or one family member moves out of the area. Also, you can't move an individual to an "inactive," "non-resident," or "deleted" file if all the names are on the one card.

One advantage in your record-keeping process of using a family record is that, for any address or telephone number change, information only has to be entered on one card, rather than on each family member's card.

Whatever your preference, either the individual record card or the family record card will help you maintain the membership records of your church.

This roll is the historical record of all persons who have joined a church. The form (Figure 13) should be reproduced on 3-hole punched, 8½ × 11-inch paper, with non-tear (or Mylar reinforced) edges. Keep the sheets in a sturdy binder. It is filled out, as follows:

1. Membership Number. Starts with "1"; names are numbered consecutively
2. How Received:
    L *Letter.* The person joins by letter from another church of the same denomination.
    B *Baptism.* The person is baptized in your church.
    S *Statement.* The person joins on a statement, or profession, of faith, from a church of a different denomination.
    W *Watchcare.* This is used in some churches when a person lives in an area for part of the year, but has another church "back home." Watchcare gives certain privileges of membership to persons who otherwise would be away from a church for a lengthy period of time.
3. Prior Church-Date of Baptism. Record the name and the location of the member's prior church if he or she has joined by letter. If joined by Baptism, write date of Baptism in this space.
4. Date Received or Dismissed. Enter date person has joined or the date you remove the person from the roll.
5. Name (address is not necessary).
6. Birthdate (to locate the correct individual in case of duplicate names).
7. Current Status. Use this column for the members' current status, making light notations in pencil:
    A *Active*
    I *Inactive*
    N *Nonresident*
8. How Dismissed:
    L *Letter.* Individual has joined a church of the same denomination.
    O *Other denomination.* Person has joined a church of a different denomination.
    D *Death.*
    R *Request.* Member has requested that his or her name be removed from the roll.
    P *Purged.* After all efforts to locate an inactive member are exhausted, and a lengthy period of time, such as three to five years, has lapsed, some churches elect to delete these members from their rolls. In these cases, this code is used.
9. New Church-Comments. Enter the name and location of the church to which you send the member's letter of recommendation. Also you can make light pencil notations for inactive or nonresident members, for example, "In the Navy," or "Attending mission church."
10. Dismissal Number. Start with "1," and continue in ascending order.

The letters in the Status column are totaled at the bottom of each page, lightly, in pencil. Each time you delete someone from the rolls, or change their status, you make the appropriate change beside that person's name; also change your totals at the bottom of the page. At all times the grand totals of the status codes on all pages should equal the membership number minus the dismissal number.

Figures 14 and 15 show two pages from a roll book, page 18, covering the period November through March 1980, and page 75 (the last page of the roll book).

Consider, as an example, that 625 persons have joined your church. The Membership Number will be 625. Suppose 122 have left the church over the years. Your last Dismissal Number is 122. Therefore, 625 minus 122 equals 503, which is the total membership.

Total all the pages for each A (active), I (inactive), and N (nonresident) member. The total membership must equal 503. This cross-referencing of your membership total will check your accuracy in record keeping.

Setting up the Chronological Roll

For a new church or one that is fairly new, the system is easy to set up. But what about the churches where membership records have not been kept?

When I started as church secretary at Cypress Lake, there were no membership records. Since the church was only seven years old, it was possible to gather membership information and start from scratch in chronological order. Ann and Jim, a retired couple

CHRONOLOGICAL MEMBERSHIP RECORD

Membership Number	How Received	Prior Church or Date of Baptism	Date Received or Dismissed	Name	Birthdate	Current Status	How Dismissed	New Church or Comments	Dismissal Number
121	L	Waverly Hills Baptist	11/8/79	Goode, Bill	4/7/21	A			
122	L	"	11/8/79	Goode, Ruth	8/18/22	A			
123	L	Riverside Baptist	11/8/79	Ratliff, Barbara	9/13/44	A.			
124	B	11/8/79	11/23/79	Smith, Kim	12/9/60	I			
125	B	11/8/79	11/23/79	Smith, Robbie	2/17/64	I			
126	L	First Baptist Ft. Myers	11/23/79	Hutchinson, Lee	2/14/38				(126)
127	L	"	11/23/79	Hutchinson, Grace	4/11/39				(127)
128	B	11/30/79	11/23/79	Hutchinson, Jimmy	9/17/68	N		in the Navy	
129	B	"	11/23/79	Hutchinson, Carol	1/5/71				(123)
130	B	2/11/80	2/11/80	Bayes, Dennis	8/27/58	A			
131	L	First Baptist West Pt., Georgia	2/11/80	Doyle, Jim	5/13/48	I		Divorced	
132	L	"	2/11/80	Doyle, Susan	8/28/47	I		"	
133	L	First Baptist Bonita Spgs	2/11/80	Pickett, Florence	4/26/18	A			
134	S	Covenant Presbyterian	2/22/80	Miller, William	5/31/25	A			
135	S	"	2/22/80	Miller, Verda	2/8/31	A			
136	L	North Palm Baptist Hialeah	2/22/80	Pratt, David	12/28/36	N		in California	
137	L	"	2/22/80	Pratt, Karen	1/4/37	N		"	
138	L	West Hills Baptist	3/21/80	Conn, Donn	5/12/44	A			
139	L	"	3/21/80	Conn, Pat	1/2/48	A			

Figure 14   A = 9   I = 4   N = 3

CHRONOLOGICAL MEMBERSHIP RECORD

Membership Number	How Received	Prior Church or Date of Baptism	Date Received or Dismissed	Name	Birthdate	Current Status	How Dismissed	New Church or Comments	Dismissal Number
621	L	Calvary Baptist Cleburne, Texas	3/2/8	Mattingly, Bill	6/20/44	A			
622	L	"	3/2/8	Mattingly, Shelia	2/19/43	A			
(126)	—	—	3/26/85	Hutchinson, Lee	—		L	Central Baptist, F.M.	120
(127)	—	—	3/26/85	Hutchinson, Grace	—		L	Central Baptist, F.M.	121
(129)	—	—	3/26/85	Hutchinson, Carol	—		L	Central Baptist, F.M	122
623	S	Central United Methodist	3/ /8	Groome, Lucy	6/2/13	A			
624	L	First Baptist Bonita Springs	3/31/85	Harvey, George	1/3/47	A			
625	L	"	3/31/85	Harvey, Beverly	10/13/48	A			

A = 5   I = __   N = __

Figure 15

who volunteered to help, spent three summer months compiling decision cards gathered from desk drawers, deacons' homes, file boxes, and the church office. Jennie, the church clerk and a charter member, met with Ann and Jim to answer questions and help compile the list. Finally, with their help, I was able to assemble the chronological roll.

This was a large project. If you do not have the help available, if your church is older, or if you do not have the records available, you would want to handle this task in the following manner:

1. Gather all the records you can.
2. Contact longtime members of the church who would remember details of people joining and leaving the church and perhaps the current church clerk or former clerks. Ask people to help you compile a list.
3. Don't worry about anyone who is no longer a member of the church. Enter your current members' names in alphabetical order. (Use black, permanent ink. Remember, this is a historical record book, and the information is permanent).
4. Assign membership numbers in consecutive, ascending order.
5. Make an individual record card for each member on the chronological roll. Use the individual card as described above.

To maintain the chronological membership roll when a member is dismissed from the roll:

1. Use red ink to write the person's name. This makes it easy to count names of members on a page. You would automatically skip over those in red.
2. Complete the rest of the person's line of information in black ink. Assign the next consecutive dismissal number.
3. Cross reference the membership and dismissal numbers:
   (a) Under the Membership Number column, put the person's original membership number, but write it very small and put a circle around it.
   (b) Find the person's name on the chronological list. Draw a straight, thin line through the name. Under the Dismissal Number column, write the person's dismissal number, but write it very small and put a circle around it. Remember that you want to provide a track for future staff workers and church historians who may want to trace an individual back through the roll. This cross-referencing avoids confusion.
   (c) Change the totals at the bottom of the last page and the page on which the person's original record is written.

6

Membership Records

INCOMING MEMBERS

In one 100-member church, people join the church by visiting the pastor in his office. After their session with the pastor, he gives their names to the secretary. She then records their names and other information on 4 × 6 cards and files the cards in a box. During service the following Sunday, the pastor introduces the new members to the congregation.

In another church with 1,000 members, an invitation is given by the pastor at the end of the worship service, and at that time a deacon talks with the people who came forward and helps them complete a four-part membership application form. The information is then turned in to the church office, where it is recorded.

Whether simple or complex, the process for recording incoming members must be consistent.

The first thing to do is to determine the flow of information pertaining to new members. If you don't know what procedures to follow, ask your church leaders or other staff for help. Even in churches of major denominations, for which there are specific guidelines, a different interpretation can alter the way a process is followed in any given church.

Figure 16 shows one way that the flow of information can be followed, a flowchart for processing new members in a 1,000-member church.

The Membership Application, or Decision Card, for this particular church is printed on four-part NCR paper (no carbon required), in four colors: white, pink, yellow, and goldenrod (see Figure 17). The forms are collated and there is a special glue at the top, so the individual sets of four colors are handy to use. A supply is kept in the church, readily available for use at the end of each service.

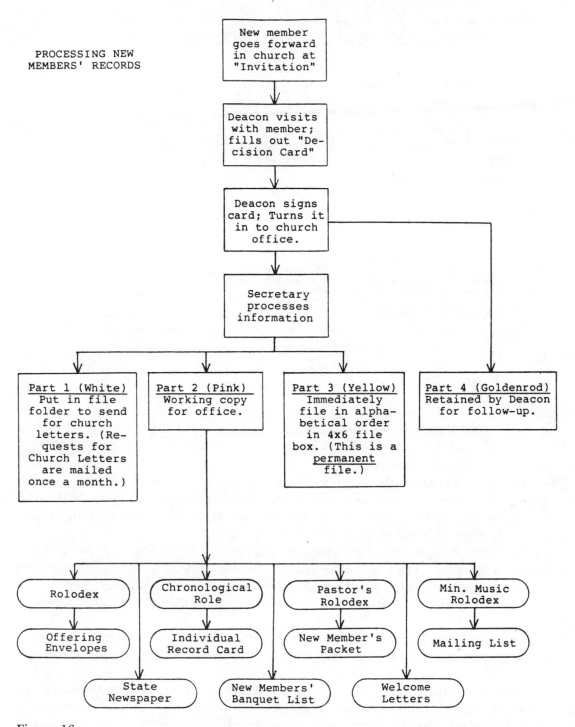

Figure 16

When prospective new members come forward in church, a deacon, not the people, fills out the form. This is done because prospective members, in the excitement of joining, tend to omit information. They also may not use a ballpoint pen, and the

```
┌─────────────────────────────────────────────────────────────────┐
│   PRESS FIRMLY WITH BALLPOINT PEN - YOU ARE MAKING 4 COPIES       │
│                        DECISION CARD                              │
│  MR/MRS/MISS_____ DATE_____       │
│                                                                   │
│  Address_____ Birthdate(s)_____        │
│  _____ Zip Code_____         │
│                                                                   │
│  Phone: Home_____ Work_____         │
│  MARITAL STATUS:  ( )Married  ( )Widowed  ( )Divorced  ( )Single   │
│  OTHER FAMILY MEMBERS:  NAME                      DATE OF BIRTH    │
│                         _____   _____   │
│                         _____   _____   │
│                                                                   │
│  DECISION:                                                        │
│  ( ) Accepts Christ as Personal Saviour and Lord                  │
│  ( ) Desires Membership in this Church:                           │
│        By Baptism_____     By Statement_____            │
│  ( ) Desires Membership in this Church by Letter from:            │
│        Name and Address of Church_____         │
│                                                                   │
│  ( ) Other Decision_____          │
└─────────────────────────────────────────────────────────────────┘
```

Figure 17

information is not visible on the bottom copies because they don't press firmly enough. The deacons, being experienced, fill out the cards correctly. (This form is printed in the back of this book. Any local instant-print shop will copy it as is, or will change information to suit your church's needs.)

Using the flowchart example shown in Figure 16, prepare a chart for your church. Although this may seem complicated, the proper preparation of this chart will make your paperwork procedures easier for everyone associated with record keeping. It has to be done only once and will save a lot of time.

After you have completed your flowchart, you are ready to make a checklist for processing new members. Look at the flowchart. Under Part 2—Pink Copy, all the places where the new member's name is to be added are shown. By determining where information is used, and planning it out on a flowchart, you can make a New Members' Checklist (Figure 18).

This form is not a permanent record, but rather a tool to assist you in maintaining accurate membership records. After you have finished with a page, it can be thrown away.

Across the top of the form, check each place the person's name is to be added. In the columns on the left, enter the person's name, address, and telephone number, as well as the birthdate and the date the person joined. The birthdate eliminates any confusion should the same name be entered (for instance, father and son).

This checklist allows you to complete one thing at a time. If you process a half-dozen new members, oftentimes there is not time to enter their information everywhere it is needed. By using the checklist, you can, for instance, just enter the information on your Rolodex, and later a volunteer can come in and add the names to the pastor's and minister of music's Rolodex. As your schedule permits, you can complete the process

NEW MEMBERS' CHECKLIST

NAME & ADDRESS	PHONE	DATE JOINED	BIRTHDAY	Chron Role	Indiv Rec Card	Rolodex	Pastor's Rolodex	Music Rolodex	Mailing List	Welcome Letter	Envelopes	Packet	Banquet	Newspaper			

Figure 18

without missing an item. As you enter information in any given area, check off that place on the checklist.

A New Member's Packet should be given to each new family or member that joins your church. This packet is a large envelope that contains at least the following:

1. Offering Envelopes. A box for the current year, or, if you use a monthly mailed system, enough blank envelopes for use until the imprinted envelopes for that member arrive. If you know what the envelope number will be, write it down.

2. Survey Sheet. This form lists interests and talents for members of the church. Ideally the form is used when it is time for the nominating committee to look for workers or when volunteer help is needed. If you are not going to look at the form to use the talents of members, don't enclose it. On one occasion, a new member phoned his pastor, quite upset because he had not been called on to work in the area he had indicated on his survey. He had taken the survey very seriously and had waited for a call that never came. (The survey sheets were filed in a drawer and had never been looked at).

3. Sunday School schedule. List classes, teachers, classroom numbers, ages, and specific information about each class. Include any information that would encourage a new member to join the Sunday School.

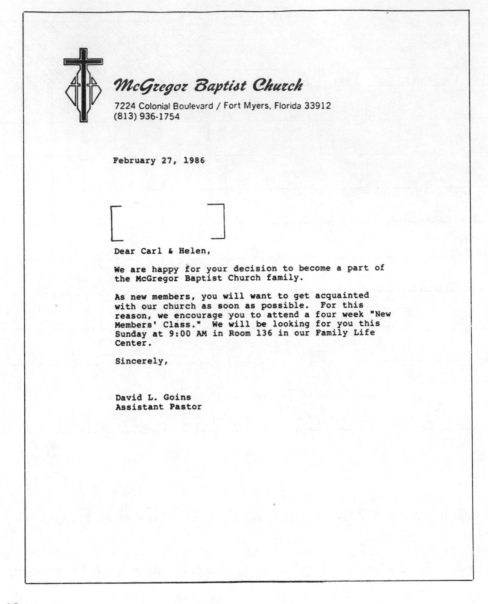

McGregor Baptist Church

7224 Colonial Boulevard / Fort Myers, Florida 33912
(813) 936-1754

February 27, 1986

[   ]

Dear Carl & Helen,

We are happy for your decision to become a part of
the McGregor Baptist Church family.

As new members, you will want to get acquainted
with our church as soon as possible. For this
reason, we encourage you to attend a four week "New
Members' Class." We will be looking for you this
Sunday at 9:00 AM in Room 136 in our Family Life
Center.

Sincerely,

David L. Goins
Assistant Pastor

Figure 19

4. Programs and Ministries Information. All activities of the church should be included.

It is very nice if someone delivers this packet in person, thereby providing a personal call and offering warmth and fellowship to the new member. If this is not possible, the church office worker is responsible for mailing the packet.

An individually typed letter to welcome new members is an additional way of saying to that person "We care about you, and are glad you're here."

Don't be like one church in which a mimeographed letter mailed to new members started out, "Dear Friend, Welcome to our church. We love you. . . ." No one who receives such a letter addressed to "Dear Friend" is going to believe that much love is behind that letter.

If the letter is brief, as is the one shown in Figure 19 (now in use at McGregor), it is no problem to send an individually typed letter each time a new member joins.

In addition to adding a new member's name and address to files and rolls, you will want to send for the new member's church letter.

SENDING FOR CHURCH LETTERS

On the flowchart (Figure 16), Part 1 of the membership application is placed in a file for use in sending for church letters. This is usually done by the church clerk, membership secretary, or church secretary.

In each church in which I've served, I've used Broadman's Form 4394-09, as shown in Figure 20.

It is used as follows:

1. Fill out the left side of the form with:
   (*a*) Name and full address of prior church. Obtaining the address of a church can sometimes be a problem. Some denominations have directories of all their churches, which is an invaluable source of names and addresses. For example, a "Directory of Southern Baptist Churches" that includes all Southern Baptist churches is available. If you need an address of a local church, use the telephone book. Call the new member to request an address for an out-of-town church.
   (*b*) Name of new member(s).
   (*c*) Date request is sent.
2. Fill out the right side of form with:
   (*a*) Name of prior church.
   (*b*) Town and state.
   (*c*) Name of member(s).

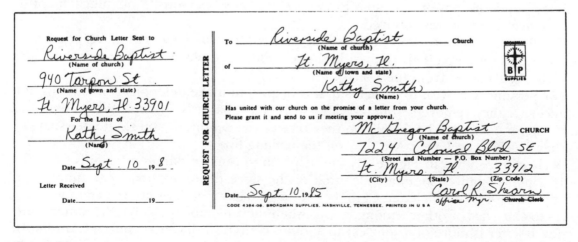

Figure 20

(d) Name and address of your church.

(e) Date sent.

(f) Your name (signature).

3. Address envelopes to churches and mail letters. If more than one request goes to a church, mail all the forms in one envelope.

OUTGOING MEMBERS

Jennifer, a secretary at McGregor, mails the monthly newsletter to the congregation. Every other month, or once a quarter, she includes "Address Correction Requested" on the face of the envelope. The Post Office will then make any address corrections necessary and return the newsletter with the corrected address shown. This way Jennifer can keep up with the individuals who move without notifying the church office of their changes of address.

Some members move away and become nonresident members. Others simply disappear, leaving no forwarding address. What should be done about those members who drop out of sight and leave no forwarding address? Are they carried on the roll indefinitely? Are their names dropped?

Some churches cross off the names of persons who have not attended for a period of six months, others even sooner. If your church or denomination does not have a specific method of deleting members, you should decide on a way to update your rolls.

One church advertises in the newsletter, listing all the names of all members who have been inactive for more than a year. Very often active members of the congregation will know the whereabouts of these persons. After three consecutive years, if the individual has not been found, the person's name is then dropped from the roll.

In one church in which I served, letters were sent to all inactive members, along with a stamped, self-addressed return envelope. (This is very important, because most people will send a stamped envelope back immediately; otherwise they may put it aside and forget about it.)

The many responses surprised us. Some persons asked to be kept on the roll, and others even returned to active membership. Several people had not attended because of illness, and the pastor was able to minister to those persons. And much helpful, constructive criticism was received.

Finally, those persons who wanted to be deleted, for whatever reason, responded to the letter and returned their request in the self-addressed envelope. We were then able to delete their names from the roll.

For persons who wish to be deleted, it is helpful to make deletions consistently. For instance, are they removed from all rolls—secretary's, pastor's, other's? What about the choir roll, or Sunday School roll? Do they receive the denomination's state newspaper? Do they receive envelopes? Are they on the mailing list?

A checklist, shown in Figure 21, will help you to remove names efficiently.

If a person moves to another church of the same denomination, that church will usually send for a church letter. Churches of major denominations are reluctant to grant letters to churches of other denominations when their members change denominations. A church letter is more of a courtesy to another church so that that church can remove the person from its roll.

KEEPING TRACK OF PEOPLE

Name	Date Deleted																		Comments

Figure 21

Sometimes when I write churches for letters, I receive a full-page letter explaining that "we are sorry, but we do not transfer members to other denominations. However, we will remove them from our rolls."

That is what the request for the church letter accomplishes in the first place. Of all the pastors I talked with, there was not one who said his church would not accept a new member if his or her prior church did not send a letter of recommendation.

So the time wasted for a secretary to type a letter explaining the church's policy could have been spent doing something else, if she had filled out the form provided. Why waste time quibbling over denominational differences? For the purposes of record keeping, a preprinted form saves time and avoids confusion.

I have used Broadman Supplies "Letter of Recommendation," Form 4384–08 (see Figure 22). These forms are postcards, which save postage.

Send Letters of Recommendation as follows.

1. Fill out the left side:
   (a) New church's name and complete address.
   (b) Person's name.
   (c) Date sent.
2. Fill out the right side:
   (a) Your church's name and state.
   (b) New church's name. (Although there is a place for the new church's town and

Letter of Recommendation

Letter issued to

Southside Christian
Name of church

5523 W. 55th St.
Name of town and state

Orlando, FL
Recommending

Jim & Ann Johnson

Date Jan. 11 1986

Reception Acknowledged

Date _____ 19 ___

The McGregor Baptist _____ Church
of Ft. Myers, Fl. _____
(Name of town and state)
to the Southside Christian _____ Church
(Name of church)

_____
(Name of town and state)

This is to Certify, That Jim & Ann Johnson are ~~is a~~ members of this church in regular standing, and, in compliance with their request is given this letter cordially recommending them to your fellowship.

By order of the church Jan. 11 1986

Carol R. Shearn
Office Mgr. ~~Church Clerk~~

CODE 4384-08. BROADMAN SUPPLIES. NASHVILLE, TENNESSEE. PRINTED IN U.S.A.

Figure 22

MEMBERSHIP UPDATES

Date	Name & Address	Information To Be Changed	Comments								

Figure 23

state, it really isn't necessary to complete the blank. The new church knows where they are located).

    (c) Person's name.

        (1) If more than one person, cross out *is a* and write in *are,* and add an *s* to *member.*

        (2) Put the proper pronouns in the blanks.

    (d) Sign your name.

UPDATING MEMBERSHIP RECORDS

"Keeping membership records up-to-date is the most frustrating thing I have to do," says one volunteer. "I wish people would quit moving around. Just when I get the records changed for this person, she moves again. I can't remember what records have been changed."

As in adding or deleting membership records, a checklist (Figure 23) will help you make your changes consistent. Add names to this list in chronological order, and keep the list in a file or notebook. If a person moves frequently, this list will help you keep track of him or her.

After all the information has been recorded appropriately, discard the notes, letters, and scraps of paper. It isn't necessary to save every piece of paper that passes through the office. Letters of recommendation, once recorded, can also be discarded. Some church officer workers have a problem with throwing away any sort of paper that has any membership information on it. Don't be a packrat. Get rid of the clutter. If the information is recorded properly, you don't need to save "originals."

7

Maintaining Visitors' Records

A 1,500-member Lutheran church requests visitors to stand during the worship service. Ushers give each visitor an information card to fill out and place in the offering plate.

In one Methodist church, a $5\frac{1}{2} \times 8\frac{1}{2}$-inch pad is provided at the end of each pew, and Sunday worshippers sign their names each week. A volunteer looks over the lists on Monday morning and makes out a visitation card for each visitor.

At McGregor, visitors' cards are in the pew pockets, where visitors can readily take them, fill them out, and place them in the offering plate.

This example of the card used at McGregor (Figure 24) shows the type of information requested by the church, as well as information about the church for the visitor. The card is perforated, so the visitor can tear off and keep the part that gives information about the church.

After the visitors' cards are turned in to the church office, then what? In many churches, the cards are put in a box so that somebody may call on the visitor. Other churches have an active visitation program, but often lose track of the visitation cards.

Visitors should be visited and nurtured, not only for the church to grow but also to minister to the visitors' needs.

A simple record-keeping system provides a method for following up with your visitors. The method is very basic, yet very effective.

To follow the method, you will need a supply of 4×6-inch, three-part visitation forms. Broadman's Form 4388-04 (Figure 25) is shown. The top copy is white, the second yellow, and the third pink.

The white copy is for the pastor. The yellow copy is given to the person who will be making the visit, and the pink copy is filed alphabetically in the church office.

OUR MINISTRIES:

PRIMETIMERS: Tues. - (Age 55 and over) Inspiration, fellowship, and Bible study
YOUTH: Wed. - (Grades 6 - 12) Joy Explosion
CHILDREN: Sun. - (Grades 1 - 5) Children's Church
Wed. - (Grades 1 - 6) Mission activities
SINGLES: Fellowship and Inspiration
Thu. - (Over 35)
Fri. - (Under 35)
MUSIC: Choirs for all ages: orchestra
COUNSELING: By trained professionals

(Call 936-1754 for Schedule and Details)

Welcome to our Guests

McGregor Baptist Church
Rt. 25, 7224 Colonial Blvd. S E
Fort Myers, FL 33912
(813) 936-1754
Jim Holbrook, Pastor

We really are glad that you have visited McGregor Baptist. Please let us know if we can help you in anyway. So that we may have a record of your visit, please complete this card below and drop in offering plate or hand to usher or minister.

Name _____ Date _____

Address _____ Phone No. _____

City _____ State _____ Zip Code _____

I am a Guest of_____

Member of What Church _____ Where _____

☐ Visitor For First Time   ☐ Would Like To Know More About Church
☐ New In Community   ☐ Would Like Minister To Call
☐ Would Like To Unite With Church   ☐ I Am A Winter Visitor

Please Circle Your Age Group Or School Grade

Age
0-3 4 5

School Grade
1 2 3 4 5 6 7 8 9 10 11 12

Age
18-23 24-29 30-34 35-39 40-44 45-49 50-54 55-59 60 up

FOR YOUR INFORMATION:
OUR SUNDAY SERVICES:

BIBLE STUDY .... 9:00 A.M.
A well staffed class for every age group

MORNING WORSHIP SERVICE .... 10:30 A.M.
Positive Inspiration from God's Word

EVENING PRAISE SERVICE .... 7:00 P.M.
An Informal and In-Depth Approach to Worship

RADIO BROADCAST .... Live over WKZY-AM - 77.0
12:00 Noon over WSOR-FM - 95.3

McGregor Baptist Church
Rt. 25, 7224 Colonial Blvd. S.E.
Fort Myers, Florida 33912
(813) 936-1754

God Loves You and So Do We

Figure 24

ARNOLD GRAPHIC INDUSTRIES

CRC A

PROSPECT VISITATION ASSIGNMENT AND REPORT

NAME_____ DATE _____
(IF UNDER 17 YEARS OF AGE GIVE PARENTS NAME)_____

RESIDENCE ADDRESS _____ PHONE _____

BUSINESS ADDRESS _____ PHONE _____

DATE OF BIRTH: MONTH _____ DAY _____ YEAR _____ CHRISTIAN?_____

CHURCH MEMBER? _____ MEMBER OF WHAT CHURCH?_____

WHERE _____

SPECIAL INFORMATION FOR VISITOR _____

DATE ASSIGNED_____

☐ S S   ☐ CT DEPARTMENT_____   CLASS OR UNION_____

☐ MUSIC   CHOIR OR DIRECTOR_____

☐ BAPTIST WOMEN   ☐ BAPTIST MEN_____

VISITED BY	RESULTS OF VISITS	DATE VISITED

PLEASE VISIT, RECORD RESULTS AND RETURN SLIP PROMPTLY
FORM 120 CODE 4388 - 04. BROADMAN SUPPLIES. NASHVILLE. TENN. PRINTED IN U S A

Figure 25

On Mondays, prepare the visitation forms, using the completed visitors' cards from Sunday's services.

Place the pink copies in the file immediately. This alphabetical file of visitors is a source of information when you are looking up spellings of names, verifying addresses, or trying to call a visitor.

One secretary said, "When the pastor says he can't find the phone number of someone who visited a couple of months ago, I can look up that person in this file, and give him the information immediately. It makes me look good."

Also each week, type an alphabetical list of visitors, as shown in Figure 26, listing all information that is shown on the visitor's card.

Even though McGregor is a large church, and we use a computer, Pastor Holbrook prefers this typed list. He keeps his copy of the list in a three-ring notebook, and carries it with him at all times. After visits to individuals' homes are made, he makes notes on the page (see Figure 27), which serves as a quick reference for help with visitation.

VISITORS - 29 Sept. 1985

ALLEN, Wayne and Ruth April Blake-3rd. Gr. Betsy Blake-5th. Gr.	1528 Medford Pl. Lehigh -36 S.S. Nash	369-9747
BERTOLOTTE, Reba	1317 S.E. 11th. Terr. CC 04 First time visitor	574-3153
BIEBER, Dick & Karen	13437 Caribbean Blvd. S.E. EFM - 05 - S.S. Chesnut	694-7861
CAREY, Tommy (Gr. 10)	1915 Coronado Rd. FM 01 First time visitor - would like to know about church	334-1595
COHEN, Seth (Gr. 12)	1029 El Valle Ave. FM 07 Visited Joy Explosion 9/25	481-1226
DRENNON, Ruth	6126 Deer Run Rd. S.W. FM 07 S.S.	433-4772
DUNAWAY, Susan	P.O. Box 1817 FM 02 Would like to join church - guest of Jackie Pope	433-1649
GASCON, Margaret	4315 S.W. 3rd. St. S.E. Lehigh - 36	369-7723
GLOVER, Ron	21600 Indian Bayou FMB 31 S.S. Tremaine	463-8779
HALL, Richard	2180 Barry D FM 07 First time visitor - would like to know about church	275-9951
MONGOMERY, Heather (Gr. 10)	145 Vermount - EFM 05 First time visitor	694-4545
SERAFINI, Jean	6205 Markland Dr. EFM -05	332-4865
SMITH, Mary Eric (Gr. 6)	6915 Harbor Ln. FM 07 First time visitor	936-3660
STRATTA, Anthony	658 Oleander Ave. FM 01	332-7800 (Work)
UPTON, Ann (Gr. 7)	12934 Cherrydale Ct. FM 07 S.S.	481-8606
VISSER, Laura (Mrs.)	Shell Point Village - #229 FM 08 First time visitor	

Figure 26

"I like it because I can look back over prior weeks, and quickly scan for follow-up calls that need to be made," he says.

In another church in which this system is used to keep track of visitors, a copy of the list is placed on the bulletin board in the vestibule of the church, and members use the list to look up names of people to visit. Outreach is expanded by placing this list where everyone can see it, as Sunday school teachers use the list to invite the visitors to the appropriate classes.

VISITORS - 29 Sept. 1985

ALLEN, Wayne and Ruth
    April Blake-3rd. Gr.
    Betsy Blake-5th. Gr.
See Aug 11 - Pastor
1528 Medford Pl. Lehigh -36
S.S. Nash *Lehigh lst*
369-9747
*** Joined*

BERTOLOTTE, Reba
Dave - Really enjoyed - in hurry - Ph. 12/19 -T
1317 S.E. 11th. Terr. CC 04
First time visitor
574-3153
★

BIEBER, Dick & Karen
13437 Caribbean Blvd. S.E.
EFM - 05 - S.S. Chesnut
694-7861
Members

CAREY, Tommy (Gr. 10)
Central-Shopping
1915 Coronado Rd. FM 01
First time visitor - would
like to know about church
334-1595

COHEN, Seth (Gr. 12)
1029 El Valle Ave. FM 07
Visited Joy Explosion 9/25
481-1226
Cypress

DRENNON, Ruth
Peter Lord's Church Everett
6126 Deer Run Rd. S.W. FM 07
S.S.
433-4772
wrong # ? *★ ★*

DUNAWAY, Susan
*10/10 Susan -
12/19 Answer Phone -*
P.O. Box 1817 FM 02
Would like to join church -
guest of Jackie Pope
433-1649
★★

GASCON, Margaret
*ph - T
Hedde left note,*
4315 S.W. 3rd. St. S.E.
Lehigh - 36
369-7723

GLOVER, Ron
*Dave 10/2
Riverside - uninterested*
21600 Indian Bayou FMB 31
S.S. Tremaine
463-8779
Delete

HALL, Richard
ph. - Dave - Talked to sister - Lives with girlfriend - not here
2180 Barry D. FM 07
First time visitor - would
like to know about church
275-9951
?

MONGOMERY, Heather (Gr. 10)
145 Vermount - EFM 05
First time visitor
694-4545

SERAFINI, Jean
ph - T Bill + Bruce - note
6205 Markland Dr. EFM -05
Ch. of Rel. Science
332-4865

SMITH, Mary
    Eric (Gr. 6)
6915 Harbor Ln. FM 07
First time visitor
936-3660

STRATTA, Anthony
Bruce + Bill - note
658 Oleander Ave. FM 01
(332-7800 (Work)

UPTON, Ann (Gr. 7)
12934 Cherrydale Ct. FM 07
S.S.
481-8606
Delete

VISSER, Laura (Mrs.)
Shell Point Village - #229
FM 08 First time visitor
?

Figure 27

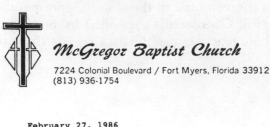

McGregor Baptist Church

7224 Colonial Boulevard / Fort Myers, Florida 33912
(813) 936-1754

February 27, 1986

[   ]

Dear Jim,

We are so glad that you visited our Church. We hope
that you found a positive lift from the message and
an encouragement from the fellowship with other
Christians.

It is our desire to "Lift up Christ, so that He
might draw all men to Himself." We hope that you
have met Christ as your personal Savior, and are
experiencing His abundant life. Let us be of help in
any of these areas. We believe we can!

Come back and see us soon.

Sincerely,

James O. Holbrook

James O. Holbrook
Pastor

Figure 28

A personal letter to visitors from the pastor will broaden the outreach of your church. Send an individually typed letter to all visitors who live in your area. A typical McGregor letter is shown in Figure 28.

MESSAGE

We are so glad you visited our church. We hope you found spiritual food and the blessing of fellowship with other Christians. It is our desire to "lift up Christ so that He might draw all men to Himself". We pray that you have met Christ as your personal Saviour, and have been strengthened in order to live a life that is pleasing to Him. Do plan to be with us again.

James O. Holbrook
Pastor
McGregor Baptist Church

Figure 29

Acknowledge the presence of out-of-town visitors by sending a postcard (Figure 29).

PART THREE

HANDLING THE CHURCH'S MONEY

God expects churches to manage their money as wisely and as efficiently as possible. Church operations are not managed the same way business operations are: The church body or finance committee adopts a budget for twelve months, usually January through December, and this budget guides spending by groups or individuals in the church. Offerings to the general budget provide the church's main income, money designated for specific funds must be accounted for and paid as indicated, and there are no accounts receivable.

Policies and guidelines for disbursing money must be carried out by the person or persons who keep the records. Oftentimes the secretary serves as bookkeeper, although she has had little or no training for the job. Or a layperson in the church becomes the treasurer, disbursing funds and signing checks. Again, there is a minimum of training.

This section describes a system of financial record keeping for small- to medium-sized churches, with limited office staff and/or volunteer help. It provides a system of record keeping from the collection, to the deposit, the disbursements, posting to accounts, preparation of the financial statement, paying FICA and Social Security, and completing government reports.

The system described in these chapters deals with the unique problems of church accounting in simple terms and concepts that can be learned quickly by anyone, even if that person has had no training in accounting. Sufficient detail is provided so that the person can "follow the directions" to sound financial management through an accurate, simple, organized bookkeeping system.

Accuracy, simplicity, and *organization* are the keys of sound financial management in the church. Why?

ACCURACY

Accurate financial record keeping allows the pastor to concentrate on preaching, shepherding, and other pastoral duties, relieving him of the concern of the day-to-day operation of the budget. It also keeps him from worrying about "how much money is available."

Accuracy allows the leaders of the church to concentrate on the programs of the church, knowing how much money is available in each budget account, and to plan programs that are within the budget.

And accuracy also allows the church to pinpoint excessive spending, deficits, and to prepare for large expenditures and lean months.

SIMPLICITY

Financial records must be simple because many churches have volunteer bookkeepers, financial secretaries, counting committee members, and treasurers. The system must be understandable.

The church secretary, who may have no formal accounting training, but who is often the bookkeeper, must be able to process financial information quickly and efficiently so she will also be able to perform her other duties.

ORGANIZATION

Financial records must be organized in such a way that recording is easy and retrieving of information is quick, and preparing reports is facilitated. Organization will help the bookkeeper provide the pastor with accurate financial information and provide department heads and others responsible for the spending of church money with budget information.

FINANCIAL PICTURE AT A GLANCE

1. The budget is approved.
2. Collections are received on Sunday.
3. Collections are counted and deposited in a checking account.
4. Receipts are entered in a Cash Receipts Journal.
5. Checks are disbursed for expenditures; the disbursements are recorded in a Cash Disbursements Journal.
6. Disbursements are entered in a General Ledger.
7. The bank statement is reconciled to the church checkbook.
8. A monthly financial statement is prepared.
9. Contributions are posted to individual accounts.
10. Reports are mailed to contributors quarterly, semiannually, or yearly.
11. Wage and tax reports are filed with the government.

HANDLING THE CHURCH'S MONEY

You can complete all the above tasks by following the directions in these chapters.

WHAT YOU WILL NEED

1. An interest-bearing checking account at a local bank. (One account will be sufficient for all your checking funds.)
2. Loose Checks forms.
3. Deposit slips, provided by the bank.
4. Your approved budget, provided by the finance committee or the church body. You will use this budget to set up your Chart Of Accounts.
5. A package of eight-column white ledger sheets with description column. (Wilson-Jones Form 10-8 is recommended).
6. A post binder for the ledger sheets.
7. Dividers for the post binder. You will need a divider for each main budget category, plus one each for *total Sunday offerings, designated funds, savings, investments,* and *employee withholding and Social Security taxes.*
8. One 5½ × 8½ three-ring notebook.

Equipped with all these supplies, you will be able to perform your daily bookkeeping duties.

8

Setting Up the Books

One type of check is the voucher check, which provides a stub for a description of the disbursement and also a duplicate copy of the check. For the bookkeeping system described here, a conventional check, as shown in Figure 30, is used.

THE CHECKING ACCOUNT

The first thing a church needs to do is open a checking account. It should be an interest-bearing checking account at a local bank. The interest earned will provide additional income.

If your present account is hopelessly out of balance, the best thing to do is to open

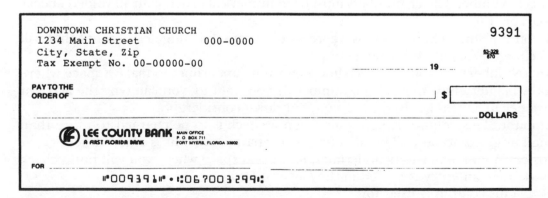

Figure 30

a new account, let all the previously written checks clear in the old account, and then close out the old account.

Your imprinted checks should include the following information:

1. Name of the church.
2. Address and zip code.
3. Phone number.
4. Tax exempt number. The inclusion of your state tax exempt number will save considerable time. If you give a church leader a check to pay for materials at a store where you don't have a charge account, there will be no hassle about obtaining the number when the sales clerk asks for one.

At the time the account is opened, decide on whether you want one person or two persons signing checks. The advantage of having two signatures is that it provides internal control. This can be very inconvenient, however, if both people are not available when a payment has to be made on short notice. In addition, when two people sign checks, there is a tendency for neither one to examine the documents as carefully as they should, since one assumes that the other has done so, and vice versa.

One method of internal control is to have the secretary prepare the bills to be paid, type the checks, and paperclip each check to its supporting document. The designated check-signer then looks over each check and its supporting documents, making sure that payments are within authorized guidelines, and signs the checks. The secretary then mails out the payments, prepares the cash disbursements register for the day, and posts the payments to the General Ledger.

In this bookkeeping system, a unique feature is the elimination of one time-consuming step: Check stubs are not used. The process of filling out the check stubs is combined with cash disbursements journal entries on one form, the Cash Disbursements Journal, as shown in Figure 31.

Cash Disbursement Journal forms should be reproduced on white paper, and three-hole-punched to fit your 5½ × 8½-inch notebook. Sheets are added to the notebook as they are typed, the latest date on top, and are grouped by month, using January through December dividers.

The seven columns of the form are for:

1. Payee. Alphabetized paid bills are listed in this column. The payee is the person or company to whom the check is made out.
2. Check Number. Check numbers must be in numerical order, with all voided checks accounted for.
3. Account Name. This column is where you indicate the budgeted account that will be charged for the disbursement.
4. No. (Number). As you type each line, enter four underlines to make a space where you will later enter the account number. If you want to, you can type the account number in as you go, but it will slow you down considerably.
5. Amount. This column is used only when a check is to be charged to more than one budgeted account. The total for each separate account is entered here.
6. Posted. Again, enter four underlines, to make a space where you will put a check mark after an entry is posted in the General Ledger.
7. *Total.* This column is used for:
   (a) The amount of the disbursement if only one budgeted account is charged.

Payee	Check No.	Account Charged			Posted	Total
		Account Name	No.	Amount		
Accent Business Products Center	1506	Printing Supplies	4.10		✓	46.50
Baptist Sunday School Board	1507	Worker Training	4.19		✓	6.00
Cobb, Dorothy	1508	Nursery thru 4/17/83	2.2		✓	65.00
Exchange Bank MMA 60342188	1509	Designated Bldg. Fund	9.6		✓	5,200.00
FRC Office Products	1510	Furnishings	7.1		✓	92.76
Florida Cities Water Co.	1511	Water & Phone	5.2		✓	25.77
Hewitt, Zennie	1512	Nursery, 4/12/83	2.2		✓	10.00
Hutchens, Becky	1513	Nursery, 4/14/83	2.2		✓	7.00
Intervarsity Press	1514	Worker Training	4.19		✓	10.91
Jolliff, Travis	1515	Transportation	4.25		✓	5.00
Jones, Nick	1516	Designated Bldg. Fund	9.6		✓	1,500.00
New York Intntl. Bible Society	1517	Jail Ministry	1.4		✓	14.49
Palm City Glass & Mirror, Inc.	1518	Building Maintenance	5.3		✓	54.00
Portable Recording Ministries	1519	Worker Training	4.19		✓	140.31
Sunday School Board	1520	Worker Training	4.19	30.99	✓	
	1520	Furnishings	7.1	270.00	✓	
	1520	Vacation Bible School	4.2	75.91	✓	
	1520	Library	4.21	29.92	✓	
	1520	Sunday School	4.1	6.74	✓	
	1520	Total				413.56
Weaver's Office Supplies	1521	Furnishings	7.1		✓	21.15

Date 4/15/83   Total Disbursed This Date   14,913.66   6

Figure 31

(b) The total of the figures in the Amount column, if more than one budgeted account is charged.

The Total column is added, with the amount being entered in the space at the bottom of the page, and on the Checking Account Balance Record. The Total column of figures will also be used to reconcile your bank statement.

CHECKING ACCOUNT BALANCE RECORD

Date	Description	Misc.	Disbursements and Debits	Deposits and Credits	Balance

Figure 32

Reproduce the Checking Account Balance Record as shown (Figure 32), using a light-colored paper. Three-hole-punch it to fit in the checking notebook. These sheets are added to the book as needed, with the latest date on top. Chapter 10 describes in detail how to use the above forms.

Now that you have a checking account and have set up the checkbook you are ready to set up the Chart of Accounts from the approved annual budget, and to prepare the General Ledger.

THE BUDGET

Even the smallest church needs a budget, for although money is not an end in itself, it is a resource that must be used wisely. The processes for establishing a budget are not defined here, but the procedures to carry out the administration of the budget are shown.

One problem area for many churches is how to arrive at the dollar figures for missions that will be included in the grand total of the annual budget.

For example, at one church, the finance committee approves the annual budget amounts for all programs and departments. They decide that 15 percent of the grand total budget will be designated to missions—Foreign Missions, 7 percent; State Missions, 5 percent; and Local Missions, 3 percent.

The assistant pastor is asked to figure the missions' totals and to have the budget prepared to present to the congregation the following evening.

"I don't know how to do this," he tells his secretary. "Our budget totals $82,400. How can I figure what the missions' totals should be?"

By using the following equation, you can figure an annual budget total, including missions' percentages.

$$\frac{A \times 100}{B} = C$$

where A is the total dollar figure of the budgeted account (in the example, it is $82,400); B is difference between 100 and the missions percentage figure (15 percent is to be sent to missions; thus, $100 - 15 = 85$), and C is the Grand Total of the new annual budget.

For example:

$$\frac{82,400 \times 100}{85} = 96,941.$$

and,

7 percent for Foreign Missions	= 6,786
5 percent for State Missions	= 4,847
3 percent for Local Missions	= 2,908
85 percent for Budgeted Accounts	= 82,400
Grand Total	96,941

After the approved budget is complete, you need to set up a Chart of Accounts.

Take a copy of the budget and number the main headings 1, 2, 3, etc. Then number the individual accounts .1, .2, .3, etc., as in Figure 33.

```
                         1983 BUDGET


        /   MISSIONS & EVANGELISM
           1.1  World Missions                      94,217
           1.2  Associational Missions              14,664
           1.3  Local Missions                         500
           1.4  Jail Ministry                          600
           1.5  Revival Expenses                       900
           1.6  Scholarship Fund                     1,200

        2   SUPPORT STAFF
           2.1  Secretary                          11,000
           2.2  Nursery Workers                     5,700
           2.3  Custodian                           4,100

        3   PASTOR
           3.1  Salary                             15,800
           3.2  Housing & Utilities                10,000
           3.3  Car Expenses                        3,500
           3.4  Hospitalization                     1,400
           3.5  Retirement                          3,000

            MINISTER OF MUSIC
           3.6  Salary                             10,200
           3.7  Housing & Utilities                10,000
           3.8  Car Expenses                        2,400
           3.9  Hospitalization                     1,400
           3.10 Retirement                          3,000

        4   ORGANIZATION/ADMINISTRATION
           4.1  Sunday School                       6,000
           4.2  Vacation Bible School                 500
           4.3  Women's Missionary Union            1,500
           4.4  Royal Ambassadors                     400
           4.5  Mission Activities                    200
           4.6  Music                               2,000
           4.7  Special Music Events                  200
           4.8  Office Supplies                       750
           4.9  Postage                               600
           4.10 Printing Supplies                     750
           4.11 Publicity                             800
           4.12 Florida Baptist Witness              650
           4.13 Nursery Supplies                      125
           4.14 Kitchen Supplies                    1,200
           4.15 Social Events                         300
           4.16 Youth                               4,000
           4.17 Flowers                               750
           4.18 Conventions                         1,600
           4.19 Worker Training                     1,000
           4.20 Recreation                            500
           4.21 Library                             1,150
           4.22 Junior Church                         300
           4.23 Puppet Ministry                       200
           4.24 Pulpit Supply                         250
           4.25 Transportation                      2,000

        5   MAINTENANCE
           5.1  Electric                            7,000
           5.2  Water & Phone                       2,000
           5.3  Building Maintenance                6,000
           5.4  Lawn Care                           2,500
           5.5  Insurance                           2,500

        6   DEBT RETIREMENT
           6.1  Exchange Bank                      20,460
           6.2  Florida Baptist Convention          2,700

        7   CONTINGENCIES
           7.1  Furnishings                         3,000
           7.2  Growth Fund                        24,400
                                              _____

                             Total                231,866
```

> The amount for each budget is the _beginning balance_ for the new year. Enter the amount for each account in Column 3 on the ledger page for that account.

Figure 33

From this numbered budget, type up a Chart of Accounts. On this page, list "Total Sunday Offerings," with January through December (or your fiscal year) typed underneath and numbered. Also list Savings, Investments, Designated Offerings (with specific designations for your church, including Miscellaneous Designated), and Tax Liability. Number and subdivide each entry, as shown in Figure 34. If you have accounts at more than one financial institution, allow a separate page for each one, and number as above. The idea is to make the system understandable for *anyone* who looks at the Chart of Accounts.

Paste the Chart of Accounts on a blank ledger page; it will be the first page of your ledger. You will use the Chart of Accounts every time you post disbursements; and it also serves as a table of contents for the General Ledger.

1. MISSIONS & EVANGELISM

1.1	World Missions
1.2	Assoc. Missions
1.3	Local Missions
1.4	Jail Ministry
1.5	Revival Expenses
1.6	PBAC Scholarship Fund

2. SUPPORT STAFF

2.1	Secretary
2.2	Nursery Workers
2.3	Custodian

3. STAFF

	Danny Harvey:
3.1	Salary
3.2	Housing & Utilities
3.3	Car Expenses
3.4	Hospitalization
3.5	Retirement
	Glenn Saunders:
3.6	Salary
3.7	Housing
3.8	Car Expenses
3.9	Hospitalization
3.10	Retirement

4. ORGANIZATION/ADMINISTRATION

4.1	Sunday School
4.2	Vacation Bible School
4.3	WMU
4.4	RAs/Brotherhood
4.5	Mission Activities
4.6	Music
4.7	Special Music Events
4.8	Office Supplies
4.9	Postage
4.10	Printing Supplies
4.11	Publicity
4.12	Fla. Baptist Witness
4.13	Nursery Supplies
4.14	Hospitality
4.15	Church Training

4. (Continued)

4.16	Youth
4.17	Flowers
4.18	Conventions
4.19	Worker Training
4.20	Recreation
4.21	Library
4.22	Junior Church
4.23	Puppet Ministry
4.24	Pulpit Supply
4.25	Transportation

5. MAINTENANCE

5.1	Electric
5.2	Water & Phone
5.3	Building Maintenance
5.4	Lawn Maintenance
5.5	Insurance

6. DEBT RETIREMENT

6.1	NCNB
6.2	Fla. Baptist Conv.

7. CONTINGENCIES

7.1	Furnishings
7.2	Growth Fund

8. TOTAL SUNDAY OFFERINGS

8.1	January
8.2	February
8.3	March
8.4	April
8.5	May
8.6	June
8.7	July
8.8	August
8.9	September
8.10	October
8.11	November
8.12	December

9. DESIGNATED OFFERINGS

9.1	Lottie Moon
9.2	Annie Armstrong
9.3	State Missions
9.4	Harvest for the Hungry
9.5	Benevolent Fund
9.6	Building Fund
9.7	Other Designated

10. SAVINGS

10.1	Regular Savings Acct.

11. CD'S & MONEY MARKET FUNDS

11.1	CD's
11.2	NCNB Money Markets
11.3	Barnett Money Markets
11.4	Coast Certificate

12. TAX LIABILITY ACCOUNT

12.1	Judy Davis
12.2	Robert W. Culp
12.3	Dorothy Cobb
12.4	Fran Hoffman
12.5	Total Liability Balance

Figure 34

A special feature of the General Ledger is that it uses eight-column ledger sheets. (Such sheets are usually three columns.) The eight-column sheets, however, have an advantage in the church office because there is room to show debits, credits, balance, the accounting month, and totals of monthly budget, monthly actual, year-to-date budget, and year-to-date actual figures for the budgeted accounts (see Figure 35).

This will allow you to keep all the information together for any given account. You can see at a glance:

1. The date of the transaction.
2. The payee (person or company to whom the check is written) if amount is subtracted (debited) or the source if amount is added (credited).
3. The check number.
4. The amount of the debit or credit.
5. The account balance.
6. The amount of the budget allocated for one month.

Sunday School

Wilson Jones Form 10-8

	Date		Payee	Ck #	Debit (1)	Credit (2)	Balance (3)	(4)	Month Budget (5)	Month Actual (6)	Y-T-D Budget (7)	Y-T-D Actual (8)
1	Jan	1					6000 –					
2		12	Christ Centered B+M	1225	47 58 ✓		5955 42					
3		12	The Parable	1236	27 15 ✓		5928 27					
4		12	Sunday School Board	1241	9 38 ✓		5918 89					
5		12	" " "	CR		12 60 ✓	5931 49					
6		12	Nancy Nelson	1235	34 67 ✓		5896 82					
7		12	The Parable	1236	5 60 ✓		5891 22					
8		26	Christ Centered B+M	1264	1 75		5889 47					
9		26	Sunday School	1274	25 20 ✓		5864 27					
10		26	Weavers	1282	2 65 ✓		5861 62					
11		31	From Designated	—		25 20	5886 82					
12		31	Postage for January (Tax .19)	—	7 80 ✓		5879 02					
13		31	Petty Cash (Scissors) .48	—	6 22 ✓		5872 80					
14								Jan.	500 –	127 20	500 –	127 20
15	Feb	16	Artmaster	1345	7 40		5865 40					
16		16	The Parable	1355	1 50		5863 90					
17		28	Petty Cash	—	5 80		5858 10					
18		28	Postage for February	—	15 98		5842 12					
19		28	Printing for February	—	2 00		5840 12					
20								Feb.	500 –	32 68	1000 –	159 88
21	Mar	1	Material Services Dept.	1385	591 89		5248 23					
22		3	Bonnie Huntington	1393	12 50		5235 73					
23		9	Dussault Stationery Co.	1406	10 66		5225 07					
24		9	The Parable	1413	38 75		5186 32					
25		16	Sunday School Board	1437	16 08		5170 24					
26		31	Postage for March	-	10 40		5159 84					
27								Mar	500 00	680 28	1500 00	840 16
28	Apr	6	Christ Centered B+M	1478	5 20		5154 64					
29		6	Dussault Stationery	1483	6 29		5148 35					
30		6	D el greco's	1494	4 99		5143 36					

Figure 35

7. The total amount actually spent for the month.

8. The amount budgeted for the account for the year-to-date.

9. The total amount actually spent for the account for the year-to-date.

By having the totals together in the ledger, you can easily verify your work. For instance, in the example shown (Figure 35):

1. The previous month's balance (Column 3, Line 13), less this month's expenditures (Column 6, Line 20), must equal the current balance (Column 3, Line 19).

2. The previous month's year-to-date budget amount (Column 7, Line 14), plus the current month's budget amount (Column 5, Line 20), is the new budget year-to-date (Column 7, Line 20).

3. The previous month's year-to-date actual amount, the amount actually spent for the year (Column 8, Line 14), plus the current month's actual amount (Column 6, Line 20), equals the new year-to-date actual amount (Column 8, Line 20).

All totals—monthly and year-to-date budget and actual figures—are completed and checked before being transferred to the financial statement (Chapter 11).

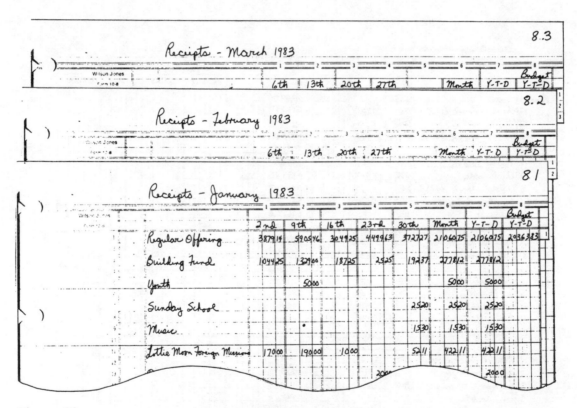

Figure 36

You will be able to double-check work for the whole year, if necessary, because all information is immediately available. If your books are checked by a volunteer committee or if department leaders want to look at their accounts, as is the case in many churches, they will be able to track the figures without having to dig into the files for records.

Another advantage of the eight-column ledger sheet is that it provides room for an entire month's offerings to be recorded and totaled. Prepare a page for each month, as shown in Figure 36, writing the date for each Sunday at the top of the columns.

Prepare one page for each designated fund. In addition, prepare one page for Miscellaneous Designated, which will be used to enter all monies that are not ordinary designated funds (see Figure 37).

Misc. Designated

9.7
Page 1

Wilson Jones
Form 10-8

					1	2	3	4	5	6	7	8
					Debit	Credit	Balance					
1	Jan	9	Youth Dept.	✓		50—	50—					
2		16	Dental Health Kits			30—	80—					
3		16	Revival Expenses	✓		50—	130—					
4		14	Danny Harvey	✓		10—	140—					
5		16	Newspaper Ad (Revival)	✓		185—	325—					
6		16	Counseling	✓		15—	340—					
7		23	Counseling	✓		100—	440—					
8		23	Detention Center	✓		20—	460—					
9		26	To Youth Dept.	—	50—		410—					
10		26	To Revival Expenses	—	50—		360—					
11		26	" " " (Ad.)	—	185—		175—					
12		21	David Gregory	1259	100—		75—					
13		30	Love Off - Revival	✓		1610—	1685—					
14		30	Revival Advertising	✓		420—	2105—					
15		30	Dental Kits	✓		5—	2110—					
16		30	Sunday School Budget	✓		25 20	2135 20					
17		30	Music Budget	✓		15 30	2150 50					
18		31	To Revival Expenses	—	420—		1730 50					
19		31	To Sunday School	—	25 20		1705 30					
20		31	To Music	—	15 30		1690—					
21		27	Joe Helms	1287	625—		1065—					
22		27	Dick Onarecker	1288	625—		440—					
23		29	Dr. Claude Rhea	1291	350—		90—					
24			Disbursed in January:				Music	Youth	Rev. Exp.	Rev. Love	Coun. ed.	S.S.
25							15 30	50—	50—	625—	100—	25 20
26									185—	625—		
27									420—	350—		
28							15 30	50—	655—	1600—	100—	25 20
29			Summary of Monies				D. Harvey	Counseling	Det. Center	Love Off.	D.H. Kits	
30			in Designated 1/31/83:				10—	15—	20—	10—	35—	

Figure 37

Prepare a page for each employee from whose payroll Withholding and Social Security (FICA) is deducted, and a page for total tax liabilities. Until payment is made by the church, this money is owed and must be accounted for in your record-keeping process. And finally, prepare separate pages for each savings account or investment fund. See Figure 38 for examples of the above.

At the top of each page in the General Ledger, write the name of the account and its corresponding number from the chart of accounts.

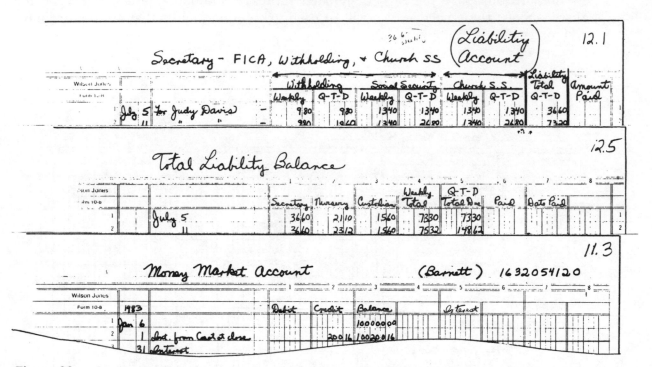

Figure 38

You will save considerable time in posting and retrieving information if you trim the pages as shown (Figure 39) to make a thumb index. Within each budget category, there should not be more than thirty subdivisions, so after you trim each page, it will be easy to find the page you are looking for quickly. Then arrange the pages in the post binder, using labeled dividers to separate each category (Figure 40).

The setup of the checkbook and the General Ledger provides ways of verifying your work, daily and monthly. With your adding machine, and the careful entry of figures, you will be able to keep an accurate record of your church's finances, easily reconcile the bank statement monthly, and produce a financial statement that will balance to the penny.

Figure 39

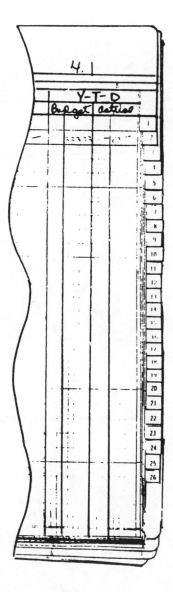

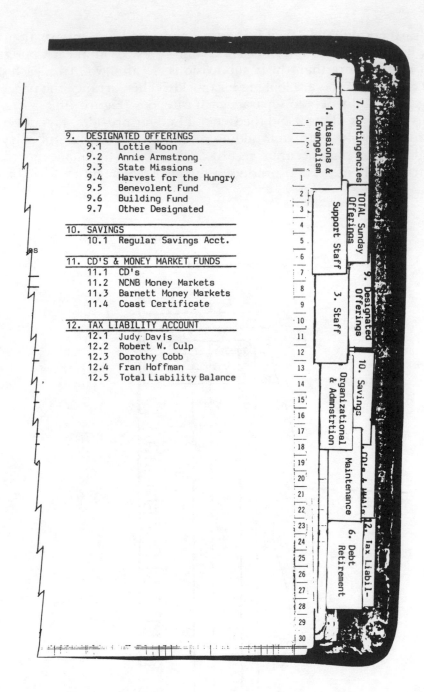

9.	DESIGNATED OFFERINGS	
	9.1	Lottie Moon
	9.2	Annie Armstrong
	9.3	State Missions
	9.4	Harvest for the Hungry
	9.5	Benevolent Fund
	9.6	Building Fund
	9.7	Other Designated

10.	SAVINGS	
	10.1	Regular Savings Acct.

11.	CD'S & MONEY MARKET FUNDS	
	11.1	CD's
	11.2	NCNB Money Markets
	11.3	Barnett Money Markets
	11.4	Coast Certificate

12.	TAX LIABILITY ACCOUNT	
	12.1	Judy Davis
	12.2	Robert W. Culp
	12.3	Dorothy Cobb
	12.4	Fran Hoffman
	12.5	Total Liability Balance

Figure 40

9

Receipts

Worshippers drop their tithes and offerings into the collection plate as it is passed. Sunday School members pass their envelopes to the class secretary. A dozen persons drop by the church office during the week to pick up a cassette tape of the pastor's sermon, and they each hand you $2.75. Seventy-five members attend the weekly fellowship supper and pay $1.50 each. Offering envelopes, with a note saying, "Sorry, I forgot my tithe on Sunday," arrive in the mail during the week.

Money is received in the church in many ways. How do you, as the bookkeeper, keep track of it? What can the church body and lay volunteers do to help in the record-keeping process?

CONTRIBUTION ENVELOPES

One church gives each member a box of numbered, predated envelopes to use for one year.

This system has certain advantages. The envelopes provide privacy (the person can prepare the offering at home), the individual can note what Sundays have not yet been given (a personalized calendar of giving), the numbers on the envelopes facilitate posting by the financial secretary, and the envelopes are not expensive.

The major disadvantage of this system is that some members lose their boxes of envelopes and "forget" to contribute.

Another church provides members with monthly sets of envelopes, which are mailed to their homes a week or two before the start of the new month. The envelopes, which are numbered and dated, also include the members' names and addresses, which personalizes the system (Figure 41).

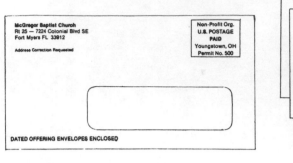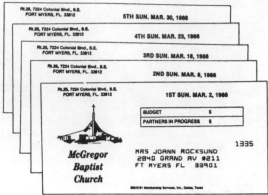

Figure 41

Although this method costs more, it quickly pays for itself because it reminds members monthly of their responsibility to support their church and its work. It is more extra work for the record keeper, however, because people constantly move and new members join and others leave, so updates, additions, and deletions must constantly be sent to the envelope service company.

Whichever system your church chooses, members should be very strongly encouraged by those in leadership to use their envelopes since they provide discipline in stewardship. Envelopes also make record keeping easier. Most people have the idea that the offering goes to the office and that the pastor, or the financial secretary, examines each check and posts the offerings from the checks on Monday morning. The congregation must be made to understand that this is simply not so. In almost every church surveyed, the financial secretary never sees the checks.

All too often, someone jots an intended designation on the corner of a check and drops it in the offering plate. Then the counting committee misses the notation, and when the committee brings the report back to the office, there is no indication that the money was earmarked for a special fund.

Then six months later, when a member receives his contribution record, he is upset that his special gift went into the general budget.

To avoid any possible error, encourage all members to use envelopes; to write any special designations on the envelopes; and to make sure that their name, date, and the amount(s) enclosed are clearly indicated on the envelope.

Some people don't like to write the amount(s) on the envelope because they are afraid someone might look through the collection and see how much they have given. Inform your church members that this wastes valuable time when the money is being counted. Encourage their assistance in the record-keeping process by requesting that they fill out their envelopes completely.

There will always be a handful of individuals who insist on putting loose checks in the offering plate, while other members and visitors put in loose bills and coins.

Some churches have a separate Sunday school offering and then a Sunday morning and a Sunday evening offering. Each offering is counted separately and then totaled on one form. In addition, Envelope, Loose Check, and Cash designations add to the confusion of counting the money.

HANDLING THE CHURCH'S MONEY

The tithes and offerings all end up in the same place—the checking account—and they are posted to the same budgeted or designated accounts. There really is no reason for keeping the offering bags separate to count the money. What is important is to:

1. Keep track of any designated monies.
2. Make sure envelopes have names and offering amounts recorded on them.
3. Count carefully, checking and double-checking all figures and totals.

MISCELLANEOUS RECEIPTS

All monies received in the church office during the week can be included with the deposit the following Monday morning. The procedure described in this chapter accounts for all designated funds, including reimbursements to budgeted accounts.

If you receive money during the week:

1. Make out a duplicate receipt for cash, and give one copy to the individual. (Receipts books are available from your office supply store.)
2. Put the money in an envelope and indicate the purpose for the money and the total enclosed. (For example, "*Tapes—$27.50.*" (One envelope for each category is sufficient.)
3. Make out an envelope for each loose offering check, and put the check in the envelope.
4. Put all the above in a bank bag and lock it up securely each evening.

On Sunday, the persons taking the bags to the bank will also take this bag. Give the individual responsible for removing the bag from the locked location a key.

COUNTING THE MONEY

In one church, the ushers pass the collection plate on Sunday morning and again in the evening. Each time, they place the offerings in a bank bag (provided by the bank), which is locked, and delivered by two persons to the bank's night depository. Two authorized counting committee members arrive at the bank on Monday morning to pick up the bags and, in a room provided by the bank, count the money.

In another church, the ushers deliver the collection to members of the finance committee, who, in turn, lock the offerings in the church safe. On the following morning, two persons come to the church, count the money, and take it to the bank.

The offerings should be either taken to the bank and deposited in the night depository or locked securely in the safe at church. Never take money home. Suspicion could be cast on persons taking money home, or they could be robbed. Even when the individual is trusted beyond a shadow of a doubt, it is not fair that such a responsibility is placed on his or her shoulders.

If the money is counted at church, be sure it is in a secured area and that at least two persons are present, not of the same family (this protects the family from any possible accusations should there be shortages).

In a small church, it is often difficult to build in a system of checks and balances.

In one church, where the same woman has been the financial secretary for ten years, a troublesome situation exists. The woman takes the money home after church, counts it herself, takes it to the bank herself, and makes the deposit.

No one in the church, except the new pastor, feels the need to make a change. "That's the way we've always done it" is the general opinion. This system places a burden on the person and gives no internal control of the church finances.

It is very important that counters do not rush through the counting process. "We really got done fast today," boasts one counter to the other. The natural inclination to "see how fast we can get done today" often results in errors. The main emphasis must be on careful, deliberate work.

MONEY-COUNTING PROCEDURES

Whether counted at the church or the bank, the following procedures will ensure accurate record keeping:

1. Empty the contents of the offering bag(s) onto the table. Separate into three piles: envelopes; loose checks; and loose bills and coins.
2. Work first on the envelopes. Open each one and verify that the amount written on the envelope is correct. (If it is not correct, write the correct amount on the envelope; circle and initial it as shown in Figure 42.) If the envelope has cash inside, write the word *Cash* on the envelope. Write the contributor's name on the envelope if it isn't there. Put the cash with the other loose cash, and place the checks in a separate pile.
3. What do you do about checks that are not in envelopes? There are two ways of accounting for these checks:
   (*a*) The first method is used when most of the congregation uses envelopes and there are very few loose checks. Use old budget envelopes (keep a supply with the counting committee's supplies, with outdated numbers and dates crossed out). Make an envelope for each loose check. Include name, amount, date, and any special designations that may be on the check.
   (*b*) When many contributors do not use envelopes, it is time-consuming to make

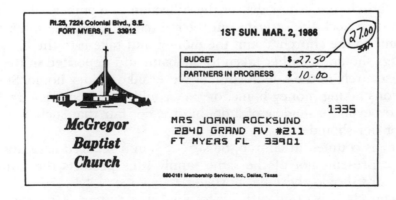

Figure 42

up an envelope for each one. In this case, the counters will place the loose checks in alphabetical order and list them on a Loose Checks form (see Fig. 43). It is very important to alphabetize the checks so the financial secretary can post these contributions quickly, without having to sort back and forth through the contribution records. Posting in alphabetical order reduces the possibility of error. Some volunteers complain that insufficient work space provided by the bank limits their ability to alphabetize the checks. (See Chapter 4 to learn how to alphabetize in a confined area.)

4. What about several designations being included in the same check or on the same envelope? Circle each designation and amount in red. (Red ink stands out, and red, if used consistently for items to be noted, will signal the financial secretary to pay special attention to what is listed.)

5. On a Designated Receipts form (printed on the back of the Counting Committee Report or on a separate sheet), make a heading for each designated offering (Building Fund, Benevolent, Children's Home, etc.). Then list each name and

			LOOSE CHECKS			
			Date 3/3/86			

| Name | Amounts | | | | | |
	Budget		PIP		Other	
Ackermann, Opal	15	-				
Adams, Erin	5	-				
Bisson, Scott	5	-				
Burton, Paulette	23	75	10	-	5	-
Cannon, Kelly	6	-				
Capps, Melissa	20	-				
Curry, Jim	20	-				
Daniel, Kathy	10	-	10	-		
Darby, Jim	25	-	15	-		
Edwards, Bob	35	-				
Eland, Bob	18	-	5	-		
Dober, Nicky	160	-	40	-		
Hayes, Tom	25	-	10	-		
Heathe, Dinny	5	-				
Holland, Dawn	3	-				
Jansen, Jill	10	-				
Johns, Daniel	12	-				
Kamp, Jeannie	5	-				
Kraus, Michella	5	-				
Lee, Scott	25	-				
Livingston, Sharon	30	-	20	-		
Mattingly, Pete	55	20	15	-		
McCullough, Bill	100	-				
McDowell, Roy	125	-				
Ocho, Bill	10	-	10	-		
Pack, Darlene	7	-	7	-		
Painter, Carol	25	-				

Figure 43

amount of offering as shown in Figure 44. Also indicate if the gift was paid by check or as cash. This is very important. The financial secretary has to have all the help she can get to make sure receipts and contributions are posted correctly.

	Date 1/16/83		
DESIGNATED RECEIPTS			
Amount	Name	Cash	Check
	Building Fund		
100.00	Kapple, Ted		✓
15.00	Wyman, Phil	✓	
20.00	Morris, Barnard	✓	
5.25	Conn, Debbie	✓	
7.00	Sperry, David		✓
40.00	Turner, Ralph		✓
187.25			
	Lottie Moon		
10.00	Morris, Barnard	✓	
10.00			
	Dental Health Kits		
10.00	Cohen, Elizabeth		✓
15.00	Smith, Paul		✓
5.00	Kalfleish, Edna		✓
30.00			
	Love Offering		
10.00	Morris, Barnard	✓	
10.00			
	Counseling		
15.00	Trotter, Carll		✓
	Revival (Advertising)		
185.00	Blackman, Betty		✓
	Revival Expenses		
50.00	Saunders, Glenn		✓

Figure 44

6. Total each fund. Write each designated amount on the Counting Committee Report, beside the name of the fund, as shown in Figure 45.

```
COUNTING COMMITTEE REPORT

Date            Jan. 16, 1983

Regular Offering                    _____
Designated Offerings'
   Building Fund            187.25
   Benevolent              _____
   Tapes                   _____
   Annie Armstrong         _____
   Lottie Moon               10.00
   Flowers                 _____
   Counseling-RPBCC        _____
   Dental Health Kits        30.00
   Love Offering             10.00
   Counseling (D.H.)         15.00
   Revival (Advertising)    185.00
   Revival (Expenses)        50.00
                           _____
                           _____
                           _____

TOTAL DESIGNATED OFFERINGS          _____

GRAND TOTAL OFFERINGS (Deposit)     _____

COMMITTEE:
                    _____
                    _____
                    _____
```

Figure 45

COUNTING COMMITTEE REPORT

Date _____Jan. 16, 1983_____

Regular Offering _____

Designated Offerings

Building Fund	187.25
Benevolent	
Tapes	
Annie Armstrong	
Lottie Moon	10.00
Flowers	
Counseling-RPBCC	
Dental Health Kits	30.00
Love Offering	10.00
Counseling (D.H.)	15.00
Revival (Advertising)	185.00
Revival (Expenses)	50.00

TOTAL DESIGNATED OFFERINGS → (487.25) ←

GRAND TOTAL OFFERINGS (Deposit) _____

COMMITTEE:

_____
_____
_____

Figure 46

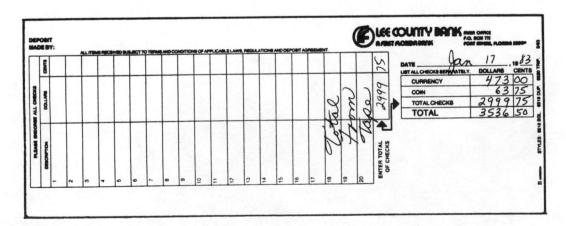

Figure 47

7. Total the designated money (Figure 46).
8. Count the currency twice to ensure accuracy and write the total on the deposit slip. Count the coins and enter the total. Then make an adding machine tape of all checks and enter that figure on the deposit slip. Total all three figures. (Note: Some banks require an itemized list of each check on the back of the deposit slip. However, most will accept a totaled adding machine tape, along with a deposit slip as shown in Figure 47. Check at your bank to see what is required.)
9. The grand total of the deposit, less the total of the designated offerings, is the amount of your budget offering. Add the budget and designated figures. Be sure that the total on the deposit slip equals the total on the counting committee report (Figure 48).
10. Use a rubber stamp, provided by the bank, to stamp the back of all checks. Generally the rubber stamp reads like this:

Pay to the order of
DOWNTOWN CHRISTIAN CHURCH
First National Bank
Account Number 123–456

11. Date and sign the Counting Committe Report (both committee members must sign).
12. Return the bag to the church office, along with three copies of the report. These are for the pastor, the financial secretary, and the treasurer. (If your church has a combination financial secretary-treasurer, make out the report in duplicate.)

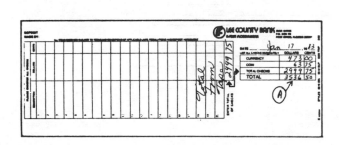

$$A - B = C$$
$$A = D$$

Figure 48

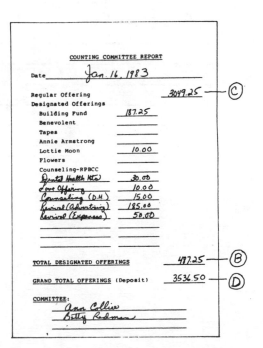

At this point, the financial secretary (or bookkeeper or church secretary) verifies the figures:

1. Deposit Slip and Counting Committee Report: Grand total agrees.
2. Designated Receipts Form: Each fund total is correct.
3. Counting Committee Report: Designated funds' totals have been recorded correctly and added correctly.
4. Loose Checks Form and Adding Machine Tape: Individual figures agree.
5. Offering Envelopes: All designated funds indicated on the Designated Receipts form are accounted for on the envelopes.

After this is completed, the envelopes and loose checks forms are ready to be posted to the contributors' records. Put them away until you are ready to post them.

Immediately enter the total deposit amount in the Checking Account Balance Record (see Figure 49).

CHECKING ACCOUNT BALANCE RECORD

Date	Description	Misc.	Disbursements and Debits	Deposits and Credits	Balance
					2,682.27
1/2/83	Deposit			5,093.39	+ 5,093.39
					7,775.66
1/5/83	Disbursements		698.02		− 698.02
					7,077.64
1/7/83	"		1,804.20		− 1,804.20
					5,273.44
1/9/83	Deposit			7,474.46	+ 7,474.46
					12,747.90
1/12/83	Disbursements		1,894.37		− 1,894.37
					10,853.53
1/13/83	"		1,695.72		− 1,695.72
					9,157.81
1/16/83	Deposit			3,536.50	+ 3,536.50
					12,694.31

Figure 49

HANDLING THE CHURCH'S MONEY

8.1

Receipts - January 1983

Wilson Jones Form 10-8

	2nd	9th	16th	23rd	30th	Month	Y-T-D	Budget Y-T-D
Regular Offering	3879.14	5905.46	3049.25					
Building Fund	1044.25	1329.00	187.25					
Youth		50.00						
Sunday School								
Music								
Lottie Moon Foreign Missions	170.00	190.00	10.00					
Dental Health Kits			30.00					
Revival Expenses			50.00					
Love Offering			10.00					
Counseling			15.00					
Detention Center								
Revival Advertising			185.00					
	5093.39	7474.46	3536.50					

Figure 50

Enter the total offering on the "Total Sunday Offerings" page in the General Ledger. List the budget offering and each designated amount. Write the total in pencil at the bottom of the column, as shown in Figure 50. (At the end of the month, all penciled totals across the bottom of the page must equal the total of Column 6. This is a cross-reference for accuracy.)

For designated money, enter each amount on its fund page in the ledger. If money has been received as a reimbursement for a budgeted account, enter the amount on the Miscellaneous Designated page (Figure 51). (Transferring the money to the budgeted accounts will be covered in Chapter 10.)

Keep your copy of the Counting Committee Report in a three-ring notebook or a file.

The final step in handling receipts is knowing how much of the money in the checking account is available to spend.

Whereas some churches are fortunate enough to have an adequate cash flow, very often this is not the case. For example, one pastor says that he often has to "rob Peter to pay Paul," and although there might be a $5,000 balance in the checking account, $3,500 is designated, and he has $3,000 worth of bills to pay.

The form shown in Figure 52 enables you to keep track of available cash in the checking account. Make it out as follows:

1. Enter the checking account balance on the top line.
2. Go through the designated pages in the ledger, including the Total Tax Liability page (which shows that Withholding and Social Security payments have been

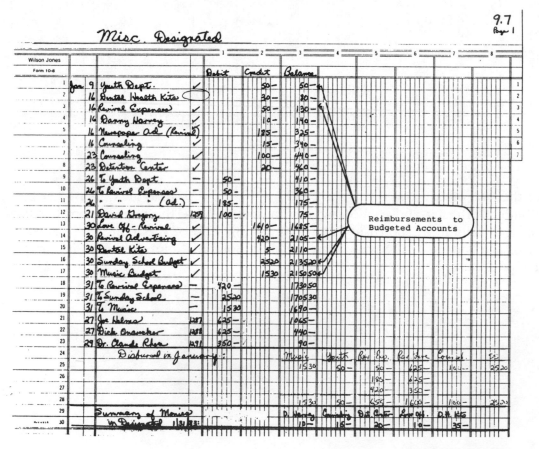

Figure 51

HANDLING THE CHURCH'S MONEY

```
Checking Balance          12,694.31

Designated:
Building Fund              6,212.00
Missions                   3,173.50
Children's Home              —
Memorial                      50.00
Benevolence                   67.50
Taxes                        112.00
Misc. Designated             450.00
_____         _____
_____         _____

Total Designated          10,065.00
  (Subtract from
  checking balance)

= Money Available          2,629.31


To Pay This Week           2,593.86




Date    1/17/83
Initials  CW
```

Figure 52

deducted from wages but not yet paid to the Internal Revenue Service). Write the amounts of each on the form.

3. Add the total designated.
4. Subtract the total designated from the checking balance. This is the amount you have available to spend.
5. Add up the total of the bills to be paid for the week. Enter the amount on the form.
6. Compare the results and note whether you will have enough available or whether you will have to hold off paying some bills until the following week.
7. Date and initial the form, and clip it inside the front cover of the checking notebook.

If you prepare this form every Monday morning after the money has been deposited and the entries are made on appropriate ledger pages, you will always know where the church stands financially.

10

Disbursements

Payments should be made by check for all goods and services. The only exception would be a Petty Cash fund used for small purchases or in emergencies.

PETTY CASH

The postman delivers a letter to you with postage due. A nursery worker gives you a receipt for $1.75 for a package of cookies for the children. The custodian, who has been cutting the lawn, rushes in to tell you he has run out of gas for the mower and has no cash to buy more.

An established Petty Cash fund, from $10.00 to $25.00, allows you to pay these small amounts without taking money out of your pocket or having to write a check.

To set up the fund, write a check for an agreed-upon amount (for example, $25.00). Charge the Miscellaneous account, or, if you do not have such an account in your budget, charge Office Supplies. At the end of the month, you will credit (add back into) this account, and debit (subtract from) the actual accounts for which the amounts were used.

Make the check out to Petty Cash. Request small bills and several dollars worth of change from the bank teller.

Order a supply of Petty Cash vouchers from an office supply store. One such voucher is the Ampad Efficiency Line 23-140, as shown in Figure 53.

Keep the money and vouchers in a small cash box, zippered bank pouch, or a large envelope, which is locked up when you are not in the office.

The fund is kept separate from all other monies in the church office. For instance if you have a tape ministry and someone pays cash for a tape, you would not put that money in Petty Cash.

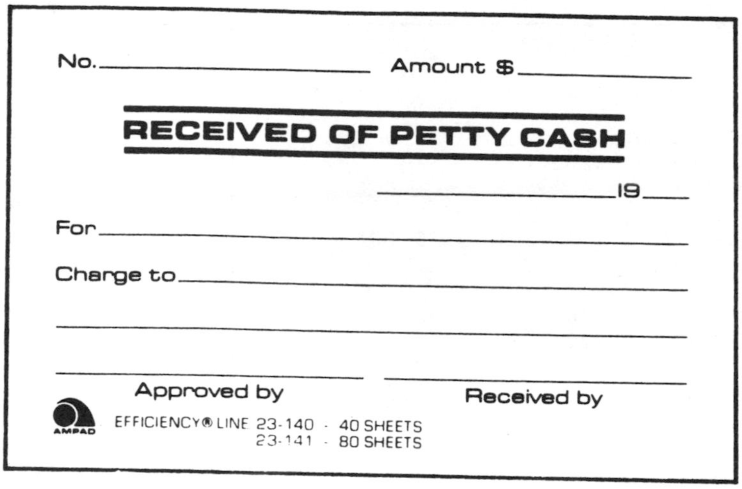
No. ____________ Amount $ ________

RECEIVED OF PETTY CASH

____________ 19___

For ____________

Charge to ____________

____

Approved by ____________ Received by ____________

AMPAD EFFICIENCY® LINE 23-140 · 40 SHEETS
23-141 · 80 SHEETS

Figure 53

At the end of the month, the Petty Cash account is reconciled and included on the financial statement (treasurer's report). One secretary who had been at a church for many years had the habit of dumping all loose change into the Petty Cash fund, including postage reimbursements and tape money, and she did not account for the monies. Her financial statement, therefore, was never accurate. Following an examination by an audit committee, it was decided that the church should hire another secretary who would be more careful with the church's money.

For each withdrawal from Petty Cash, a voucher must be filled out; it must include the amount, the date of withdrawal, the purpose of the payment, and the account to be charged. The slip must be signed by the person who receives the money.

This fund should be handled by one person only. A newly hired secretary in one church was amazed to find that the youth pastor and his adult workers freely dipped into Petty Cash, which was kept in a drawer that was open during Sunday School and evening services. Frequently cash was missing and not accounted for by a voucher. The workers had the misconception that the money was available for "whatever they needed," even pizza for the youth after the evening service.

At the end of the month, total the Petty Cash vouchers. Subtract this total from the beginning balance (in this example, $25.00). The balance must equal the actual remaining cash. If it does not, the account originally charged (in this case, Miscellaneous) absorbs the difference. Determine to be more careful about filling out Petty Cash vouchers in the future.

Total the vouchers for each account to be charged and prepare a statement. For the example shown in Figure 54 when entries are made in the ledger:

1. The total $7.97 is added back into the Miscellaneous account.
2. Each account charged, Building and Grounds, Postage, and Nursery Supplies, has the amount subtracted from its budgeted amount.

Some churches wait until the Petty Cash fund is completely depleted before reimbursing it. Others write a check at the end of each month in the amount of the depletion.

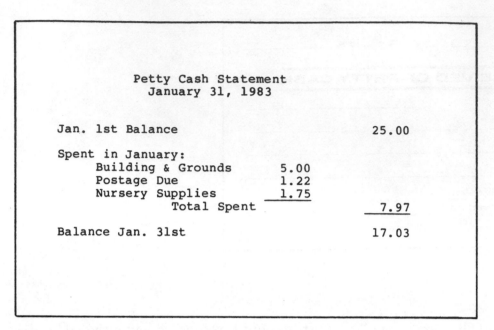

```
                    Petty Cash Statement
                     January 31, 1983


      Jan. 1st Balance                          25.00

      Spent in January:
           Building & Grounds        5.00
           Postage Due               1.22
           Nursery Supplies          1.75
                     Total Spent                 7.97

      Balance Jan. 31st                         17.03
```

Figure 54

If the amount spent is small, you may prefer to reimburse the account every other month or when it falls below a predetermined level.

INVOICES AND DELIVERY SLIPS

Invoices arrive daily in the mail. Delivery persons and church members drop delivery slips on your desk. Monthly statements and bills accumulate, waiting to be paid.

How do you handle the paperwork associated with accounts payable? Shuffling papers is a tremendous waste of time. Here is a way to eliminate shuffling and to handle paperwork only when necessary:

1. Purchase file pockets. These are file folders with closed sides that will keep small pieces of paper from falling out (Fig. 55). You will need six pockets.
2. With a black marker, label one pocket Delivery Slips and Invoices, where you will put the slips and invoices that will be paid when a monthly statement is mailed to you.
3. Number the remaining pockets 1 through 5, as shown in the figure. These numbers correspond to the weeks in the month.
4. In pencil, lightly write the dates for the current month beside the numbers.
5. Place the six folders in your desk drawer or in a desk-top file, and keep it at your fingertips. The current week should be in front. Suppose it is the second week of January. The figure shows how the file pockets should be arranged.
6. Place delivery slips, and invoices for which a monthly statement will be mailed to you, into the Delivery Slips and Invoices pocket. When a monthly statement comes

HANDLING THE CHURCH'S MONEY

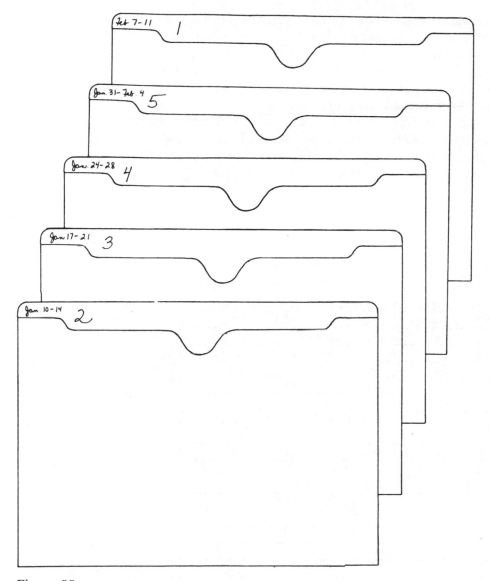

Figure 55

in, pull the slips from this pocket, match to the invoices listed on the statement, and staple them to the back of the statement.

7. For statements with supporting delivery slips and invoices attached and for invoices to be paid that will not have a monthly statement mailed to you, determine when the bill is to be paid and place that bill in the appropriate pocket. For example, if you receive an electric bill that will not be paid until the fourth week of the month, and it is only the second week, you would drop that bill in "4." You will not always use the fifth pocket. In the figure, the final day of the month is the fifth Monday, so the pocket is used.

8. For payments that have no bill or supporting document, such as bank loans or payroll, prepare a page for each payable, which then rotates as the disbursement

is made for each period. For example, one church has a monthly mortgage payment. The bank has supplied a book of coupons, one of which is to be mailed each month with the payment, but there is no supporting document for the church's file. Figure 56 shows how the record of the payment is kept.

Figure 57 is a payroll record that shows payments to the church secretary; it illustrates how the form is used over and over again. It is very easy to see, at any time, exactly what has been paid, the date it was paid, and the check number.

These multiple-use vouchers are rotated through the Payables Pockets. After payments are entered on the Cash Disbursements Journal pages, the vouchers are put into the pockets for the next week or month to be paid.

Paid To:	First National Bank		
	P. O. 12345	Account Charged	Debt Reduction
	Fort Myers, FL 33911	Account Number	7.1

-----Date Due-----	-----Amount-----	-------Date Paid-------	---Check Number---
1/20/85	1,704.20	PAID JAN 1 6 1985	1269
2/20/85	"	PAID FEB 1 8 1985	1343
3/20/85	"	PAID MAR 1 8 1985	1425
4/20/85	"	PAID APR 1 7 1985	1497
5/20/85	"	PAID MAY 1 6 1985	1550
6/20/85	"	PAID JUN 1 8 1985	1637
7/20/85	"	PAID JUL 1 8 1985	1708
8/20/85	"	PAID AUG 1 8 1985	1774
9/20/85	"	PAID SEP 1 7 1985	1856
10/20/85	"	PAID OCT 1 8 1985	1932
11/20/85	"	PAID NOV 1 8 1985	1998
12/20/85	"	PAID DEC 1 8 1985	2078

Figure 56

HANDLING THE CHURCH'S MONEY

Paid To _Judy Davis_   Account Charged _Secretary_

                                                    Account Number _2.1_

1985

Date Due	Gross Pay	--WH--	--SS--	*-C-SS-	-Net Pay-	------Date Paid------	Check -Number-
Jan 4	289.00	22.00	20.52	20.52	246.48	PAID JAN 2 1985	1207
11	289.00	22.00	20.52	20.52	246.48	PAID JAN 9 1985	1239
18	289.00	22.00	20.52	20.52	246.48	PAID JAN 16 1985	1255
25	289.00	22.00	20.52	20.52	246.48	PAID JAN 23 1985	1280
Feb 1	289.00	22.00	20.52	20.52	246.48	PAID JAN 30 1985	1294
8	289.00	22.00	20.52	20.52	246.48	PAID FEB 6 1985	1313
15	289.00	22.00	20.52	20.52	246.48	PAID FEB 13 1985	1333
22	289.00	22.00	20.52	20.52	246.48	PAID FEB 20 1985	1356
Mar 1	289.00	22.00	20.52	20.52	246.48	PAID FEB 27 1985	1368
8	289.00	22.00	20.52	20.52	246.48	PAID MAR 6 1985	1394
15	289.00	22.00	20.52	20.52	246.48	PAID MAR 13 1985	1416
22	289.00	22.00	20.52	20.52	246.48	PAID MAR 20 1985	1436
29	289.00	22.00	20.52	20.52	246.48	PAID MAR 27 1985	1450
Apr 5	289.00	22.00	20.52	20.52	246.48	PAID APR 3 1985	1458
12	289.00	22.00	20.52	20.52	246.48	PAID APR 10 1985	1445
19	289.00	22.00	20.52	20.52	246.48	PAID APR 17 1985	1494
26	289.00	22.00	20.52	20.52	246.48	PAID APR 24 1985	1505
May 3	289.00	22.00	20.52	20.52	246.48	PAID MAY 1 1985	1526
10	289.00	22.00	20.52	20.52	246.48	PAID MAY 8 1985	1533
17	289.00	22.00	20.52	20.52	246.48	PAID MAY 15 1985	1553
24	289.00	22.00	20.52	20.52	246.48	PAID MAY 22 1985	1569
31	289.00	22.00	20.52	20.52	246.48	PAID MAY 29 1985	1588
Jun 7	289.00	22.00	20.52	20.52	246.48	PAID JUN 5 1985	1616
14	289.00	22.00	20.52	20.52	246.48	PAID JUN 12 1985	1625
21	289.00	22.00	20.52	20.52	246.48	PAID JUN 19 1985	1642
28	289.00	22.00	20.52	20.52	246.48	PAID JUN 26 1985	1657

* Church's Portion; Not deducted from Gross Pay.

Figure 57

PAYING THE BILLS

Paying the bills does not have to be a frustrating experience. Prepare your current week's payables before you begin to write checks:

1. For each item, be sure supporting invoices or delivery slips have been attached.
2. Write on each item what account is to be charged. If you are unable to determine the account to be charged, do not pay the bill until you are certain that the purchase was made by someone with the authorization to do so.
3. If multiple accounts are to be charged, indicate the individual accounts and the amounts, and be sure the total is accurate. For example, you receive a monthly statement for $582.00 from the Christian bookstore. Invoices, which you have attached to the statement, indicate the following:

Music Department	155.00
Sunday School Literature	325.00
Youth Supplies	62.00
Office Supplies	12.00
Library	33.00
Total	582.00

You will use the figures for each budgeted account when you prepare a Disbursement Journal sheet for the day's payments.

4. For each payment, detach any remittance copy, prepare an envelope (if one has not been included with the bill), and clip the remittance copy and envelope behind the papers.

5. For any payments that do not have a statement or invoice, it is absolutely necessary to prepare a source document for your files. For example, the youth minister asks you for a check to pay for pizza for the Sunday night afterglow, but he doesn't have a bill or receipt. Request for Check forms are available at any office supply store, or you can use the form shown in Figure 58, which is the one currently used at McGregor.

6. Alphabetize the bills according to whom the check will be made out. You are now ready to write checks.

WRITING CHECKS

If possible, write checks at a certain time of day. By avoiding interruptions and concentrating on the task at hand, you will avoid errors that could be caused by distractions.

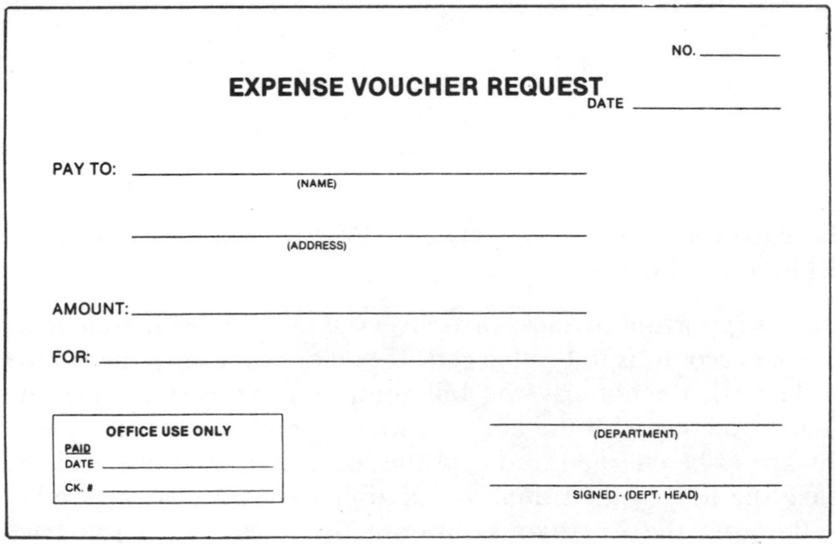

Figure 58

HANDLING THE CHURCH'S MONEY

Checks can be written by hand, or, preferably, typed, as shown in Figure 59, following this procedure:

1. Enter the date, which should be today's date.
2. "Pay to the order of" should be completed by filling in the name of a person or company shown on the bill. (Never make checks payable to "cash," because if the check is lost, whoever found it would be able to cash it. The only exception is for Petty Cash).
3. Immediately beside the dollar sign, write the total in numerals. Do not leave space between the dollar sign and the first numeral. Use a decimal point and enter the cents; enter zeroes if the amount is for an exact dollar figure.
4. On the next line, beginning at the extreme left, spell out the total amount. For cents, indicate a fraction, with the actual cents over 100. Use a straight line or wavy line or dashes to fill in the unused part of the line.
5. On the Memo line, write the statement or invoice number.
6. Attach the check to the support document, by sliding it under the paperclip that holds the envelope and remittance copy together.
7. As you finish each check and attach it to the document, turn the document face down, so the bills remain in alphabetical order.

After you have finished typing or writing all the checks, mark each document paid, indicating the date the payment was made. A date stamp is available at your local office supply store, similar to those shown in Figure 60, on which the word *PAID* is included with the date

First, go through the disbursements and stamp all bills (red ink makes the date stand out). As you do this, glance over the checks, looking for errors.

Second, go through the pile again. Write the check number on each document, beside the "paid" stamp. Again, verify that the amounts are correct.

Have the checks signed, or sign them yourself, keeping the documents in alphabetical order.

This careful, methodical system allows you to avoid errors in preparing checks and eliminates the frustration of trying to find errors when you are reconciling your bank statement or preparing a financial statement at the end of the month.

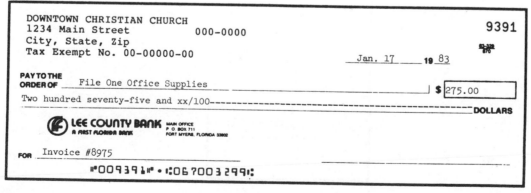

Figure 59

P A I D FEB 2 7 1986

IDL Dial-A-Phrase Dater   X-Stamper Dater & Paid

Figure 60

After the checks are signed, place them in their envelopes, along with any remittance copies. Keep the supporting documents in alphabetical order.

CASH DISBURSEMENTS JOURNAL

It is very important to immediately prepare the Cash Disbursements Journal sheet for the checks you have written. As mentioned before, for this system, check stubs are not used. The Cash Disbursements Journal sheet allows you to make detailed entries of all accounts being charged; check stubs do not. Just as you would immediately fill out a check stub, you must also immediately complete this form.

Before you begin typing the Cash Disbursements Journal sheet, make an adding machine tape of all payments to be made (Figure 61).

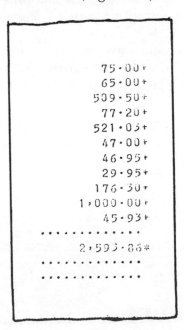

Figure 61

Fill out the Cash Disbursements Journal sheet (Figure 62) as follows:

1. Payee: Enter the name of the person (last name first, followed by first name) or company to whom the check is made out. *The* is not considered an alphabetical part of the name. Place it at the end of the name, preceded by a comma.
2. Check Number: This is the number you have written on the document.
3. Account charged:
   (*a*) Account Name. Enter the name of the budgeted account to be charged. Note that for each account charged, you will make a separate one-line entry.
   (*b*) No. (Number). This refers to the number of the budgeted account shown on your chart of accounts. On each line an account name is entered on, type or draw a line. These lines will be used later when you are ready to post the accounts in the ledger. Do not use this column for a Total line.
   (*c*) Amount. If a check is charged to only one account, leave this column blank. If a check is to be charged to more than one account, however, enter the amount for each account beside the account charged.
   (*d*) Posted. Type or draw a line. These lines will be used when you post accounts to the ledger. Do not use this column for a Total line.
4. Total: If a check is charged to one account, the amount is entered here. If the check is charged to more than one account, the total amount of the check is entered here.
5. Add any figures in the Amount column on the Cash Disbursements Journal sheet and verify that the Total figure for that payee is correct (Figure 63).

CASH DISBURSEMENTS JOURNAL

Payee	Check No.	Account Charged			Posted	Total
		Account Name	No.	Amount		
Burkhart, Stan	1617	Custodian thru 1/14/83	——		——	75.00
Cobb, Dorothy	1618	Nursery thru 1/14/83	——		——	65.00
Elgin Company	1619	Furnishings	——	350.00	——	
	1619	Printing Supplies	——	128.00	——	
	1619	Building Maintenance	——	31.50	——	
	1619	Total				509.50
Eli-Witt Company	1620	Kitchen Supplies	——	66.80	——	
	1620	Building Maintenance	——	10.40	——	
	1620	Total				77.20
Florida Power & Light Co.	1621	Electric	——		——	521.03
Postmaster	1622	Postage	——		——	47.00
Quickprint	1623	Office Supplies	——		——	46.95
Radio Shack	1624	Worker Training	——		——	29.95
Sullivan, Janet	1625	Secretary thru 1/21/83	——		——	176.30
		10.30 WH & 13.40 SS				
		13.40 Church SS	——		——	
Trevor's Glass Shop	1626	Building Fund	——		——	1,000.00
Weaver's	1627	Office Supplies	——		——	45.93

Date __Jan. 18, 1983__   Total Disbursed This Date ___2,593.86___   8

Figure 62

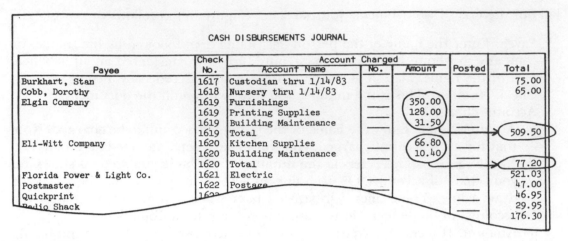

| Payee | Check No. | Account Charged | | | Posted | Total |
		Account Name	No.	Amount		
Burkhart, Stan	1617	Custodian thru 1/14/83	—		—	75.00
Cobb, Dorothy	1618	Nursery thru 1/14/83	—		—	65.00
Elgin Company	1619	Furnishings	—	350.00	—	
	1619	Printing Supplies	—	128.00	—	
	1619	Building Maintenance	—	31.50	—	
	1619	Total				509.50
Eli-Witt Company	1620	Kitchen Supplies	—	66.80	—	
	1620	Building Maintenance	—	10.40	—	
	1620	Total				77.20
Florida Power & Light Co.	1621	Electric			—	521.03
Postmaster	1622	Postage			—	47.00
Quickprint	1623				—	46.95
Radio Shack						29.95
						176.30

CASH DISBURSEMENTS JOURNAL

Figure 63

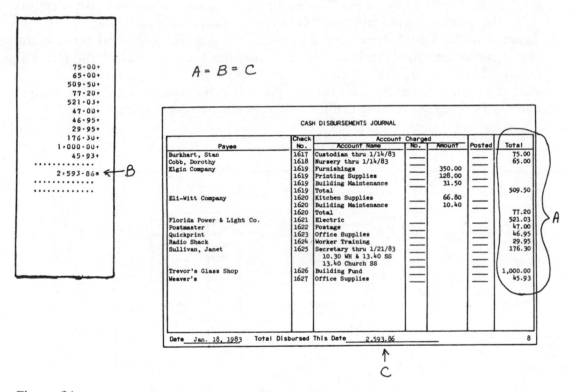

$A = B = C$

```
   75·00*
   65·00*
  509·50*
   77·20*
  521·03*
   47·00*
   46·95*
   29·95*
  176·30*
1·000·00*
   45·93*
············
2·593·86*   ← B
············
············
```

| Payee | Check No. | Account Charged | | | Posted | Total |
		Account Name	No.	Amount		
Burkhart, Stan	1617	Custodian thru 1/14/83	—		—	75.00
Cobb, Dorothy	1618	Nursery thru 1/14/83	—		—	65.00
Elgin Company	1619	Furnishings	—	350.00	—	
	1619	Printing Supplies	—	128.00	—	
	1619	Building Maintenance	—	31.50	—	
	1619	Total				509.50
Eli-Witt Company	1620	Kitchen Supplies	—	66.80	—	
	1620	Building Maintenance	—	10.40	—	
	1620	Total				77.20
Florida Power & Light Co.	1621	Electric			—	521.03
Postmaster	1622	Postage			—	47.00
Quickprint	1623	Office Supplies			—	46.95
Radio Shack	1624	Worker Training			—	29.95
Sullivan, Janet	1625	Secretary thru 1/21/83	—		—	176.30
		10.30 WH & 13.40 SS	—		—	
		13.40 Church SS	—		—	
Trevor's Glass Shop	1626	Building Fund	—		—	1,000.00
Weaver's	1627	Office Supplies	—		—	45.93

CASH DISBURSEMENTS JOURNAL

Date Jan. 18, 1983   Total Disbursed This Date ___ 2,593.86 _____   8

↑
C

Figure 64

6. Add the Total column, and verify that it agrees with the total of the adding machine tape (Figure 64).

7. When you're sure that all amounts are correct, enter the total disbursed this date at the bottom of the page, as shown in the figure.

8. At the lower left-hand corner, put today's date. If more than one page is used for a date, enter "Page 1 of ___," etc., below the date. Also if more than one page

is used, do not put the total at the bottom of the first page; enter it on the last page.

9. At the lower right-hand corner of the page, enter the page number. Pages are numbered consecutively, beginning with "1" at the start of each month.

10. Finally the total at the bottom of the page is entered on the Checking Account Balance Record, as shown in Figure 65, and subtracted from the checking account balance.

If you make a mistake and a check must be voided, keep that check with your source documents. Its number must be entered on the Cash Disbursements Journal sheet be-

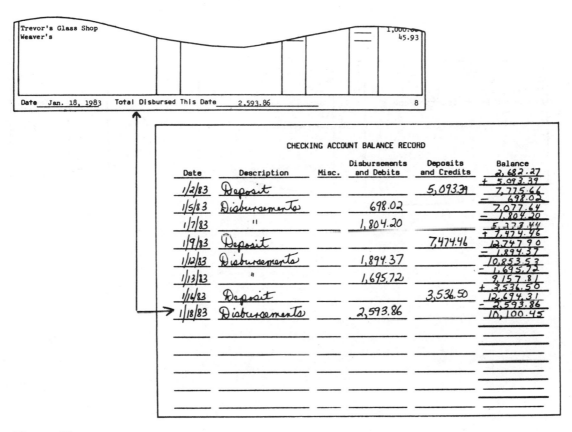

Figure 65

cause all check numbers must be accounted for. For a voided check, write VOID in the Payee and the Account Name columns (Figure 66)

Put the Cash Disbursements form in the checking notebook, before the previously entered page.

File the disbursement records, the supporting documents, in the Accounts Paid file.

You are now ready to post the disbursements to the General Ledger. This does not have to be done immediately, though. Do your posting when you have time, but be sure to complete this task weekly, so your book-keeping records are up-to-date.

CASH DISBURSEMENTS JOURNAL

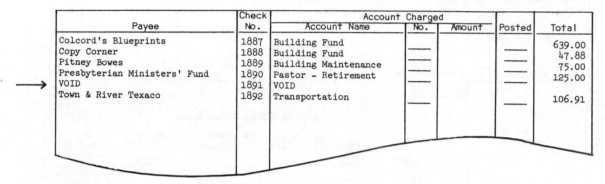

Payee	Check No.	Account Charged			Posted	Total
		Account Name	No.	Amount		
Colcord's Blueprints	1887	Building Fund	___		___	639.00
Copy Corner	1888	Building Fund	___		___	47.88
Pitney Bowes	1889	Building Maintenance	___		___	75.00
Presbyterian Ministers' Fund	1890	Pastor - Retirement	___		___	125.00
VOID	1891	VOID	___			
Town & River Texaco	1892	Transportation	___		___	106.91

Figure 66

HANDLING THE CHURCH'S MONEY

11

Preparing the Financial Report

Church members have a right to know if the money they have contributed has been wisely spent. Now that you have recorded the receipts and paid the bills, how is the congregation told about the current financial status of the church?

The preparation of a Financial Statement conveys this information. The Financial Statement, also called the Treasurer's Report, is prepared monthly. In some churches, the report is presented to the entire church body at a business meeting; in other churches, financial reports are reviewed only by the financial committee or administrative board.

In preparation for this report, it is necessary to:

1. Post all disbursements to the General Ledger.
2. Reconcile the bank statement.
3. Enter in the General Ledger any adjustments found when reconciling the bank statement, such as errors in addition or subtraction, bank charges, and credits.
4. Enter in the General Ledger any petty cash or other miscellaneous adjustments.
5. "Close" the ledger sheets.

POSTING TO THE GENERAL LEDGER

All disbursements must be posted in the General Ledger. This is easily accomplished by following these instructions:

1. Referring to the Chart of Accounts, write the account numbers on the Cash Disbursements Journal sheets, as shown in Figure 67.
2. On the corresponding page in the ledger, enter the payee, the check number, and

		CASH DISBURSEMENTS JOURNAL				

| | Check | Account Charged | | | | |
Payee	No.	Account Name	No.	Amount	Posted	Total
Burkhart, Stan	1617	Custodian thru 1/14/83	2.3		___	75.00
Cobb, Dorothy	1618	Nursery thru 1/14/83	2.2		___	65.00
Elgin Company	1619	Furnishings	7.1	350.00	___	
	1619	Printing Supplies	4.10	128.00	___	
	1619	Building Maintenance	5.3	31.50	___	
	1619	Total				509.50
Eli-Witt Company	1620	Kitchen Supplies	4.14	66.80	___	
	1620	Building Maintenance	5.3	10.40		
	1620	Total				77.20
Florida Power & Light Co.	1621	Electric	5.1		___	521.03
Postmaster	1622	Postage	4.9		___	47.00
Quickprint	1623	Office Supplies	4.8		___	46.95
Radio Shack	1624	Worker Training	4.19		___	29.95
Sullivan, Janet	1625	Secretary thru 1/21/83	2.1		___	176.30
		10.30 WH & 13.40 SS	12.1		___	
		13.40 Church SS	12.1			
Trevor's Glass Shop	1626	Building Fund	9.6		___	1,000.00
Weaver's	1627	Office Supplies	4.8		___	45.93

Date___Jan. 18, 1983___   Total Disbursed This Date___2,593.86___   8

Figure 67

the total charged to the account. For disbursements, the Debit column is used to enter these figures, which are subtracted from the budgeted total (Balance).

3. As you make each entry in the ledger, place a check mark on the line under the Posted column on the corresponding line on the Cash Disbursements Journal page.

Notice that in the example given in Figure 68, the payment to Elgin Company has been entered on the ledger pages for Furnishings, Printing Supplies, and Building Maintenance.

Note also that the secretary's disbursement (Figure 69) includes two additional lines. The first one shows the amounts of Withholding and Social Security deducted from her gross pay. The second line indicates the amount of the church's

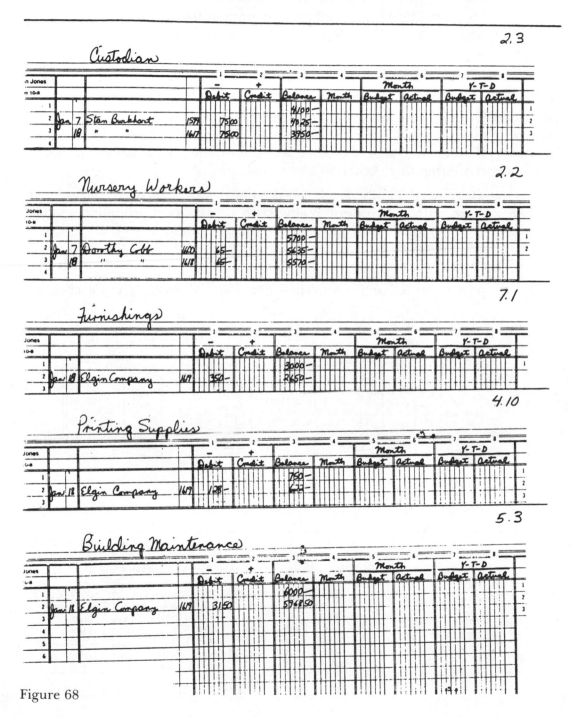

CASH DISBURSEMENTS JOURNAL

Payee	Check No.	Account Charged			Posted	Total
		Account Name	No.	Amount		
Burkhart, Stan	1617	Custodian thru 1/14/83	2.3		✓	75.00
Cobb, Dorothy	1618	Nursery thru 1/14/83	2.2		✓	65.00
Elgin Company	1619	Furnishings	7.1	350.00	✓	
	1619	Printing Supplies	4.10	128.00	✓	
	1619	Building Maintenance	5.3	31.50	✓	
	1619	Total				509.50
	1620	Kitchen				

Figure 68

portion of Social Security that is to be paid to the Internal Revenue Service. These two lines do not have any dollar amounts indicated in the Amount or Total column, because these payments were not made then. The inclusion of this information serves as a reminder to enter the amounts on the secretary's Tax Liability page (Figure 70), where the Withholding and Social Security that have been deducted from earnings, but that have not yet been paid to the Internal Revenue Service, are kept. (This information shows how much money in the checking account is designated for taxes. The church is responsible for all money withheld for taxes until it is paid to the Internal Revenue Service. It is very important not to spend this money.)

If taxes are withheld for more than one employee, it is helpful to have one page that shows all due taxes (Figure 71), although this is optional.

Designated Funds, those monies given to the church that are apart from regular budgeted funds, is a fly in the ointment for many financial workers. As discussed in Chapter 8, a separate page should be set up for each regular category, that is, a designated offering that occurs on a regular basis.

Occasional Designated Funds do not need to be kept on separate pages. (For example, at one church, an offering designated for the local juvenile detention home is given by the Sunday School class two or three times a year. Or a revival is held, and one member gives $185.00 to pay for advertising in the local newspaper. This money coming into the church is designated for a specific cause.)

Set up one page in the ledger for Miscellaneous Designated funds. For each entry

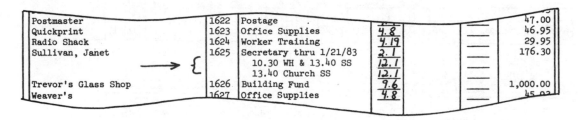

Figure 69

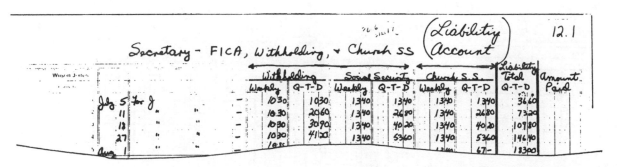

Figure 70

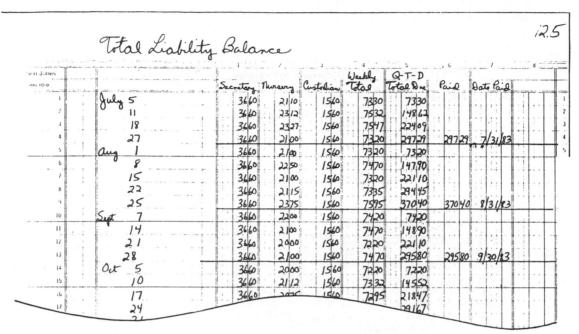

Figure 71

Figure 72

where money is added, enter the figure in the Credit column, and add the amount to the balance, but leave the Check Number or Budget column blank, as shown in Figure 72.

When the money is disbursed, an entry is made on the page to indicate the payee, and the check number is entered in the Check Number or Budget column (see Figure 73).

A check mark (√) is then placed in the column on the line where the amount was credited (see Figure 74). Enter the disbursed amount in the Debit column, and enter the new balance.

When money is a Reimbursement to a Budgeted Account, as when a youth leader reimburses the Youth account for cash advanced by the church, the entry is made on the Miscellaneous Designated page. Figure 75 shows an entry on January 9th (Line 1).

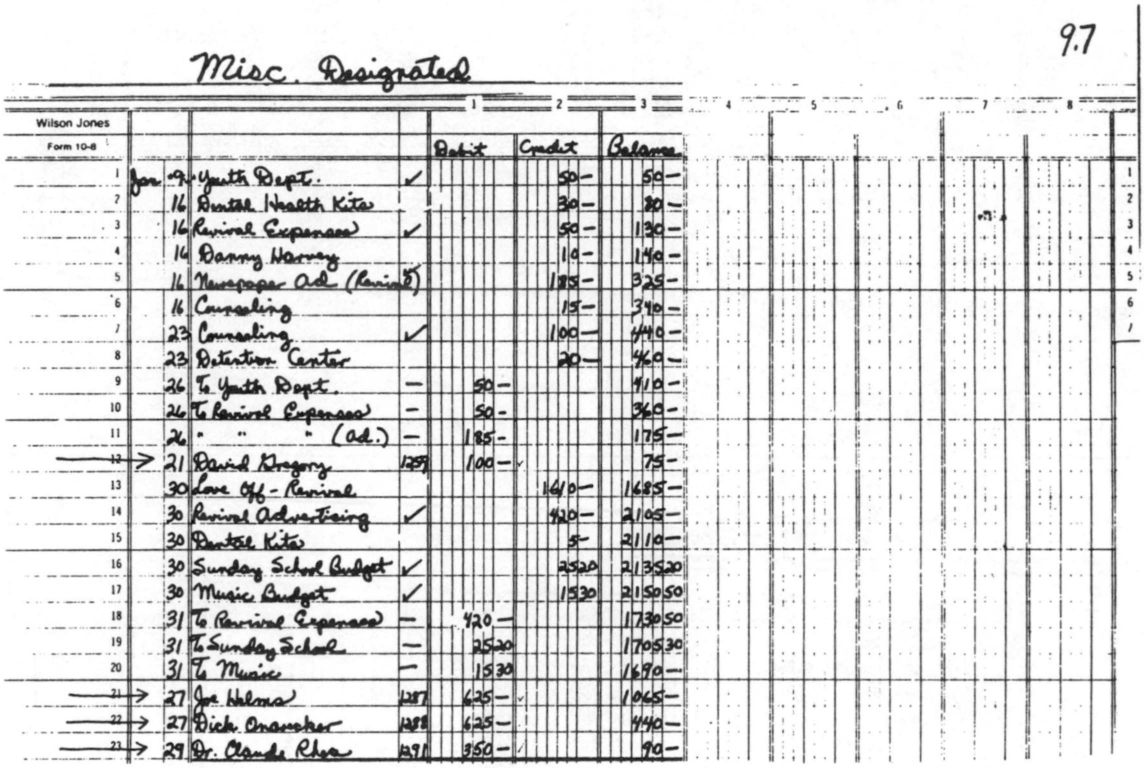

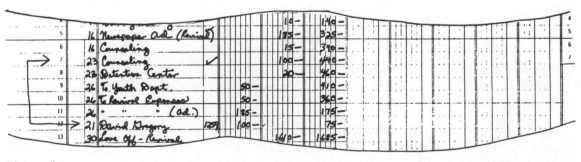

Figure 73

Figure 74

HANDLING THE CHURCH'S MONEY

On another line, To Youth is entered, with the amount in the debit column and subtracted from the balance. A dash (—) indicates that no check has been written. A check mark is placed in the same column on the line where the payment was first entered. These transactions are shown in Figure 76.

4. On the ledger page for Youth, From Designated is entered, the amount is added in the credit column, and the new balance is entered (see Figure 77).

By entering all designated monies on either a specified individual page or on the Miscellaneous Designated page, all designated funds are recorded. If you were to omit

Figure 75

Figure 76

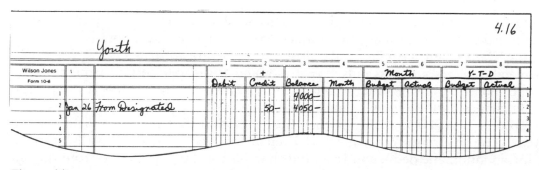

Figure 77

entering amounts on the Miscellaneous page, the probability of not posting and disbursing funds would be high.

Every entry on the Miscellaneous Designated page must be either:

1. A reimbursement to a budgeted account, which is transferred to that account, or
2. A designation paid by check.

Be sure that all disbursements are posted to the General Ledger before you attempt to prepare a financial statement.

RECONCILING THE BANK STATEMENT

Each month the bank mails a statement that indicates deposits made, checks deducted from the church's account, interest paid to the account, and any other charges or credits. Included with the statement are the canceled checks.

The amount shown on the statement as the ending balance is not the balance in your checkbook. Outstanding checks—those not yet paid by the bank—have not been subtracted from the bank's total balance. Also if the church made a deposit after the date the statement was prepared, that amount would not be included. It is your responsibility to account for these outstanding checks and deposits by reconciling the bank statement with the church's checkbook. When you are through, the amounts must be equal.

Judy, a new secretary at a 500-member church, phoned me one evening. "Please help me with the financial statement," she pleaded. "The business meeting is tomorrow, and I can't get the amounts to balance."

"Did the checkbook balance," I queried.

"Oh, yes," she replied, "It balanced right away."

After two hours of searching through the General Ledger for an error that would turn up the discrepancy, I decided to look at the checkbook and bank statement. An automatic bank draft for the pastor's hospitalization had not been entered in the checkbook. In addition, Judy had failed to enter the interest amount.

When Judy could not find the reason for the difference in the checkbook and bank statement, she "pulled a figure out of the air" to equalize the amounts. She didn't understand that this error would turn up when she attempted to prepare an accurate financial statement.

Remember, you cannot start with the wrong information and end up with the right answer.

During my first week at one church, the bank statement arrived in the mail. "Who usually reconciles the bank statement," I asked the minister of education.

"No one," he replied. "We just make sure the checks are returned."

Fortunately the account was only a year old, and I was able to go through all the checks, one month at a time, and reconcile the statements. When I was through, the checkbook balance and the bank balance were equal.

The process revealed that the pastor's hospitalization had not been paid for the entire year. The insurance company had been authorized to issue a bank draft—a request for an automatic deduction from the church's checking account—from the old checking account. After the new account was opened, the insurance company issued the draft to the bank. It was quickly returned to the company because the old account had been closed and the company canceled the insurance.

The former church secretary had subtracted the automatic insurance payment from the checking balance each month. But because no one ever reconciled the bank statement, the cancellation of the insurance was not detected. It had not occurred to anyone to issue a change of bank account number to the insurance company.

Fortunately for the pastor and his family, hospitalization had not been necessary for the year. Had there been an emergency, however, they would have been left with a tremendous debt.

Reconciling the year's bank statements also revealed many errors in addition and subtraction, and double entries and omissions in the checkbook. Three letter-sized pages listed the errors, ranging from 2¢ to $2,000. In the end, over $3,000 had been added incorrectly, and over $2,000 had been subtracted incorrectly. The resulting balance of approximately $1,000 had to be subtracted from the final checkbook balance, and the account was up-to-date.

Fortunately for the church body, the actual balance in the checkbook never fell below the amount required to cover checks at the bank, which would have resulted in bounced checks and much embarrassment.

At this same church, the person who prepared the financial statement "made it balance" each month, by plugging in a figure to balance the grand total. This is unfair to the church body. It is the responsibility of the financial secretary, or whoever keeps the books, to keep accurate financial records.

Here is how you can reconcile your bank statement with your checkbook:

1. Look over the bank statement (Figure 78, left) and note any debits or credits not entered in your checkbook. Examples are interest earned, charges for new checks, and automatic payments.
2. Enter these amounts in your checkbook. Place an X in the Misc. Column. This denotes an item for which a check was not written, and which is not posted in your General Ledger.
3. On the Checking Account Balance Record (Figure 78, right) verify that all deposits have been entered, placing a red check beside each deposit amount on the records and beside each deposit amount on the statement.
4. Verify that all daily disbursement totals for the month are entered on the checking account balance record. Place a red check beside the totals on the disbursement sheets and on the balance record sheets.
5. Add the bank interest earned. Place an X in the Misc. Column. In red, check off the interest shown on the record and on the statement.
6. Deduct bank charges. Place a red check beside the amounts on the checking account balance record and on the bank statement. Place an X in the Misc. Column.
7. Arrange the canceled checks—those checks paid by the bank and returned to you—in numerical order.
8. On the Cash Disbursements Journal Sheets (Figure 79, left) place a red check beside the total amount of each canceled check. As you come to check numbers that have not been canceled and returned, write each check number and its amount on the back of the statement (Figure 79, right) in the place provided.

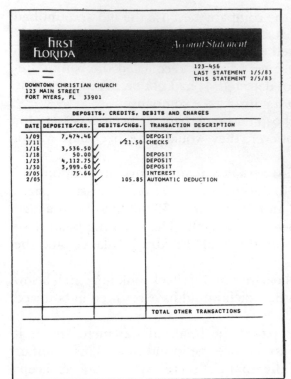

FIRST FLORIDA — *Account Statement*

123-456
LAST STATEMENT 1/5/83
THIS STATEMENT 2/5/83

DOWNTOWN CHRISTIAN CHURCH
123 MAIN STREET
FORT MYERS, FL 33901

DEPOSITS, CREDITS, DEBITS AND CHARGES

DATE	DEPOSITS/CRS.	DEBITS/CHGS.	TRANSACTION DESCRIPTION
1/09	7,474.46 ✓		DEPOSIT
1/11		✓21.50	CHECKS
1/16	3,536.50 ✓		DEPOSIT
1/18	50.00 ✓		DEPOSIT
1/23	4,112.75 ✓		DEPOSIT
1/30	3,999.60 ✓		DEPOSIT
2/05	75.66 ✓		INTEREST
2/05		105.85 ✓	AUTOMATIC DEDUCTION
		TOTAL OTHER TRANSACTIONS	

CHECKING ACCOUNT BALANCE RECORD

Date	Description	Misc.	Disbursements and Debits	Deposits and Credits	Balance
					2,682.27
1/2/83	Deposit			5,093.39 ✓	+5,093.39
					7,775.66
1/5/83	Disbursements		698.02		-698.02
					7,077.64
1/7/83	"		1,804.20		-1,804.20
					5,273.44
1/9/83	Deposit			7,474.46 ✓	+7,474.46
					12,747.90
1/12/83	Disbursements		1,894.37		-1,894.37
					10,853.53
1/13/83	"		1,695.72		-1,695.72
					9,157.81
1/16/83	Deposit			3,536.50 ✓	+3,536.50
					12,694.31
1/11/83	Check Printed	X	21.50 ✓		-21.50
					12,672.81
1/18/83	Deposit (Atlantic Stevens)			50.00	+50.00
					12,722.81
1/17/83	Disbursements		2,593.86		-2,593.86
					10,128.95
1/23/83	Deposit			4,112.75 ✓	+4,112.75
					14,241.70
1/25/83	Disbursements		1,963.00		-1,963.00
					12,278.70
1/30/83	Deposit			3,999.60 ✓	+3,999.60
					16,278.30

CHECKING ACCOUNT BALANCE RECORD

Date	Description	Misc.	Disbursements and Debits	Deposits and Credits	Balance
					16,278.30
2/05/83	January Interest	X		75.66 ✓	+75.66
					16,353.96
2/05/83	AD - Insurance	X	105.85 ✓		-105.85
					16,248.11

Figure 78

CASH DISBURSEMENTS JOURNAL

Payee	Check No.	Account Name	No.	Amount	Posted	Total
Burkhart, Stan	1617	Custodian thru 1/14/83	2.3		✓	75.00
Cobb, Dorothy	1618	Nursery thru 1/14/83	2.2		✓	65.00
Elgin Company	1619	Furnishings	7.1	350.00	✓	
	1619	Printing Supplies	4.10	128.00	✓	
	1619	Building Maintenance	5.3	31.50	✓	
	1619	Total				509.50
Eli-Witt Company	1620	Kitchen Supplies	4.4	66.80	✓	
	1620	Building Maintenance	5.3	10.40	✓	
	1620	Total				77.20
Florida Power & Light Co.	1621	Electric	5.1		✓	521.03
Postmaster	1622	Postage	4.9		✓	47.00
Quickprint	1623	Office Supplies	4.8		✓	46.95
Radio Shack	1624	Worker Training	4.19		✓	29.95
Sullivan, Janet	1625	Secretary thru 1/21/83	2.1		✓	176.30
		10.30 WH & 13.40 SS	12.1		✓	
		13.40 Church SS	12.1		✓	
Trevor's Glass Shop	1626	Building Fund	9.6		✓	1,000.00
Weaver's	1627	Office Supplies	4.8		✓	45.93

Date Jan. 18, 1983   Total Disbursed This Date   2,593.86   8

Please Reconcile This Statement at Once.
This form is provided to help you reconcile your bank statement.

Month Jan 19 83

Bank Balance on This Statement	Your Bank Book Balance	Checks Outstanding Not Charged to Account	
$ 20,573.11	$	Number 1600 $	75.00
		1613	3250.00
Add +	Add +	1626	1000.00
Deposits Not Credited in This Statement (if Any)	Interest		
$	$		
$			
	Total		
Subtract −	Subtract −		
Total Checks Outstanding	Service Charge		
$ 4,325.00	$		
Balance = These Balances Should Equal	Balance =	Total Checks Outstanding $	4325.00
$ 16,248.11	$ 16,248.11		

Figure 79

9. Add the outstanding checks.
10. Enter the bank balance shown on the front of the statement; also list any deposits not credited by the bank. Add these amounts.
11. Subtract the oustanding checks.
12. The balance should equal the amount shown in your checkbook.

"Great," you say, "but it doesn't!" Now what?

Unless your bank is very inept, it is generally safe to assume that the bank's computer is not at fault. I can recall only one time in my life when a bank error caused a discrepancy in my checkbook and bank statement balances. And even then the error was mine, for a hastily written ".06" looked like ".00," and the bank did not read my writing correctly.

First, go over your checkbook. Go back to the point where you last reconciled the statement, when your balance was in agreement with the statement. (When you reconcile the statement, and the amounts have balanced, you should initial, date, and mark "OK" beside the amount, so you will have a point of reference the following month. Figure 80.)

From this point on, using your adding machine, go over each addition and subtraction, being sure your entries were written correctly.

Next, compare the Disbursements and Debits or Deposits and Credits Column amounts with the Balance Column amounts. Sometimes numbers are transposed when they are written, so be sure that the two amounts for each entry agree.

After you have found the error, do you refigure the Balance Column, making the necessary change? No. Circle errors in red, and write the correct amount beside the error. Then, at the end of the checking account balance record, enter the amount to correct the error.

This method of making corrections in the checkbook saves a lot of time, and the pages look better and are easier to read without having amounts scratched out and written over.

If you still have not determined why your totals don't balance, look at each canceled check. Compare the figure written on each check with the amount encoded by the bank in the lower right-hand corner of the check. Sometimes the error is here, as in the case of my missing six cents.

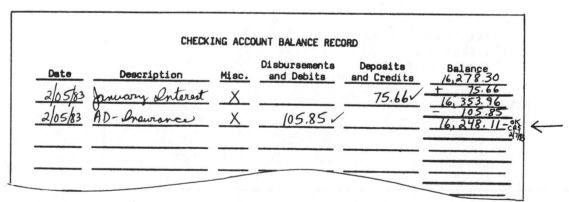

Figure 80

Verify that each check total on the disbursements sheets agrees with the actual amount written on the check.

And finally, recheck your addition and subtraction on the bank statement.

If you've followed all these steps and you are still out of balance, go through the procedure one more time. Then if the discrepancy is still not cleared up, consult your bank.

ENTERING ADJUSTMENTS

After you've reconciled the bank statement with the checking account balance, transfer all credits and charges to the General Ledger. For example, a bank error in your favor would be added to the receipts total, on the Total Receipts page. Similarly, a charge for checks imprinted would be subtracted from office supplies or treasurer's supplies. Be sure to account for all charges and credits.

As discussed, Petty Cash disbursements are adjusted at the end of the month, and a statement issued (Figure 81):

1. The Building and Ground, Postage, and Nursery Supplies budgets each have the amounts above subtracted from their accounts.
2. The Office Supplies budget, from which the original $25.00 was deducted, has the amount of $7.97 added back into its budget.

The ledger page in Figure 82 shows Petty Cash credits on Lines 6, 10, 20, and 24. The charge for new checks is shown on Line 15. Bank service charges, for returned checks, were charged to office supplies (Lines 1 and 4).

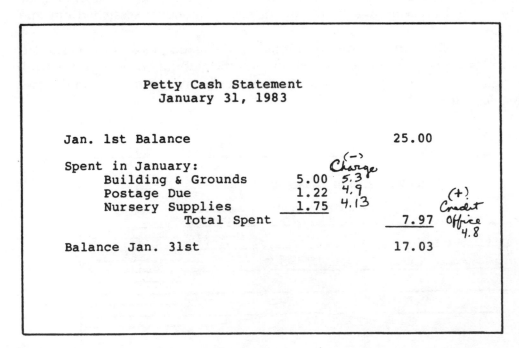

```
                    Petty Cash Statement
                     January 31, 1983


Jan. 1st Balance                             25.00

Spent in January:                        Charge (-)
    Building & Grounds        5.00   5.3
    Postage Due              1.22    4.9
    Nursery Supplies         1.75    4.13        Credit (+)
               Total Spent          7.97    Office
                                                 4.8
Balance Jan. 31st                           17.03
```

Figure 81

Office Supplies

		Debit	Credit	Balance		Month Budget	Month Actual	Y-T-D Budget	Y-T-D Actual
30	NSF Massey (SC) —	200		472.79					
	Apr					6250	3324	250—	39721
5	Petty Cash 1566	25—		447.79					
6	NSF Service Charge —	200		445.79					
25	Quickprint 1623	46.95		398.84					
31	Petty Cash Credits —		8.37	407.21					
	May					6250	6558	31250	34279
1	Weaver's Office Supplies 1693	39.31		40328					
27	The Very Idea 1705	44.95		39833					
30	Petty Cash —		23.20	421.53					
	June					6250	(1432)	375—	32847
11	Weaver's Office Supplies 1745	1.185		40968					
13	Walgreens 1753	3—		406.68					
31	Petty Cash Credits —		5—	411.68					
31	Checks Printed auto	21.50		390.18					
	July					6250	3135	43750	35982
8	Dussault Stationery 1812	9.95		380.23					
22	Plastic Letters + Signs 1856	6.75		373.48					
22	Quill Corporation 1857	75.23		298.25					
31	Petty Cash Credits		15.25	313.50					
	Aug					6250	7668	500—	43650
2	Carol R. Shearn 1880	3.53		309.97					
14	Dussault Stationery 1908	2.98		306.99					
30	Petty Cash Credits		7.45	314.44					
	Sept					6250	(94)	56250	43614
5	Quill Corporation 1977	19.74		294.70					
27	Quill Corporation 2044	3.78		290.92					
	Oct					6250	2352	125000	45908
14	Communication Resources 2005	19.95		270.97					
14	Dussault Stationery 286	2.74		268.23					

Figure 82

CLOSING THE LEDGER SHEETS

For each account in the General Ledger, in pencil:

1. Draw lines as shown.
2. Enter the month in Column 4.
3. Enter the month budget and actual and year-to-date budget and actual figures.

Now you are ready to prepare the Financial Statement.

FINANCIAL STATEMENT

What is the purpose of the Financial Statement? For the church leaders, it is a track to run on. It tells how much has been received, how it has been spent, and how much is available to run the programs of the church.

For the individual members, it indicates that their tithes and offerings are being spent wisely, or not so wisely.

The following basic Financial Statement provides information on monthly and year-to-date figures for receipts, disbursements, individual account balances, designated receipts and payments, petty cash balance, checking and savings balances, and investments.

Examine the two sides of the statement.

The back of the Financial Statement (Figure 83) includes all budgeted accounts. The figures in the first four columns are taken off the ledger pages. Simply copy the figures on the ledger pages, add the columns, and this section is done.

The front of the Financial Statement (Figure 84) is the Income and Expense statement.

The procedure is as follows:

1. Income
   (a) Beginning Balances for Checking, Savings, and Petty Cash. Enter these amounts first. These figures are the ending balances from the month before.
   (b) General Receipts. Turn to the Total Sunday Offerings page. This is the total of all regular, or budgeted, offerings for the month.
   (c) Interest Income. Enter checking and savings only. (Account for investment interest at the bottom section of the page).
   (d) Adjustments. Enter any adjustments that increase the church's income.
   (e) Designated Gifts. Include reimbursements to budgeted accounts. Total the designated gifts and enter the amount in the right-hand column.
   (f) Petty Cash In. Enter any amount that was received for the month.
   (g) Add the figures. This gives you the "Total Available."
2. Expenditures:
   (a) Enter the Budgeted Expenditures. This is the total Spent This Month, at the bottom of the second column of the back page.
   (b) Designated Expenditures. Include Petty Cash Out, which includes all monies paid out of the Petty Cash fund. Also include reimbursements to budgeted accounts that were transferred to those accounts.
   (c) Total the designated expenditures and enter the amount in the right-hand column.
   (d) Add the right-hand column. This gives you the Total Expenditures.
3. Balance of Cash on Hand:
   (a) Subtract the total expenditures from the total available. The Balance is your cash on hand in Checking, Savings, and Petty Cash.
   (b) Enter the actual cash amounts for these three funds:
       (1) Checking. The actual balance shown on your Checking Account Balance Record.
       (2) Savings. The actual amount shown on the ledger page for the savings account, after interest has been added.
       (3) Petty Cash. The actual amount of cash in the Petty Cash fund.
   (c) Add the account balances, as shown in Figure 85. This total must equal the difference between your income and expenditures—your Balance on Hand. If it doesn't, you are "out-of-balance."
   (d) If you are out-of-balance, recheck your work carefully. Look for transposed

	BUDGETED THIS MONTH	SPENT THIS MONTH	BUDGETED THRU 3/31	SPENT THRU 3/31	TOTAL 1983 BUDGET
1. MISSIONS & EVANGELISM					
World Missions	2,851.41	2,313.61	8,554.23	7,541.13	34,217.00
Associational Missions	1,222.00	991.54	3,666.00	3,231.90	14,664.00
Local Missions	41.66	−	124.99	−	500.00
Jail Ministry	50.00	15.75	150.00	149.17	600.00
Revival Expenses	75.00	−	225.00	975.04	900.00
PBAC Scholarship Fund	100.00	−	300.00	−	1,200.00
TOTALS	4,340.07	3,320.90	13,020.22	11,897.24	52,081.00
2. SUPPORT STAFF					
Secretarial Services	916.68	950.65	2,750.00	3,168.77	11,000.00
Nursery Workers	475.00	575.25	1,425.00	1,498.00	5,700.00
Custodial Services	341.67	375.00	1,025.00	975.00	4,100.00
TOTALS	1,733.35	1,900.90	5,200.00	5,641.77	20,800.00
3. PASTOR					
Salary	1,316.66	1,316.66	3,949.98	3,949.98	15,800.00
Housing & Utilities	833.33	833.33	2,499.99	2,499.99	10,000.00
Car Expenses	291.67	291.67	875.01	875.01	3,500.00
Hospitalization	116.67	113.45	350.00	216.66	1,400.00
Retirement	250.00	158.34	750.00	475.02	3,000.00
TOTALS	2,808.33	2,713.45	8,424.98	8,016.66	33,700.00
4. MINISTER OF EDUCATION/YOUTH					
Salary	850.00	850.00	2,550.00	2,550.00	10,200.00
Housing & Utilities	833.33	833.33	2,499.99	2,499.99	10,000.00
Car Expenses	200.00	200.00	600.00	600.00	2,400.00
Hospitalization	116.67	−	350.01	328.41	1,400.00
Retirement	250.00	250.00	750.00	750.00	3,000.00
TOTALS	2,250.00	2,133.33	6,750.00	6,728.40	27,000.00
5. NEW STAFF MEMBER					
Salary	1,041.66	−	3,124.98	−	12,500.00
TOTALS	1,041.66	−	3,124.98	−	12,500.00
6. ORGANIZATION/ADMINISTRATION					
Sunday School	500.00	680.28	1,500.00	840.16	6,000.00
Vacation Bible School	41.67	−	83.33	84.50	500.00
WMU	125.00	84.98	375.00	201.08	1,500.00
RAs	33.33	293.12	99.99	293.12	400.00
Mission Activities	16.67	−	33.33	−	200.00
Music	166.67	112.55	500.00	822.98	2,000.00
Special Music Events	16.67	−	50.00	−	200.00
Office Supplies	62.50	74.11	187.50	243.97	750.00
Postage	50.00	(23.60)	150.00	161.32	600.00
Printing Supplies	62.50	38.97	187.50	592.14	750.00
Publicity	66.67	53.40	200.00	200.58	800.00
Florida Baptist Witness	54.16	52.80	162.48	135.63	650.00
Nursery Supplies	10.41	63.62	31.23	88.66	125.00
Kitchen Supplies	100.00	199.24	300.00	254.74	1,200.00
Social Events	25.00	67.89	75.00	174.60	300.00
Youth	333.33	687.00	999.99	661.16	4,000.00
Flowers	62.50	−	187.50	−	750.00
Conventions	133.33	−	399.99	28.00	1,600.00
Worker Training	83.33	116.25	249.99	195.96	1,000.00
Recreation	41.66	−	124.98	−	500.00
Library	95.83	182.95	287.49	343.19	1,150.00
Junior Church	25.00	−	75.00	−	300.00
Puppet Ministry	16.67	−	50.00	−	200.00
Pulpit Supply	20.83	−	62.49	−	250.00
Transportation	166.67	19.00	500.00	251.05	2,000.00
TOTALS	2,310.40	2,702.56	6,872.79	5,572.84	27,725.00
7. MAINTENANCE					
Electric	583.33	476.43	1,749.99	1,425.69	7,000.00
Water & Phone	166.67	182.30	500.00	537.52	2,000.00
Building Maintenance	500.00	109.98	1,500.00	1,217.68	6,000.00
Lawn Care	208.33	237.50	624.99	615.00	2,500.00
Insurance	208.33	−	624.99	1,082.00	2,500.00
TOTALS	1,666.66	1,006.21	4,999.97	4,877.89	20,000.00
8. DEBT RETIREMENT					
Exchange Bank	1,705.00	1,704.20	5,114.00	5,112.60	20,460.00
Florida Baptist Convention	225.00	222.05	676.00	666.15	2,700.00
TOTALS	1,930.00	1,926.25	5,790.00	5,778.75	23,160.00
9. CONTINGENCIES					
Furnishings	250.00	46.87	750.00	164.84	3,000.00
Growth Fund	2,033.33	1,652.58	6,099.99	5,441.12	24,400.00
TOTALS	2,283.33	1,699.45	6,849.99	5,605.96	27,400.00
GRAND TOTALS	20,363.80	17,403.05	61,032.93	54,119.51	244,366.00

Figure 83

```
                    MONTHLY FINANCIAL STATEMENT
                         FOR MARCH 1983

                     (Presented April 13, 1983)


INCOME THIS MONTH
    Beginning Balances
        Checking                                        6,511.71
        Savings                                         2,933.02
        Petty Cash                                         20.66
    General Receipts                                   16,525.80
    Interest Income
        Checking                                           35.74
        Savings (CD 100.41, 1st Qtr. Interest 29.00)      129.41
    Adjustment to Checking (Void #290, dated 3/10/82)     182.60
    Designated Gifts
        Youth                                  50.00
        Camp                                  300.00
        Worker Training                        19.00
        Printing Supplies                      15.00
        Counseling                             15.00
        Annie Armstrong                     1,135.00
        Petty Cash In                          34.00
        Building Fund                       2,362.30
            TOTAL DESIGNATED                              3,930.30

            TOTAL AVAILABLE                              30,269.24

EXPENDITURES THIS MONTH
    Budgeted Expenditures                              17,403.05
    Designated Expenditures
        To Youth Budget                        50.00
        To Printing Supplies                   15.00
        Counseling                             15.00
        Detention Center                       26.00
        To Worker Training                     19.00
        Youth Camp                            850.00
        To MMA from Checking (Designated Bldg. Fund) 2,614.73
        To MMA from Savings (Growth Fund)   2,500.00
        Petty Cash Out                         51.42
            TOTAL DESIGNATED                              6,141.15

            TOTAL EXPENDITURES                           23,544.20

BALANCE (TOTAL AVAILABLE LESS TOTAL EXPENDITURES)         6,725.04

ACCOUNT BALANCES
    Checking                                6,159.37
    Savings                                   562.43
    Petty Cash                                  3.24

            TOTAL CASH BALANCE                            6,725.04

BUDGET SUMMARY                              THIS MONTH    THIS YEAR
    General Receipts                        16,525.80    53,865.28
    Less Actual Budget Expenditures        -17,565.54   -52,895.66
        RECEIPTS OVER (UNDER) ACTUAL EXPENDITURES (1,039.74)  969.12

    General Receipts                        16,525.80    53,865.28
    Less Projected Budget Expenditures     -20,363.80   -60,916.25
        RECEIPTS OVER (UNDER) PROJECTED BUDGET (3,838.00) (7,050.97)

BUILDING FUND                              THIS MONTH     TO DATE
    Actually Given                          2,362.30   211,222.60
    With Growth Fund                        4,014.88   229,296.39

CDs & MONEY MARKET ACCOUNTS (MMA)
    Beginning Balance                                   249,976.59
    From Growth Fund, Designated Building Fund,
        and Savings                         8,903.27
    Interest for March (MMAs)               1,201.48
        TOTAL INTO INVESTMENTS                           10,104.75

        TOTAL IN CDs & MONEY MARKET ACCOUNTS            260,081.34
```

Figure 84

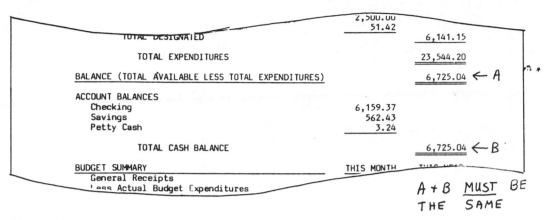

Figure 85

numbers or errors in addition or subtraction. If you have followed the system to carefully enter and post your work, you should have very little trouble in balancing these figures.

The figures at the bottom of the page, showing the Budget Summary, Building Fund recap, and Investment Holdings, can be adapted to suit the needs of your church.

12

Reports

Although the Financial Report presents the financial standing of the church to the congregation, two other areas of responsibility in reporting are:

1. Regular reports of individual giving records to the members of the congregation.
2. Payroll and income tax reports to the Internal Revenue Service.

CONTRIBUTION RECORDS

After the morning worship service each week, James, an active member, goes into the church office where the ushers are sorting the contents of the offering plate. As the ushers separate tithes and offerings, dinner reservation slips, and prayer requests, James enters the room.

"Can I get a hundred dollars worth of change?" he asks. "I need it for my business. I'll write you a check for that amount."

"Sure," an usher replies, quickly counting out small bills and loose coins.

This seemingly innocent transaction, in one year's time, turned into a $5,200 tax deduction for James, when he used his canceled checks as proof that he contributed that amount of money to his church.

The practice is widespread. At a seminar I attended several years ago, no less than eight church secretaries spoke of a similar problem in their churches.

Internal Revenue Service audits of individuals' tax returns have uncovered this false representation of donations, and as a result the Service is more strict about the requirements of church record keeping to substantiate the claims of the church members; canceled checks are no longer adequate. Therefore the church is responsible for providing its members with an annual statement of giving. Some churches prefer to provide quarterly or semiannual statements, which also remind its members to catch up on their pledges, tithes, and offerings.

The high cost of postage, however, can prohibit quarterly mailings. If this is the case for your church, perhaps statements could be given out after service on Sunday.

At Cypress Lake, the finance committee decided to send semiannual statements to the congregation. The form used (Figure 86) has columns for the general budget, the building fund, and special gifts. It is printed on NCR paper (no carbon required), in three parts: white, yellow, and pink.

In July of each year, the back (pink) copy is mailed to members and, in January, the completely filled out top (white) copy is mailed as the annual statement of giving. The middle (yellow) copy is retained for church records.

Two columns are sufficient if you do not have a building fund. The Other column is used to record all cash designated for other than building or budget.

Here is the procedure for preparing contribution statements:

1. Before the start of a new year, for each member or regular contributor, type the person's or couple's name on the statement. Keep statements in alphabetical order.
2. Each week, enter the contributions on the statements:
   (a) Alphabetize offering envelopes, if this has not already been done by the counters.
   (b) Examine each envelope carefully as you enter information on the statement. (The counters should have circled any designated amounts in red so you can

Cypress Lake Baptist Church

3755 Cypress Lake Drive   Fort Myers, Florida 33907

	BUDGET	BUILDING FUND	SPECIAL GIFTS		BUDGET	BUILDING FUND	SPECIAL GIFTS		BUDGET	BUILDING FUND	SPECIAL GIFTS		BUDGET	BUILDING FUND	SPECIAL GIFTS
JAN				APR				JUL				OCT			
2				2				2				2			
3				3				3				3			
4				4				4				4			
5				5				5				5			
FEB				MAY				AUG				NOV			
2				2				2				2			
3				3				3				3			
4				4				4				4			
5				5				5				5			
MAR				JUN				SEP				DEC			
2				2				2				2			
3				3				3				3			
4				4				4				4			
5				5				5				5			
QTR				QTR				QTR				QTR			
				+				+				+			
				=				=				=			

NAME _____

CONTRIBUTIONS RECORD FOR JAN. 1 TO DEC. 31, YEAR: **198**___

GRAND TOTAL

Figure 86

quickly note and record the amounts.) You would not include the following amounts on a contribution statement:

(1) Reimbursements to budgeted accounts. For example, the youth group wants pizza for its Friday evening meeting. A church check is written for the total amount. That evening, the youth each pay his or her share and the total collected is turned in by Joe, the youth leader, with the Sunday offering, thereby reimbursing the youth budgeted acount.

(2) Payments for camp, outings, or similar events. If Mary Smith writes a check for $200.00 for her Billy to go to camp, that amount is not a contribution.

(3) Money paid for books, tapes, or similar items.

(One church had a problem with nondeductible payments, when members complained to the financial secretary that their records of giving did not include these payments. The financial secretary had the following rubber stamp made:

> THIS IS NOT A TAX-DEDUCTIBLE ITEM

The counting committee stamps the front of all nondeductible checks before they are deposited. There is no question about whether such a check can be used for income tax purposes.

(c) Post amounts listed on the Loose Checks form, following the guidelines given above.

(d) Wrap the envelopes and loose check forms securely, and place the date on the front.

(e) Store in a locked drawer or cabinet. These are confidential records and should not be left out for people to see.

3. At the end of each quarter, total the columns. Distribute to members quarterly or semiannually, as decided by the church body or finance committee.

4. At the end of the year, total the columns.

5. Distribute contribution records to contributors. If mailed, the statements must have first-class postage. They do not qualify for bulk mail.

What about such noncash gifts as computers, organs, VCRs, and choir robes? The following form letter (Figure 87) can be used to thank the contributor for the gift and to provide a tax-deductible receipt for the members' tax returns.

PAYROLL AND TAX RECORDS

If the church does not already have one, you must obtain an Employer Identification Number by applying to the Internal Revenue Service or Social Security Administration (SSA) offices; use Form SS-4.

Use this identification number on all forms you send to the Internal Revenue Service. This is not your state tax exempt number or your Social Security Number. The Employer Identification Number is a nine-digit number (written 00-0000000).

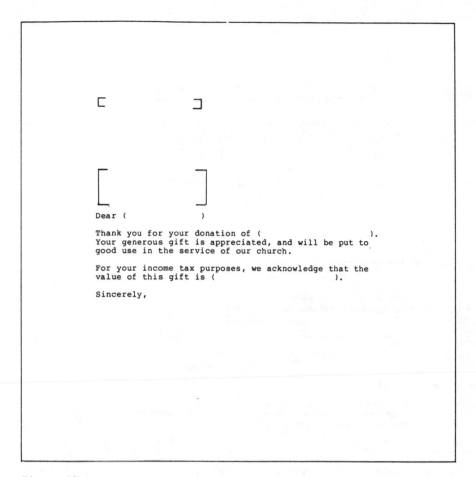

```
        ⌐          ¬



        ⌐          ¬
        │          │
        └          ┘
        Dear (          )

        Thank you for your donation of (                ).
        Your generous gift is appreciated, and will be put to
        good use in the service of our church.

        For your income tax purposes, we acknowledge that the
        value of this gift is (                ).

        Sincerely,
```

Figure 87

Church workers fall into two categories: ordained and unordained, and the tax laws for ordained ministers are complex.

Ordained Ministers

At one church I served, there were two ordained ministers. They debated for weeks on the interpretation of the laws for that year, and in the end, each one did what he wanted to do when filing his return.

Another church had six ministers. In spite of a special class set up by the denomination's state office to teach tax laws, the six ministers did not agree about what the laws really meant.

I won't attempt to interpret tax laws for ordained ministers. The scope and volume of recent changes defy comprehension, and I leave this area to the experts.

One expert is B.J. Worth, who wrote *Income Tax Law for Ministers and Religous Workers* (Baker Book House, Grand Rapids, Michigan 49506).

A number of other publications dealing with the complex areas of ministers' taxes have been written by Manfred Holck, Jr., a Certified Public Accountant. For information on these publications, write to Church Management, Inc., P.O. Box 1625, Austin, TX 78767.

Nonordained Church Workers

For nonordained employees, the law is clear. It requires records of how much the employee has earned and how much has been withheld.

Certain forms must be completed. Complete instructions for each form are included in Publication 15, *Circular E, Employer's Tax Guide,* available from any Internal Revenue Service office.

1. Employee's Withholding Allowance Certificate (Form W-4; see Figure 88) is completed when an employee is hired. It determines the rate at which income tax is to be withheld from wages.

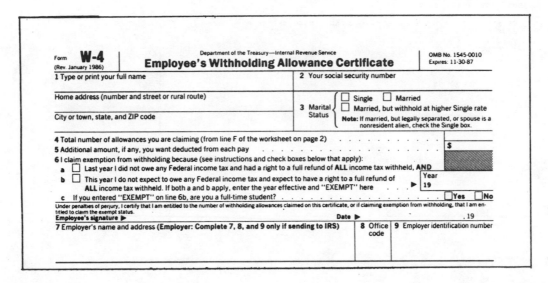

Figure 88

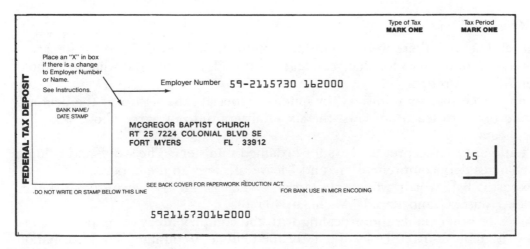

Figure 89

HANDLING THE CHURCH'S MONEY

2. Federal Tax Deposit (FTD). These coupons (Figure 89) are provided in booklet form from the IRS and are used to make a deposit to an approved agency (usually your bank where you have your checking account) on a monthly or quarterly basis. Although the following rules are not all-inclusive, they do pertain to small churches:

(a) If at the end of a quarter, your total undeposited taxes for the quarter are less than $500, no deposit is required. You may pay the taxes to IRS with Form 941 (or 941E) by the due date of the return.

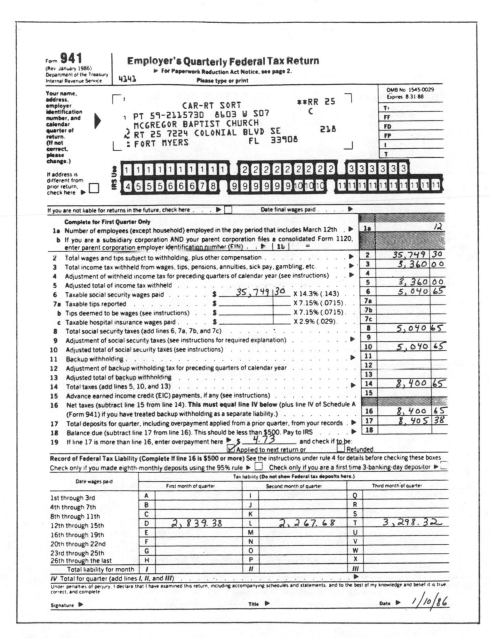

Figure 90

(*b*) If at the end of any month, your total undeposited taxes are less than $500, no deposit is required. You may carry the taxes over to the following month.

(*c*) If at the end of any month, your total undeposited taxes are $500 or more, but less than $3,000, pay the deposit to the approved agency within fifteen days after the end of the month.

3. Employer's Quarterly Federal Tax Return (Form 941; see Figure 90). This form must be filed as shown in Figure 91. If you deposit all taxes when due for the quarter, you may file the return by the tenth day of the second month following the quarter.

4. Wage and Tax Statement (Form W-2; see Figure 92). This form must be given to employees no later than January 31st for the prior year; copies are also forwarded to the Internal Revenue Service. (If an employee is terminated, the W-2 may be given at any time after that).

Churches are exempt from federal and state unemployment taxes. For state income taxes, individual churches should contact a local state office and request the latest state tax booklet.

```
When To File Form 941 (Employer's Federal Tax Return)

     Quarter          Ending        Due Date
Jan.-Feb.-Mar.        Mar. 31       Apr. 30
Apr.-May.-Jun.        June 30       July 31
Jul.-Aug.-Sept.       Sept. 30      Oct. 31
Oct.-Nov.-Dec.        Dec. 31       Jan. 31
```

Figure 91

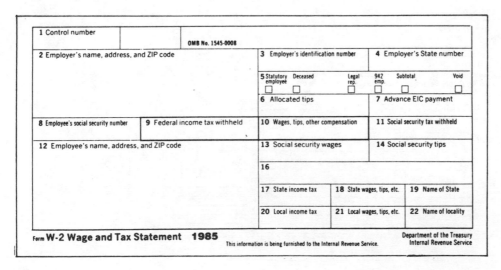

Figure 92

HANDLING THE CHURCH'S MONEY

Suppose that Jennifer is a church secretary and that her hourly rate is $5.50 per hour. Her W-4 form (Figure 93) indicates that she is married and is claiming herself as a dependent.

Jennifer is paid weekly. At $5.50 an hour for 40 hours, her salary is $220. In Circular E, find the page for withholding for the category "MARRIED Persons, WEEKLY Payroll Period" (Figure 94).

Look down the left side of the page. There is a line that reads "At least $220, But less than $230." On this line, move across the columns to the one corresponding to the number of allowances claimed on Jennifer's W-4 Form. In this case, it is the second column, with one allowance. The tax to be deducted is $19.

Next, figure the amount of Social Security from the Social Security Employee Tax Table (see Figure 95).

The scale from $0.00 to $99.99 is included on the two pages. In the lower right-hand corner of the right page, there is a scale for amounts from $100 to $1,000, in $100 increments.

To figure Jennifer's Social Security Employee Tax:

1. Determine the correct amount for the even hundred-dollar portion of her pay. Beside $200, the taxes due are $14.30.
2. The balance of Jennifer's pay, or $20.00, is taxed based on the rates shown on the two pages. Find the correct amount, within "Wages at least 19.94 But less than 20.07," on the left page. The tax to be withheld is $1.44. Therefore, her Social Security tax is $14.30 + $1.44, or $15.74.

Follow this procedure for determining the taxes of all nonordained employees.

Form **W-4** (Rev. January 1986)
Department of the Treasury—Internal Revenue Service
Employee's Withholding Allowance Certificate
OMB No. 1545-0010
Expires: 11-30-87

1 Type or print your full name: Jennifer Jannett
2 Your social security number: 123-45-6789
Home address (number and street or rural route): 45 Main Street
City or town, state, and ZIP code: Cape Coral, FL 33904
3 Marital Status: ☐ Single ☑ Married ☐ Married, but withhold at higher Single rate
Note: If married, but legally separated, or spouse is a nonresident alien, check the Single box.

4 Total number of allowances you are claiming (from line F of the worksheet on page 2) . . . 1
5 Additional amount, if any, you want deducted from each pay . . . $
6 I claim exemption from withholding because (see instructions and check boxes below that apply):
a ☐ Last year I did not owe any Federal income tax and had a right to a full refund of **ALL** income tax withheld, **AND**
b ☐ This year I do not expect to owe any Federal income tax and expect to have a right to a full refund of **ALL** income tax withheld. If both a and b apply, enter the year effective and "EXEMPT" here . . . ▶ Year 19
c If you entered "EXEMPT" on line 6b, are you a full-time student? . . . ☐ Yes ☐ No

Under penalties of perjury, I certify that I am entitled to the number of withholding allowances claimed on this certificate, or if claiming exemption from withholding, that I am entitled to claim the exempt status.
Employee's signature ▶ Jennifer Jannett **Date ▶** Feb. 10, 19 84

7 Employer's name and address (**Employer: Complete 7, 8, and 9 only if sending to IRS**) | 8 Office code | 9 Employer identification number

Figure 93

MARRIED Persons–WEEKLY Payroll Period
(For Wages Paid After December 1985)

And the wages are–		And the number of withholding allowances claimed is–										
At least	But less than	0	1	2	3	4	5	6	7	8	9	10
		The amount of income tax to be withheld shall be–										
$0	$54	$0	$0	$0	$0	$0	$0	$0	$0	$0	$0	$0
54	56	1	0	0	0	0	0	0	0	0	0	0
56	58	1	0	0	0	0	0	0	0	0	0	0
58	60	1	0	0	0	0	0	0	0	0	0	0
60	62	1	0	0	0	0	0	0	0	0	0	0
62	64	1	0	0	0	0	0	0	0	0	0	0
64	66	2	0	0	0	0	0	0	0	0	0	0
66	68	2	0	0	0	0	0	0	0	0	0	0
68	70	2	0	0	0	0	0	0	0	0	0	0
70	72	2	0	0	0	0	0	0	0	0	0	0
72	74	3	0	0	0	0	0	0	0	0	0	0
74	76	3	0	0	0	0	0	0	0	0	0	0
76	78	3	1	0	0	0	0	0	0	0	0	0
78	80	3	1	0	0	0	0	0	0	0	0	0
80	82	3	1	0	0	0	0	0	0	0	0	0
82	84	4	1	0	0	0	0	0	0	0	0	0
84	86	4	2	0	0	0	0	0	0	0	0	0
86	88	4	2	0	0	0	0	0	0	0	0	0
88	90	4	2	0	0	0	0	0	0	0	0	0
90	92	5	2	0	0	0	0	0	0	0	0	0
92	94	5	2	0	0	0	0	0	0	0	0	0
94	96	5	3	0	0	0	0	0	0	0	0	0
96	98	5	3	1	0	0	0	0	0	0	0	0
98	100	5	3	1	0	0	0	0	0	0	0	0
100	105	6	4	1	0	0	0	0	0	0	0	0
105	110	6	4	2	0	0	0	0	0	0	0	0
110	115	7	5	2	0	0	0	0	0	0	0	0
115	120	8	5	3	1	0	0	0	0	0	0	0
120	125	8	6	3	1	0	0	0	0	0	0	0
125	130	9	6	4	2	0	0	0	0	0	0	0
130	135	9	7	5	2	0	0	0	0	0	0	0
135	140	10	8	5	3	1	0	0	0	0	0	0
140	145	11	8	6	3	1	0	0	0	0	0	0
145	150	11	9	6	4	2	0	0	0	0	0	0
150	160	13	10	7	5	2	0	0	0	0	0	0
160	170	14	11	8	6	4	1	0	0	0	0	0
170	180	15	12	10	7	5	2	0	0	0	0	0
180	190	17	14	11	8	6	3	1	0	0	0	0
190	200	18	15	12	10	7	5	2	0	0	0	0
200	210	20	17	14	11	8	6	3	1	0	0	0
210	220	21	18	15	12	9	7	4	2	0	0	0
220	230	23	19	17	14	11	8	6	3	1	0	0
230	240	24	20	18	15	12	9	7	4	2	0	0
240	250	26	22	19	16	14	11	8	6	3	1	0
250	260	27	24	21	18	15	12	9	7	4	2	0
260	270	29	25	22	19	16	13	11	8	5	3	1
270	280	30	27	24	21	18	15	12	9	7	4	2
280	290	32	29	25	22	19	16	13	10	8	5	3
290	300	34	30	27	24	21	18	15	12	9	7	4
300	310	35	32	28	25	22	19	16	13	10	8	5
310	320	37	33	30	27	23	20	18	15	12	9	6
320	330	39	35	32	28	25	22	19	16	13	10	8
330	340	40	37	33	30	27	23	20	17	14	12	9
340	350	42	38	35	32	28	25	22	19	16	13	10
350	360	44	40	37	33	30	27	23	20	17	14	11
360	370	46	42	38	35	31	28	25	22	19	16	13
370	380	48	44	40	36	33	30	26	23	20	17	14
380	390	49	46	42	38	35	31	28	25	21	19	16
390	400	51	47	44	40	36	33	30	26	23	20	17
400	410	53	49	46	42	38	35	31	28	25	21	18
410	420	55	51	47	44	40	36	33	29	26	23	20
420	430	58	53	49	45	42	38	34	31	28	24	21
430	440	60	55	51	47	43	40	36	33	29	26	23
440	450	62	57	53	49	45	42	38	34	31	28	24
450	460	64	60	55	51	47	43	40	36	33	29	26
460	470	66	62	57	53	49	45	41	38	34	31	27
470	480	69	64	60	55	51	47	43	39	36	32	29
480	490	71	66	62	57	53	49	45	41	37	34	31
490	500	73	68	64	59	55	51	47	43	39	36	32

(Continued on next page)

Figure 94

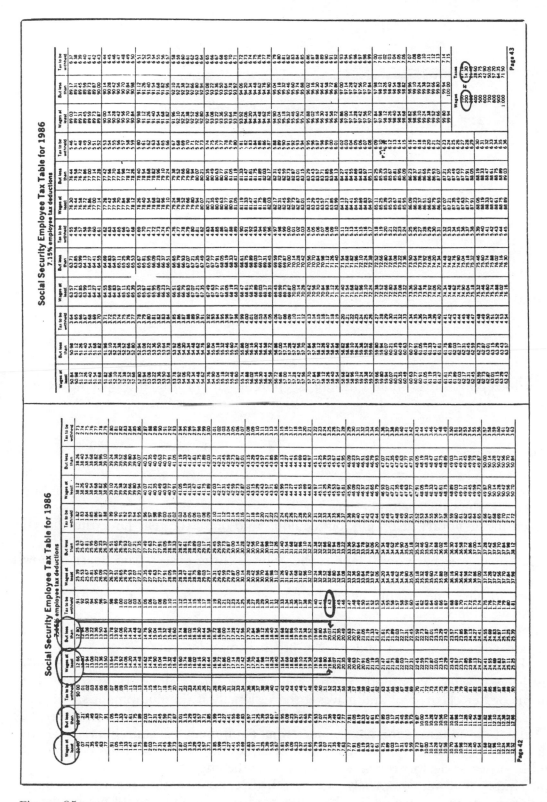

Figure 95

13

Inventory and Purchasing Records

Basic record-keeping duties should include keeping inventory lists and purchasing information.

INVENTORY RECORDS

Martha, a children's worker, calls the church office for a filmstrip projector that she needs for her Wednesday evening class.

"I looked in the library last night, but couldn't find one," she tells Jane, the church secretary.

"I don't know if we have one," Jane replies. She asks the pastor, who doesn't know either.

"We used to have one around here," he ponders. "But I haven't seen it for a long time. We'll have to look for it."

A search of the Sunday School classrooms finally turns up the missing filmstrip projector in the back of a closet under boxes of Christmas decorations.

All too often the church's equipment is not accounted for. Volunteers use the equipment and leave it where it is used. Then someone else comes along, picks it up, and uses it in his or her classroom, and leaves it there. Finally if the equipment sits in the same place for too long, the custodian picks it up and puts it in a convenient closet.

Members of the congregation have no idea what equipment the church has or where to find it. Volunteer workers are discouraged because they don't have the equipment they need in order to perform their work in serving the church.

In one church that was completely destroyed by fire, no inventory records had been made, and so a fair market value for the contents of the buildings could not be determined. Months after the insurance company had settled the claim, the pastor and members of the congregation remembered pieces of equipment that had not been accounted for.

An inventory of the church's equipment allows the congregation to know its assets and resources. In addition, the inventory provides details for insurance reimbursement in the event of fire, theft, or other casualty.

Whose responsibility is it to prepare an inventory list? In many small churches, no one's.

This is a very important task, and a member of the congregation should be responsible for maintaining the inventory list and coordinating the lists of all areas or departments. Assigning a person from each area of responsibility will ensure that all areas are covered. For example:

1. Kitchen, kitchen committee.
2. Office, secretary or pastor.
3. Maintenance equipment, custodian.
4. Musical equipment, minister of music or choir director.
5. Parsonage, pastor.
6. Sunday School classrooms, minister of education or Sunday School director.

STATIONARY
EQUIPMENT INVENTORY

Description	Location	Date of Purchase	Purchase Price	Comments	Replacement Cost

Figure 96

When taking an inventory, it is not necessary to count every paperclip holder or fork and spoon because 80 percent of the church's worth is in 20 percent of its furnishings. Only the *major* items should be counted. An insurance company would count these items, plus an additional allowance for the small things too numerous to mention and account for on an inventory list.

Take Polaroid pictures of artwork and valuable belongings. In the event of theft, the attempt by the thief to sell your valuables could be thwarted if you can provide pictures of the items to the police.

Two types of inventory lists should be maintained:

1. An inventory record (Figure 96) of all major pieces of furniture and stationary equipment. This includes typewriters, mimeographs, copiers, computers, desks, file cabinets, parsonage furnishings, classroom furnishings, pianos, and organs.
2. An inventory (Figure 97) of moveable equipment. Included on this list would be slide projectors, cameras, VCRs, film screens, and televisions. This list provides not only the information needed for the listing of assets or insurance purposes, it also informs the congregation (and secretary and pastor) where items can be located, what kind of training is necessary to operate the equipment, and who is in charge of a particular piece of equipment.

MOVEABLE
EQUIPMENT INVENTORY

Description	General Use	Special-ized Use	Trained Persons Only	Person in Charge of Equipment	Location of Equipment	Date of Purchase	Purchase Price	Replacement Cost

Figure 97

At McGregor, this list is maintained by the church librarian. Having one person in charge of overseeing all moveable equipment helps us keep an accurate record of where equipment is at all times.

For example, we have a video camera. Kelly, the director of children's ministries, wants to videotape a puppet performance that is being shown to her third-grade class. She asks the librarian, who informs her that the minister of music is in charge of that piece of equipment and that only trained persons may operate it. Kelly sees the minister of music, advising him that she has a trained worker to use the camera. He gives her the camera. When she is finished using it, she immediately returns the camera to him.

Because each piece of equipment is assigned to a certain individual, we no longer have to search through all the buildings to find a certain item.

Any inventory list should include a description, date of purchase, price, and replacement cost. The list should be updated annually, with discarded items being noted and crossed out. Add items to your inventory list as they are purchased.

A copy of the inventory list and Polaroid photographs should be kept off the church property. Keep them in a secure place, possibly a safe deposit box.

PURCHASING RECORDS

Basically a budget is adopted for a church and put into effect at the beginning of the calendar year.

One pastor of a 2,000-member Baptist church says, "We believe the budget to be a guideline . . . not a restrictive document. However, all purchases and expenses of any nature must be requisitioned and approved by the Finance Committee. A purchase order number must be used."

The pastor of a 500-member church says, "The people vote on the budget, and they've given me the authorization to approve expenditures. I extend to each department head the responsibility for approving expenditures within his or her department."

For one church that had strict purchasing policies for three years, the system proved burdensome, causing a lot of "make work" in some areas. The Finance Committee, with the congregation's approval, decided to permit expenditures of up to $50 to be made without writing a purchase order. "We found we were 'nickel and dimeing' ourselves and making a lot of paperwork unnecessarily," said the pastor.

In addition, the tendency for suppliers not to require a purchase order number, even though one is requested by the church, caused confusion within the record-keeping system.

"Ministers have a tendency to do 'after the fact' purchase orders because vendors do not insist on the numbers. We haven't mastered the problem," says the pastor.

One individual, designated as the purchasing officer for a church, can buy the supplies, equipment, and services required by the church efficiently and at the lowest possible cost. When one individual is in charge of all purchasing, it is easy to issue and maintain purchase orders.

A designated purchasing officer ensures that money will not be spent when it is not available or when the item has not been budgeted. That person will also ensure that all purchases are made to the full advantage of the church and that the charges are made to authorized accounts.

Purchase Order forms are available from office suppliers. Form No. PR73 (Figure 98) is from The Drawing Board in Dallas, Texas, and can be imprinted with your church's name and address.

In order to establish a system in which purchase orders are used, everyone involved must cooperate. Each staff member should be contacted individually, to obtain an overall idea of how purchases are being made. Unless key people are able to help set up a system, they may resist the new procedures.

A problem with the use of purchase order numbers, and having to obtain a number before a purchase is made, is that it stifles the work of church workers.

For example, Irma is a Junior Church teacher. It is Saturday afternoon and she is putting the final touches on a program for the following evening. She needs scissors, glue, and construction paper for the group to participate in a hands-on project. The necessity of having a purchase order number in advance keeps her from obtaining these supplies.

Although purchases of merchandise and services must be made in the most efficient

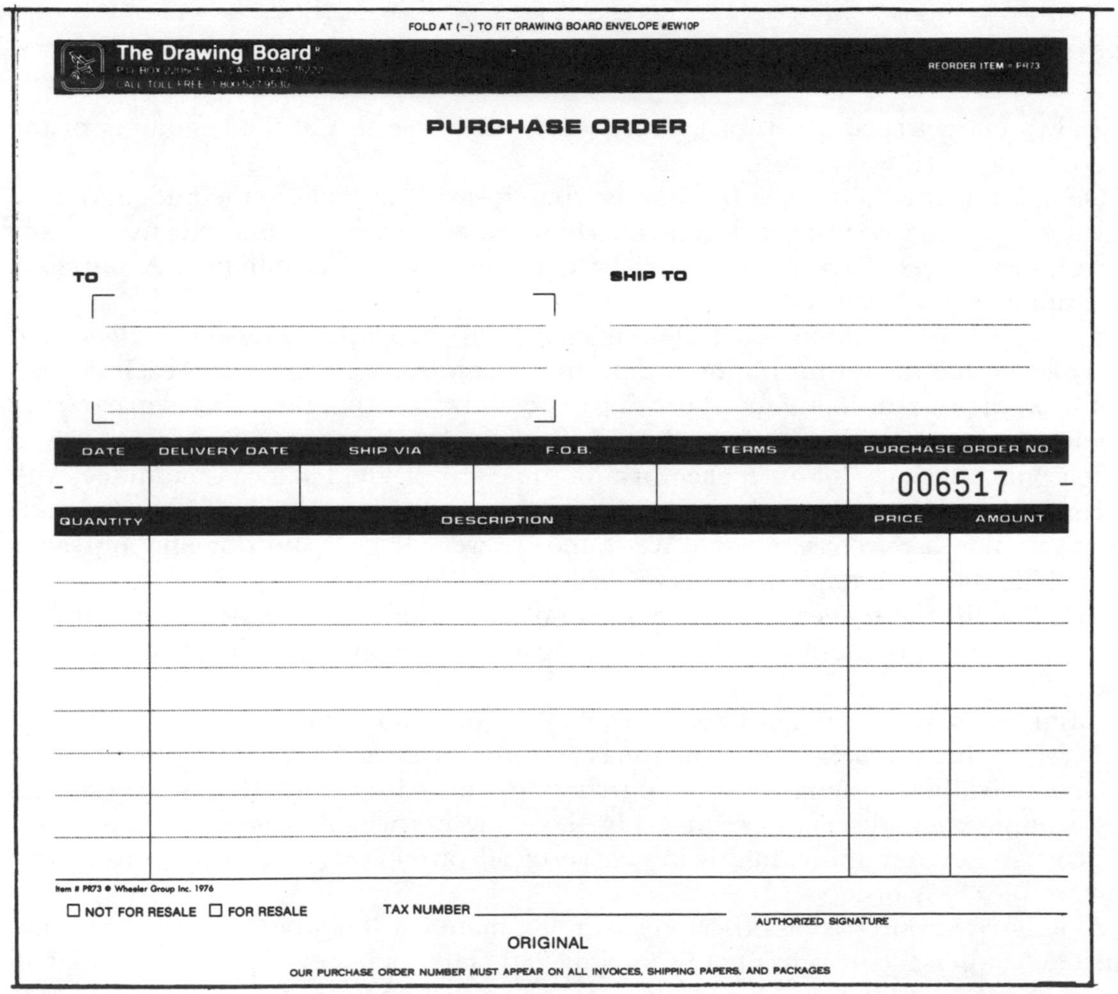

FOLD AT (–) TO FIT DRAWING BOARD ENVELOPE #EW10P

The Drawing Board®

CALL TOLL FREE 1-800-527-9530

REORDER ITEM = PR73

PURCHASE ORDER

TO

SHIP TO

DATE	DELIVERY DATE	SHIP VIA	F.O.B.	TERMS	PURCHASE ORDER NO.
					006517

QUANTITY	DESCRIPTION	PRICE	AMOUNT

Item # PR73 © Wheeler Group Inc. 1976

☐ NOT FOR RESALE ☐ FOR RESALE TAX NUMBER ______ AUTHORIZED SIGNATURE

ORIGINAL

OUR PURCHASE ORDER NUMBER MUST APPEAR ON ALL INVOICES, SHIPPING PAPERS, AND PACKAGES

Figure 98

and effective manner possible to protect the best interests of the church, for most of the churches surveyed, purchase orders were not required to make purchases.

"I just pick up the phone and order what we need," says Elizabeth, the secretary for a 150-member congregation.

Here are several suggestions for making purchases without purchase orders:

1. Small items picked up at stores by workers should be kept to a minimum.
2. All requests for reimbursements for supplies must be accompanied by a receipt for the purchases.
3. Workers should fill out a requisition form for supplies to be purchased by the church secretary or another office worker. This will save a lot of money. For example, a department leader for the children's missions group needs poster board. She sees what she wants in a national school supply catalog and orders a large supply, at $1.09 a sheet. However, she is not aware that the church receives a 25 percent discount for all office supplies and that each sheet should have cost only 69¢. If you notice shipments coming into the church office, it is your responsibility to advise the person ordering the supplies that you receive a discount from such-and-such an office supply company.
4. Look for sales. Request sale flyers from all local office suppliers. Quill Corporation, a national office supply company in Lincolnshire, Illinois has monthly sale catalogs and attractive prices for merchandise.
5. Be sure that your church receives a discount. McGregor used to get a 10 percent to 15 percent discount at several local stores but competition drove the discount up to 20 percent. However, I found that I could purchase similar items for less money through Quill. One day I happened to say to my sales representative's manager, "I really would like to buy more from Cynthia, but I have to shop for price." Cynthia called me the next day, saying that the company would give the church a full 25 percent discount on all merchandise.
6. Before ordering any supplies, be sure you know what department the purchase will be charged to.
7. Make sure that the person requesting supplies is authorized to do so. In a small church, this generally is not a problem. If you don't know, ask the department leader to approve the purchase.

Whatever system of purchasing your church uses, it is important to establish definite procedures. Whether a simple system of "picking up the phone and ordering what you need," or a complex system of requisitions, purchase orders, and finance committee approvals, definite procedures will make your record-keeping task easier.

The Requisition Form shown in Figure 99 eliminates the problem of not knowing specific details of a request for supplies. I used to find notes on my desk on Monday morning that "The children's department needs crayons" or "Order construction paper for Vacation Bible School." How many boxes of crayons? Six? Six dozen? What kind of construction paper? One color? Assorted? One package? Twenty packages? Help yourself by providing these forms to your church workers.

Suppliers of goods, equipment, and services can be very helpful. Keep an open mind when talking with them. My personal preference for choosing suppliers depends on the amount of time they are willing to spend for my church. I appreciate in-person sales calls because I can learn what new products are on the market. Also the sales

```
                    REQUISITION FORM
                                          Date_____
     Please order:

    | Quantity | Item & Description | Price | Amount | Charge To |
    |          |                    |       |        |           |
    |          |                    |       |        |           |
    |          |                    |       |        |           |
    |          |                    |       |        |           |
    |          |                    |       |        |           |

     Requested by_____    Phone_____

     Order from_____    Need by_____

       Special Instructions:
```

Figure 99

representatives can help me develop ideas about how to use products. Sales representatives willing to look through their numerous catalogs for specific products I am seeking win my respect.

Does the company deliver, or do you have to pick up the supplies? Choosing a company that will provide free delivery will save you time and money.

PART FOUR

STORING RECORDS

Written records provide a trail for all to see. The problem in many churches is that the trail leads through unorganized drawers, boxes, closets, nooks, and crannies, which makes the retrieval of information difficult.

Improper or poor organization of records can risk the destruction of needed records. Some churches, however, keep everything forever. Papers pile up, work areas are cluttered, and time is wasted looking for needed documents. Extra storage cabinets are frequently purchased to accommodate piles of useless paper.

Church files are not like business files, which close out one year and move on to the next. Committees request information from prior years, a new pastor or secretary may want to review old files for orientation, the chairman of the finance committee requests information about the budgets for the previous five years, or a loan application for the building fund requires membership and financial information for the past ten years.

But how long should records be kept? And where should they be kept? What kinds of files are necessary?

"I don't know anything about filing," says the pastor of a mission church in Fort Myers. "But we can't afford a secretary right now. I need help."

No one filing system meets the needs of all records. In Chapter 14, the general file and the accounts paid file, both very necessary in the church office, are discussed, and Chapter 15 informs about record retention and storage.

"A place for everything" will eliminate your records storage and retrieval challenges. Remember that finding records is more important than putting them away. Well-kept files are very important.

So clean the piles of paper off your book shelves, clear your desk drawers of clutter, and integrate your church's records so all information can either be made available, if needed, or disposed of, if not needed.

14

Filing Systems

"Where are the neighborhood maps we used for our area canvassing last year," Pastor Harvey asks Kathy, the church secretary.

After looking through the file drawers under "map" and "canvass," Kathy thumbs through three packed file drawers, unable to locate the missing maps.

"Look in Dan's office," the pastor says, referring to the youth minister who recently left the church. "He was in charge of the canvass last year."

Sorting through Dan's files, desk drawers, and book cases, Kathy finds records and information that should have been filed in a central location to be available to others in the church. Kathy finally finds the missing maps, and decides to coordinate all the files in a central location.

Susan, the financial secretary, receives a statement from the Christian bookstore, where the church purchases most of its literature and church supplies. She notices three items on the statement that were paid the previous month. In addition, she remembers that there was also a minor error on the statement two months earlier.

Pulling open the file drawer, she scans the file folder headings—Church Supplies, Library, Literature—"Where did I file those other statements," she says to herself. Her Accounts Paid file is arranged by budget accounts, making it difficult to locate information that might be filed in one of several folders. Within each folder, paid invoices and statements are not arranged in any particular order, which increases the time necessary to retrieve data.

Organizing and developing workable, efficient filing systems for your general files and your accounts paid file will help you and the church staff to retrieve information quickly. Files should be functional, with file groups arranged by what they do or what type of information they contain.

Each office worker—secretary, pastor, or other minister—should have a desk file drawer where personal confidential information, work in progress, and frequently used material are kept.

For retrieval of information by all staff persons and lay leaders, though, there are two types of filing systems to keep church records—the general file and the accounts paid file. If these two systems are efficiently organized, not only will it be easier to find information, it will also make your filing routine easier and more pleasant.

GENERAL FILES

There are basically four types of files. These are geographical, numerical, alphabetical, and subject. The first two types would have limited use in the church office.

An alphabetical file, containing documents in order by name, can make retrieval difficult if there is uncertainty over a name's proper spelling. Or a name on a piece of paper might not necessarily be the subject of the document.

The fourth type of file, a subject file, works very well in the church office for the general administrative files. Within the *subject file,* all items are filed alphabetically, but you are not limited to strict A-to-Z filing.

For example, one church has several different insurance policies, each one with a different company, for casualty, flood, workers' compensation, automobile, and accident. Instead of filing the policies under each company name, which makes the retrieval of information difficult, the policies are all filed under the subject Insurance.

To set up your files, you will need the following equipment.

1. *File drawers.* A minimum of one four-drawer cabinet will provide room for the general file, as well as space for the accounts paid file and merchandise catalogs. Letter-sized cabinets should be sufficient. At Cypress Lake, legal-sized cabinets were purchased. They took up too much room, and the extra width of the drawers was not needed. Rarely did I ever file documents that were longer than letter-sized, and those items could have easily been folded to fit the file folders.
2. *File folders.* Naturally for letter-sized drawers, you will use letter-sized folders. What kind will be best for you?
   (a) *Manila folders.* These are certainly all right, but they bend and slide down in the drawers easily, and the tabs tend to become dog-eared with frequent use.
   (b) *Hanging folders.* This type of folder is definitely preferred. They are more durable, the files look neater, and it is easy to slide the folders on the metal frames when you are retrieving information. There are two types of hanging folders. Both hang on the same type of frame; the difference is the way the tabs are attached to the folders.
      (1) *Vertiflex* (Figure 100). This folder has a solid metal bar across the top. The tabs clip on at any place across the bar. A disadvantage of this folder is that the tabs may slide out of place with frequent use.
      (2) *Pendaflex* (Figure 101). The label tabs for this folder have inserts that slip into slots on the file folder. These tabs stay in place.
3. *File folder labels or tabs.* If you use manila folders, you will have to purchase labels unless you are going to write directly on the folders. Typing labels on folders is messy and time-consuming, since folders are difficult to insert into the typewriter. Many kinds of file folder labels are available from your office supplier. Both

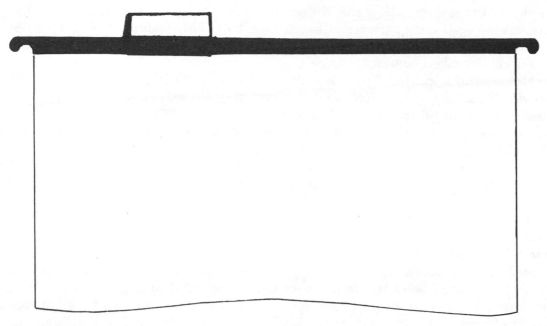

Figure 100

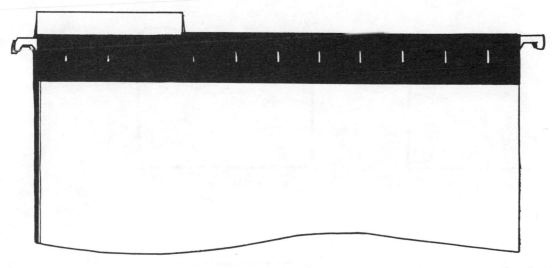

Figure 101

Vertiflex and Pendaflex file folders, as well as other brands, include a package of tabs in each box of folders. In addition, you will need an extra package of tabs because the system shown here uses more labels than the package provides.

File folders (Figure 102) are sold as half-cut, third-cut, fifth-cut, or straight cut. Half-cut, third-cut, and fifth-cut refers to the number of tabs that will fit across the top of the file folder—two, three, or five. Straight-cut refers to manila folders that have no tabs cut across the top.

People tend to arrange staggering fifth-cut file tabs, the general thought being that they are easy to read just by glancing through the files. This maneuver is more time-consuming, and more tiring on the eyes, than the maneuver required for the third-cut subject system described below.

For this system, select third-cut file folders or tabs or both (Figure 103). Third-cut tabs provide for a main subject (left side), subdivision (middle), and second subdivision (right side). Thus, all subjects are filed on the left side of the drawer.

Before organizing (or reorganizing) your files, be sure you know the needs of the church and your office. Reorganizing files requires an understanding of the church's programs, goals, and priorities. For instance, it would be difficult for a newly hired secretary to understand enough of the total scope of the church to set up comprehensive files.

Survey the needs, and then decide on categories into which the materials will be classified. The manner in which most material is requested will be your determining factor in filing records.

I waited over six months after I started at Cypress Lake before I began reorganizing the files. By that time I had a thorough understanding of the church's programs, goals, and priorities. The whole process took several months. Reorganizing three full file drawers can be an overwhelming project, but if taken bit by bit, as I took it, the task can be accomplished efficiently and thoroughly.

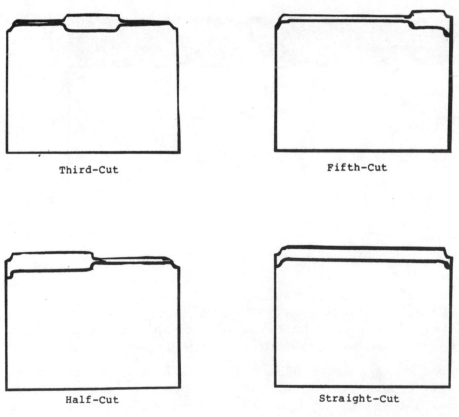

Third-Cut

Fifth-Cut

Half-Cut

Straight-Cut

Figure 102

STORING RECORDS

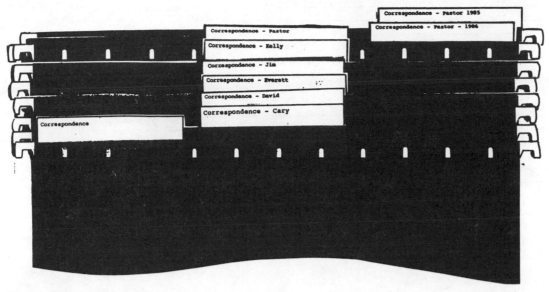

Figure 103

The largest folders were reorganized first, one at a time, and the new folders, as they were completed, were put in the file drawer along with existing files.

For example, Insurance was the first subject I tackled. Going through the files, I located and pulled out each individual insurance company folder, which included policies, forms to fill out, claims paid, premium notices due, and even expired policies.

A particular problem was that one insurance company carried several different policies for us. One week the youth were away at camp, and the youth minister called me, saying one of the youth had been injured and was in the local hospital.

"I need our insurance policy number," he said.

"Which one," I asked, "There are several in this folder." The legal jargon of the insurance policies did not clearly define which policy was our "accident policy," and the youth minister had to wait on the line for several minutes while I sorted through papers to locate the correct information.

I sorted all information, policies, and unnecessary material, discarding the latter. After each policy was sorted, I decided what information should be further divided: for example, claims already paid, forms to file a claim, the actual policies, and corresponding information. My finished file folders for "Insurance" are shown in Figure 104.

As mentioned, the third-cut subject system places all subjects on the left. The first subdivision is in the middle, the second subdivision on the right.

For subjects that are divided into categories—so that no material will be filed within the subject folder itself—in order to save on file folders, cut some folders in half at the crease (this can only be done with the hanging file folders). This will allow you to use one file folder for two file guides, saving money (Figure 105).

On the first subdivision, repeat the name of the subject and add the subdivision title. For the second subdivision, repeat the information on the first two labels and then complete it. This will prevent any misfiling of folders and will help persons who are not familiar with the files.

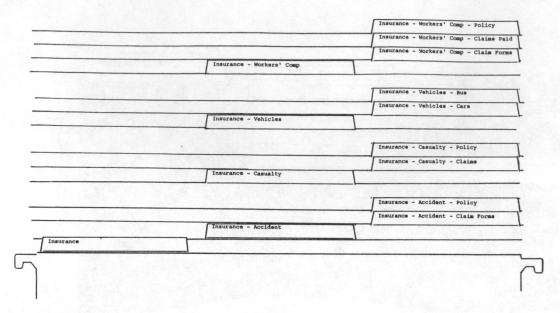

Figure 104

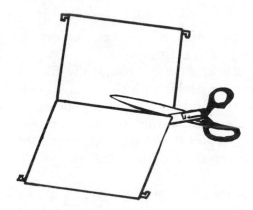

Figure 105

Repeat the above for all the remaining subjects in your file. When you are in doubt about where an item should be filed, cross-reference it. For example, magazine subscription information for the youth might be filed under Publications, but you would put a letter-sized note under Youth: *Youth Magazine—See Publications*

Each church will have its own subjects and classifications. You must decide how your own files will be organized. Be sure that the subject classifications make sense to you and to persons who will be using the file.

Filing Tips

Here are fifteen tips to make your filing tasks easier and more pleasant:

    1. Index your files. It is very important that all persons who use the files understand the system. No filing system is useful if no one else knows how to use it. If

necessary, prepare an index of your files and keep it in a 3 × 5 box or in a notebook on top of the filing cabinet.

2. File material promptly. This will keep paper from piling up in your office. You'll feel better about your work and yourself if you aren't snowed under by mountains of paperwork. It is a good practice to file at the end of each day or the first thing in the morning.

3. Type file folder labels in upper and lower case. They will be much easier to read than labels typed completely in upper case.

4. Keep papers to be filed in one place. You might have a basket or tray on top of the filing cabinet.

5. Check all clipped pages to be sure they should be together. Sometimes pages stick together, and a page may be misfiled and lost forever. After you are sure that the pages belong together, staple them.

6. File papers in date order, placing the latest one in front.

7. Mend tears, and flatten pages as much as possible.

8. As you handle each piece of paper for the general file, and before you put it in the filing basket, determine where that paper is to be filed. In pencil at the upper right-hand corner, designate the folder where it will be filed. Then when you are ready to file, you can go right to that folder and put it away.

9. Allow sufficient space in your file drawers for expansion. You will need extra space for the letters B, C, H, M, S, and W.

10. Use the telephone book as a quick reference to determine how to alphabetize.

11. Cross-reference files if there is any doubt about their contents or where material should be filed.

12. Use large file pockets for bulky items. (These are also available in hanging and manila folders.) Keep large items in subject order.

13. Don't overload the drawers. Leave three to four inches in each drawer for working room.

14. Limit the number of papers to 50 to 100 a file.

15. Fold large-size papers with printing to outside, so the page can be read easily.

Filing Catalogs

What do you do about the bulky catalogs that arrive daily in the mail?

A bottom file drawer is the perfect place to keep all catalogs. Two-inch expansion file pockets, available from your office supplier, will hold these catalogs and keep them from sliding around and bending in the drawer.

Label the pockets according to types of supplies, such as Office Supplies, Clip Art, Church Supplies and Literature, Audio Visual, and Films. Of course you will also have a Miscellaneous pocket for the dozens of small catalogs that advertise odds and ends.

When you receive a new catalog from a vendor, mark the date received on the cover, and throw away the previous issue. Keep only the most current copy. This will keep your catalog file up-to-date.

ACCOUNTS PAID FILE

Pastor Robinson received a bill from a publisher. He felt certain that the item indicated was already paid for, so he went to Mary, the financial secretary, for verification.

"Well, I don't know," Mary said. "There are several checks written to that company the past few months, and I don't know what they're for." Pulling out several large manila envelopes, she dumped them, one at a time, on her desk.

Sorting through the contents of each envelope in turn, she pulled out several receipts from the company in question. Finally after 20 minutes, Mary found the correct receipt that indicated that the bill had, in fact, been paid.

Mary's filing system for paid bills is a bottom desk drawer, into which she throws manila envelopes stuffed full of paid bills. Mary herself states that she is following the procedure the person who had the job before her followed, and she too is frustrated when she tries to find anything.

Receipts for accounts paid must be filed alphabetically, by vendor, that is, the person or company to whom the check is made out. Included in this alphabetical list would be Petty Cash, if you make checks out to Petty Cash, and Postmaster if you make checks out to the Postmaster for bulk mail deposits and postage.

Set up a folder for each vendor, employee, or any person who frequently receives payments from the church. Manila folders work well for this file. In addition, the use of file guides, A to Z, will help with the filing and retrieving of information.

For each letter of the alphabet, a Miscellaneous folder should be made. This folder will hold one-time-only or very occasional payments and is kept immediately behind the file guide for each letter. Any time there are five pieces or more to the same vendor, however, a separate folder should be made.

By filing paid bills in alphabetical order according to payee, your work as financial secretary will be greatly eased. You will be able to find or file information more quickly.

Occasionally someone will want to review all the bills paid for a given budget account. For instance, the minister of music cannot remember what music was ordered from a certain company. He can go right to the file, pull out that vendor's folder, and find the order and you don't have to waste your time looking through piles of receipts.

"What about the minister of education who wants to know everything that has been paid out of his budget?" you ask.

He would be able to refer to that budget's page in the ledger to see any other payments that have been made out of that account, and he could then quickly look up any payee's file folder to examine the payments in question, made by himself or authorized persons for the budget.

Because your paid bills were arranged in alphabetical order before payments were made, your filing task is easy. Keep your accounts paid filing up-to-date by filing at the end of the day.

15

Record Retention and Methods

Sally and Janice, two church secretaries, have totally opposite ideas about maintaining church records.

Sally believes that any papers left by mistake in the office or workroom over the weekend or in the evening should be thrown out. "When in doubt, throw it out," she laughs, "If they [Sunday school teachers, church workers] wanted them, they wouldn't leave them here," she argues.

Frequently a teacher calls the office frantically, asking for the missing papers. Sally does not hesitate to say, "I threw them away."

Sally's pastor similarly often asks for a document or letter, only to be told, "Sorry, we don't have that any more." Janice, however, has kept every piece of paper that has passed through the church office in the past twenty years. Her desk file drawer is crammed full of the dated correspondence of four or five previous pastors. Other desk drawers contain years old bank statements, receipts for paid bills, and other financial information.

The four-drawer file cabinet in Janice's office is stuffed with old calendars, contribution records and envelopes dating back twenty years, and yellowed file folders filled with useless information.

The office is cluttered, and her desk is stacked with papers, notebooks, and file folders in which she keeps her current work.

Obviously some records should be kept forever. Yes, but some records should be disposed of as soon as a transaction is completed.

Who decides what will be retained, and how long a retained document should be kept? A problem in churches is that everybody's business is nobody's business, and things that someone should do are not done by anyone. Committees come and go, pastors and secretaries come and go, and for some churches, the records pile up and inundate the office. No one takes the time to organize the church's records.

But, as in Sally's case, records often are not kept long enough. Too much clutter is more often the case, though.

Someone must be responsible for disposing of or moving outdated records. Will you be the one to organize things?

For the immediate problem of church members, Sunday School teachers, lay leaders, and staff members leaving materials around the church office or workroom, you can do two things.

First, if you know who leaves the materials, talk to that person and explain the problem. Ask where the materials belong and what the person wants you to do with them when you find them. I have found that personal contact alone will remind church workers to pick up after themselves.

Second, you might have organizer bins or drawers available in the office for the various departments to use, and you will put all materials pertaining to each department in the bins. You would also use these bins for incoming department mail.

The important thing is to move the clutter out of your way. Don't let the church office become the dumping area of the church, as happens in so many instances.

Now what about the church's records? Which records are permanent, and which should be disposed of? Some guidelines for records retention follow.

GUIDELINES FOR RECORD RETENTION

Applications for Employment. Three months. For good prospects for whom you have no immediate opening, you may want to keep applications for up to a year.

Attendance Records for Personnel. Permanent.

Audit Reports. Permanent. These are a part of the historical records. One copy of each audit report is kept in the general file.

Bank Deposit Slips and Statements. Seven years.

Bonds and Related Records. Permanent. Store in the church's safe, but keep a photocopy in the general file for immediate reference.

Budgets. One copy of each year's approved annual budget should be kept permanently in the general file. This is a historical record.

Bulk Mail Forms. Keep for a year or two in your general file.

Bulletins. Store one copy of each week's bulletin in the general file or put in a three-ring binder. After two years, place the copies in the church library.

Canceled Checks. Six to seven years.

Checkbook Register. Keep last year's book in the church office for reference. Store other books for six to seven years.

Chronological Record. Permanent. This is the historical record of membership in your church.

Constitution and Bylaws. Permanent.

Construction Records. Permanent. This includes plans, drawings, correspondence, payments to contractors, and all related materials. For any future development of church property, old construction records may be required for reference. Or should the building be sold, the records could be helpful. Store bulky records and drawings in a safe place. Notes telling where to find all such records should be in the general file.

Contribution Records (Annual statements of giving). Seven years.

Correspondence. This will vary. Generally correspondence should be kept for five years. One pastor I know, however, dictates dozens of letters a week, thanking people for this and that, offering condolences, inviting folks to evening activities, and so on. For this type of correspondence, retaining the document for more than six months is not necessary. Also if a pastor leaves the church, his personal correspondence does not have to be retained (although the new pastor may want to look through it to see if there is any information he might find helpful). Some correspondence is permanent, such as that pertaining to legal matters, administrative policies, or church history.

Decision cards. If you maintain individual membership records, the decision cards can be disposed of. If the decision card is the only record you have of a person's joining your church, however, it should be kept permanently.

Deeds. Permanent. Store originals in a safe deposit box at a bank or keep in a fireproof church safe. Make photocopies for the general file for immediate reference.

Financial Statements. One copy of each month's financial statement should be kept permanently in the general file. This is a historical record.

General Ledger. Keep last year's ledger in a convenient place. It is often necessary to refer to the previous year for information. For example, a youth minister might come to you and say, "How much did we spend for camp supplies last year?" After two years, the ledgers should be kept in a storage box, out of the church office. Keep the ledgers for at least seven years.

Guarantees and Instructions. Keep in the general file for as long as the church has the equipment described. For example, if your typewriter dies and you replace it, you can dispose of the instruction book.

Incorporation Records. Permanent. Make photocopies for the general file, and store originals in the church safe or a bank safe deposit box.

Insurance Policies. Retain in the general file as long as the policies are in force. Expired policies can be disposed of.

Inventory Records. Current copies should be kept in the general file. Some churches use a ledger book or bound notebook to record new purchases. Sold or replaced equipment is crossed out. This is a permanent record.

Invoices and Receipts. For reference, keep in the accounts paid file for two years. For small churches, this would not pose a storage problem, because there wouldn't be that much bulk for a year's worth of invoices and receipts, and it is very helpful to have last year's information available. After two years, pull the paid bills out of the file and store them. The finance committee should decide how long these records should be kept. Some could be disposed of after two years, such as those for consumable supplies. Others should be kept permanently, such as receipts for major expenditures.

Letters of Transfer or Recommendation. Keep these only until the information is recorded in your permanent records.

Licenses (Federal, State, Local). Retain in your general file until they are obsolete or superseded by new ones.

Membership Record Cards. Permanent. Retain all membership cards. The cards for persons who leave the church should be kept at the back of the file, in a "Dead File."

Minutes of Business Meetings. Permanent. Copies should be retained in the general file, with the membership secretary or church clerk retaining copies in a binder or notebook. Minutes are important historical documents.

Newsletters. One copy of each issue should be kept in the general file or in a three-ring notebook. Several churches keep bound volumes of newsletters in their libraries.

Offering Envelopes (members' individual envelopes). Seven years. In several churches, offering envelopes have been kept since the beginning of time. They take up a lot of storage space, and it is simply not necessary to retain them longer than seven years.

Payroll Records. Seven years. Although individuals only have to retain their records four years, a business is required to maintain these records for seven years. (Yes, a church is considered a business by the Internal Revenue Service.)

Personnel Records. Permanent. Keep for two years in the general file. After that, they can be moved to permanent storage.

Policies and Procedures Manual. An up-to-date manual should be kept in a three-ring notebook. Pages should be updated as needed. Those that are superseded by new pages should be disposed of.

Service Contracts. Generally these records are disposed of when they become obsolete. But you may want to retain them in your files for a year or two for reference. For example, suppose the church has a lawn service and then decides to cancel it and have the custodian cut the lawn. After a year, though, the church wants to have an outside company do the work again. Having the contract on file will help with negotiating a new contract.

Sunday School Records. Keep for at least five years. The church should decide how long these records should be kept.

Tax Exemption Certificates. Permanent. Keep in the general file.

Tax Records. Seven years.

The value of records for your church is the length of time such records are needed or used within your church. The following questions should be asked in determining the value of records:

1. What are the legal requirements for keeping this document?
2. Does this document have historical value in telling the story of the church's development?
3. Will it help the church's work today to have this particular record of the past?
4. Does the information in this document support the information in some current document?

As a guideline, your administrative board, trustees, or deacons should determine the value of organizational records. The finance committee will advise on all financial records. Advice on disposing of membership and meeting records should be given by the church clerk, pastoral staff, or elected leaders of the church. The needs of all departments using the records should be considered, and guidelines should be set forth in a procedure manual.

How long the church needs a record is one thing. How long the government thinks you should keep it is another. Laws are constantly changing, and the record retention time required by governments may change as well. If in doubt, ask someone in authority. The church body will be held responsible for noncompliance with government regulations.

For any records not included on the above list, consult church leaders, local and state authorities, or the Internal Revenue Service.

RECORDS STORAGE

Where will you keep your boxes of records?

Store them in a limited-access room, out of the way of general traffic. A closet may serve your needs.

Often, though, the space in a church is at a premium, and there is no extra room for storage. Then consider using wall space. Ask the building and grounds committee to construct shelves in a suitable location. Two or three shelves, the length of a wall and close to the ceiling, will store many boxes of records without taking up valuable floor space.

Storage boxes should be sturdy. Keep boxes from your paper supplier or buy boxes, especially made for storing records, from your office supply dealer. Be sure to:

1. Seal all boxes, since much of the material is confidential.
2. Use a black marker and write the contents on the end of each box.
3. Mark the date the contents are to be destroyed.
4. Store the boxes so that the writing is visible.
5. Maintain a log of all stored records. This log should:
   (a) Indicate the item(s) preserved.
   (b) Tell where each box is stored.
   (c) Tell how it is labeled.
   (d) State date of storage.
   (e) State date item is to be destroyed.

This will allow efficient retrieval of needed inactive records and will provide information for persons who will be responsible for records disposition some time in the future. After all, you might not still be at the church. The present committee members won't be the same committee persons three, five, or seven years from now. Help your church's future workers by providing this information.

Microfilming

Protecting records is very important, and losing records can be devastating. The use of microfilm will preserve vital church records in the event of a catastrophe.

One large Baptist church in Alabama has been completely destroyed twice by fire over the past twenty-five years. After the first fire, which destroyed all the offices and their entire contents, members had to start from scratch and reconstruct financial and membership records. It was a painstaking process.

The church learned from this costly, time-consuming lesson and decided to have their vital records microfilmed at regular intervals. Twice a year after that, all records were recorded on microfilm, and stored in a bank safe deposit box. A second fire, years after the first, destroyed the buildings and their contents, but because the vital information was on microfilm, reconstruction of the church records was easy. All necessary documents were reproduced and only the most current statements had to be obtained from the bank to complete the financial records. Membership records, minutes, bulletins, and all other records were also preserved.

Putting material on microfilm is also a method of storing records in a very limited space. Microfilm can reduce the space required by conventional files by 98 percent. If space is really at a premium in your church, this may be the answer to preserving your records.

Microfilm is one of the most valuable aids for storing and retrieving data. There are various types of microfilm, for many applications. For use in the church office, two applications are 16 mm reels and microfiche.

1. *Reels.* These are used to store inactive or permanent records. Documents are filmed in a continuous roll, containing 2,500 frames (Figure 106). Each frame holds one or more records, depending on their size. Reels of film can be stored in a safe deposit box, safe, or other secure area. To find a record on a reel, it is necessary to search through the entire reel. If documents are filmed in chronological order, however, this is not too much of a problem.
2. *Microfiche.* For quick retrieval of records, 16 mm reels are separated into individual frames and put on microfiche "jackets." This example (Figure 107), which is approximately 4 × 6 inches, contains 126 frames. The number of frames on each jacket can vary also, depending on the size of individual records. Microfiche jackets have headings that indicate the records included, and are consecutively numbered for indexing. Records are fairly easy to find on microfiche.

A service bureau will film all your records for approximately three to five cents a frame and provide either a reel or a microfiche. Copies can be stored off-site, providing security for your records.

A microfiche reader, available for under $200, allows quick access to information. A reader-printer lets you read and make a copy of a particular record.

The primary factors to consider in selecting the most appropriate form of microfilm include the nature of information you want to store, who will use the information, how often you must have access to records, and how the records are to be used.

Figure 106

STORING RECORDS

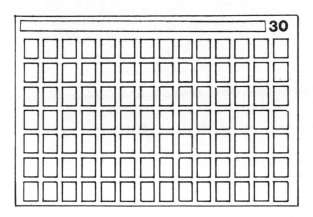

Figure 107

To learn all about microfilming, contact a local service bureau from the listings in your *Yellow Pages*. Microfilm service bureau technicians earn their living by filming. They're experts, and can answer any questions you have.

RECORDS DISPOSITION

Destroying unnecessary records can reduce the space now occupied by records by 40 percent. When it is time to dispose of the records, be sure you obtain final authority of current committee members to do so. Then do it! You don't have to suffocate in piles of paper.

PART FIVE

HANDLING THE MAIL

Handling the mail in the church office is easy. Open the mail that comes in or put stamps on the outgoing mail and put it in the mailbox. Right?

Wrong. What do you do with all the incoming mail? Who gets it if it is not addressed to anyone in particular? And what should you do with pieces of mail for Sunday School classes, the finance committee chairman, or the minister of music?

Advertisements and circulars that come into the office could be of interest to the nursery coordinator or children's workers. How can these persons each receive this information?

Finally, how does each person receiving mail want their mail handled? One youth minister adamantly opposes having any piece of mail opened by the church secretary. Another minister, the pastor of a fairly large church, likes all his mail opened and wants his secretary to dispose of the junk mail and other nonessential material.

Chapter 16, dealing with incoming mail, tells how to handle all the mail that arrives at the church office.

It is no problem to mail a letter. But do you know how to send out a large mailing the least expensive way? Do you know how much postage to put on a large envelope?

Outgoing mail is the subject of Chapter 17. It deals with sending first-class and second-class mail and third-class bulk mail. It also details the use of library rate, available for such items as books and audio- or videotapes.

16

Incoming Mail

The postman delivers the mail to the church office. Peg, the church secretary, looks through the pile, pulling out junk mail and quickly tossing it out. She sets the remaining pile on a counter near her desk. Fifteen minutes later, the pastor walks by and sorts through the stack looking for his mail. The minister of youth does the same. The remaining pile is "not for anybody," and Peg places the pile to one side, with other pieces of mail that have accumulated.

In another church, pigeon-hole type mail bins are provided for all the mail for all the ministers and lay leaders. Many of the bins are full. As the secretary looks through the bins, she sees that the organist has not picked up his mail in three months. And there is one letter that looks rather important.

One person in the church office should be responsible for picking up the mail, whether it is in the mailbox, at the post office box, or delivered in person by the mail carrier. That person should also see that the intended recipients of mail receive their mail promptly.

Mail organizer bins are very helpful for distributing mail. A person who does not receive mail very often, however, can get out of the habit of looking in the bin. In that case, the person responsible for the mail should telephone the individual and advise him or her that mail is in the office, ready to be picked up.

Often greeting cards come into the church office addressed to "So-and-so's Sunday School Class." Naturally, because the teacher isn't expecting any mail, he or she doesn't look for any in the office. Again, it is the responsibility of the person in charge of the mail to advise the intended recipient that the mail is in the office.

How should mail be handled? These twelve steps will ensure that your mail will be handled efficiently:

1. Talk to each person who regularly receives mail. Determine how that individual wants his or her mail handled. Also be sure you know how to handle incoming mail for leaders in the church. Sometimes it is very important to open mail immediately, as the following example illustrates:

   At one church, a first-class piece of mail, addressed to the finance committee chairperson, was placed in his mail slot by the secretary. He had had no occasion to be in the office for several weeks, and when he did pick up his mail, he found the first-class letter from the bank. The notice inside advised that a $10,000 CD was nearing maturity, and the ten-day grace period for cashing it would come up within the next week.

   "Always open mail addressed to me," he snapped. "Look at this! We've missed the grace period, and it's going to cost us $200 to cash the CD now." He explained that he didn't look in his box often. He was too busy on Sundays, and had been very busy at his place of business.

2. Establish a daily routine. Be sure to process each piece of mail that comes in each day.

3. Have the proper supplies on hand. These include:
   (*a*) Date stamp and stamp pad;
   (*b*) Letter opener;
   (*c*) Paper clips;
   (*d*) Stapler;
   (*e*) Tape.

4. Sort the mail into five stacks, as follows:
   (*a*) Personal or confidential.
   (*b*) First class, including, *urgent, registered,* or *airmail.* These pieces usually require prompt attention.
   (*c*) Financial mail, including bills, statements, and offering envelopes.
   (*d*) Third-class mail, including advertising and circulars.
   (*e*) Magazines, newspapers, catalogs, and periodicals.

5. Open the first-class mail (if you are authorized to do so):
   (*a*) Tap the lower edges of the envelopes on the desk so material inside will fall to the bottom.
   (*b*) Slit open the envelopes with the letter opener.
   (*c*) Remove contents, making sure that everything has been removed; tape any cuts or rips.
   (*d*) Date stamp each piece of mail.
   (*e*) Check to see if the return address is included on the letter. If it isn't, staple the envelope to the letter or write the return address on the letter and throw away the envelope.
   (*f*) Sort into stacks for each recipient.

6. Date stamp personal and confidential mail and place it on top of each stack.

7. Sort newspapers and magazines. Determine who reads which ones. Place on the bottom of the stacks of mail. A lot of sample magazines are sent to church offices. If no one wants them, they can be placed in the reception area as reading material for visitors. Attach a routing slip, similar to the one shown in Figure 108, to those magazines and newspapers that are read by everyone in the church

office. Printed routing slips save time, because a list doesn't have to be written each time publications are received and pieces are distributed. Each person on the list reads the publication, checks off his or her name, and passes it to the next person on the list.

8. Examine all the advertising material. Frequently you will find items of interest. Date stamp pieces you want, and discard the rest. Place any advertising material on the bottom of the stacks of mail.
9. Distribute the stacks of mail for the pastor and staff. Place mail on their desks, or in mail bins or drawers.
10. Put mail for everyone else in bins or drawers. If there is mail for someone who doesn't normally come into the office, let that person know that the mail is there to be picked up.
11. Tend to bills, statements, and contribution envelopes as follows:
    (*a*) Put bills and statements in file pockets marked Delivery Slips and Invoices, as discussed in Chapter 10. (Processing bills and statements is another task that should be done as soon as possible, according to instructions in Chapter 10.)
    (*b*) Place unopened contribution envelopes in a bank bag and lock it securely in a safe or file drawer.
12. Immediately attend to correpondence requiring your personal attention.

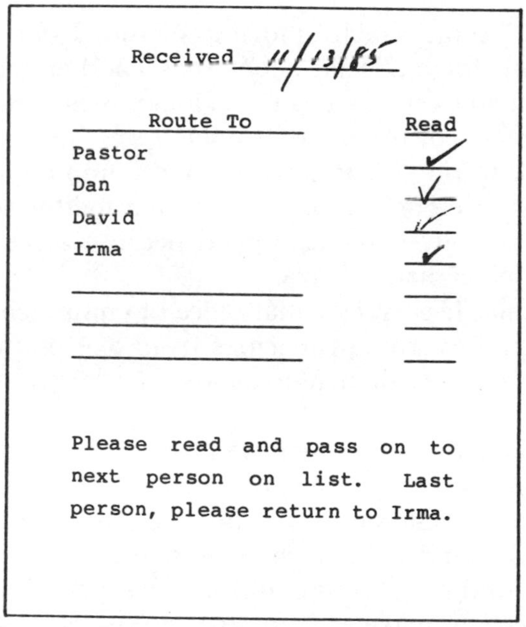
Received 11/13/85

Route To	Read
Pastor	✓
Dan	✓
David	✓
Irma	✓

Please read and pass on to next person on list. Last person, please return to Irma.

Figure 108

17

Outgoing Mail

"Let's see, that's about 22 cents' worth," murmurs Pastor Evans, as he balances a sealed envelope on the tip of his finger. "Nah, better stick another stamp on, just to be safe." Another 22-cent stamp is stuck on the envelope, and possibly wasted, because the pastor cannot determine the weight of the piece of mail.

Everyone knows how to put a first-class postage stamp on an envelope and mail it. However, determining the weight of a piece is another matter. And even for pieces that are weighed, incorrect postage is often applied because a person does not know the correct postage for first-class mail.

Purchase a postal scale. It is an essential piece of equipment. Many styles are available, ranging in maximum weighing capacities from one pound to over one hundred pounds. Smaller scales are less than ten dollars; the larger ones cost well over one hundred dollars.

A problem with the small scales, which weigh material from one-half ounce to one pound, is that the imprinted rates quickly become outdated when the postal rates change. If you have such an outdated scale, however, it is a simple matter to cover old rates with a label or sticker and write in the new rates.

Although the one-pound scale is quite useful, a five-pound maximum scale is a wiser investment. You don't have to make as many trips to the post office to mail small packages, thereby saving time and gasoline.

At McGregor, if one of the secretaries has a package to mail, she simply weighs it and then calls the post office, saying "I have a package that weighs (total weight), going to (city, state, zip code). How much is the postage?" The package is then stamped and put outside in the mailbox for pickup. The secretary does not waste her time running to the post office.

In the church office, several different classes of mailings might be used in addition to first class. These include second- and third-class bulk mailings, fourth-class (parcel post) for packages, and library rate. The fees, forms, and/or regulations for these classes of mailings confuse many church workers, and the result is that first-class postage is wasted, higher bulk rates are paid, and time is lost in preparing mailings.

To get the maximum benefit from the mails, it is essential to become familiar with postal rates, classes, and regulations.

The following minimum size standards apply to all mailable matter:

1. All mailing pieces must be at least .007 of an inch thick. For all practical purposes, you would more than likely never mail a piece this thin.
2. Pieces up to ¼ of an inch thick must be:
   (a) Rectangular in shape
   (b) At least 3½ inches wide
   (c) At least 5 inches long

When processing mail, the U.S. Postal Service separates all pieces into five categories, determined by size and shape. The categories and specifications for each are:

1. Letter Size. This refers to all pieces that conform to the following dimensions:
   (a) Length, 5 to 11½ inches
   (b) Height, 3½ to 6⅛ inches
   (c) Thickness, 0.007 to ¼ inch
   A piece does not have to be a letter to be classified as such. For example, an 8½ × 11-inch flyer or newsletter, folded in half to make a piece 5½ high by 8½ inches, would be considered a letter by the postal service.
2. Flat Size. Flat size mail consists of pieces that exceed one or more of the dimensions for letter size mail but that do not exceed any of the following maximum dimensions:
   (a) Length, over 11½ inches, but not more than 15 inches
   (b) Height, over 6⅛ inches, but not more than 12 inches
   (c) Thickness, over ¼ inch, but not more than ¾ inch
3. Machinable (Regular) Parcels. These are pieces that can be machine-processed by the postal service's parcel sorters. The dimensions are:
   (a) Length, 6 to 34 inches
   (b) Width, 3 to 17 inches
   (c) Height/Thickness, ¼ inch to 17 inches
   (d) Weight, 8 ounces to 35 pounds. (Note: Pieces weighing between 6 and 8 ounces are machinable if all their sides are rectangular. Also, for books or other printed matter, the maximum weight is 25 pounds.)
4. Irregular Parcels. These are parcels that cannot be processed by machine. Included in this category are packages with any of the following characteristics:
   (a) Length, less than 6 inches
   (b) Width, less than 3 inches
   (c) Height/Thickness, less than ¼ inch
   (d) Weight, less than 8 ounces (again the exception would be packages between 6 and 8 ounces, as long as all sides are rectangular)
   (e) Rolls and tubes, up to 26 inches long
   (f) Articles enclosed in envelopes that are not letter size, flat size, or machinable parcels.

5. Outside Parcels. This refers to those packages that because of size, shape, weight, container, or contents cannot be processed in postal sacks. These characteristics apply:
(*a*) Length, over 34 inches
(*b*) Width, over 17 inches
(*c*) Height/Thickness, over 17 inches
(*d*) Weight, over 35 pounds

FIRST-CLASS MAIL

Any mailable matter can be mailed first class, but the following items must be mailed first class: Hand- or typewritten material; correspondence; contribution records; notebooks; blank printed forms filled out in writing; any matter that contains the endorsement Postcard or Double Postcard; and printed cards or letters bearing a written date, when the date is not the date of the card but rather conveys information as to when something will occur or has occurred.

At the time of this writing, a first-class letter weighing up to one ounce is 22 cents. The postage for each succeeding ounce (up to 12 ounces), is 17 cents, not 22 cents. Thus, instead of "sticking an extra stamp on to be sure," you should weigh the piece of mail, determine the exact ounces, and use only the postage necessary. You will save a nickel on each two-ounce-or-less piece. Savings over one year's time will be considerable.

The post office carries stamps of many denominations. Keep a supply on hand to cover mailings over one ounce. At the time of this writing, stamps carried are 1, 2, 3, 4, 5, 7, 10, 14, 17, 22, 25, 30, 37, 39, 40, and 50 cents and 1, 2, and 5 dollars.

Stamps bought by the church should be used only for the church. They must be locked away when the office is closed. Stamps requested for personal use should be paid for immediately by the person requesting them. Keep an envelope marked "postage" in which you will put the cash received for personal postage used. You could put the money back into the general fund designated for the postage account, but to eliminate this bookkeeping procedure, use the cash to buy more stamps the next time you go to the post office.

LIBRARY RATE

Certain items can be mailed by churches at the fourth-class library rate. These include books, printed music, sound recordings, filmstrips, 16 mm, or narrower, width films, catalogs, bound volumes, instruments, transparencies, or microfilms.

The library rate for such items at time of this writing is:

First pound or fraction of a pound	$.50
Each additional pound or fraction through 7 pounds	.17
Each additional pound or fraction over 7 pounds	.09

Suppose a music minister from another church calls your music minister and wants to borrow fifty volumes of a youth musical from your library. The library rate will be the least expensive rate to mail these volumes.

If you have a tape ministry and are mailing packages that weigh over 3 ounces each, the library rate would be cheaper than the first-class rate.

No permit is required to use the library rate. There are certain specifications that must be followed, however. These are:

1. The identification Library Rate must be placed conspicuously on the address side of the package.
2. The name of your church, to indicate that yours is a nonprofit religious group, must be clearly marked.
3. Your return address must be included.
4. You may not include any correspondence in the package.

BULK MAIL

Some churches mail their newsletters by third-class bulk mail, others by second-class mail. What's the difference? Which one is less expensive? How are they similar? Different? Which is best for my church?

Several years ago, while working at Trinity, I asked the local post office these questions. I had noticed that many newsletters received from other churches had been mailed second class, but I knew nothing about the rates or regulations that would apply.

"You don't want to be bothered with that," the clerk told me. "It costs $220 just to apply, and that's non-refundable. If your application isn't approved, you don't get the money back."

The thought of losing $220 of the church's money frightened me, and I dismissed the idea. The following year, after moving to a new city and a new church, I called the local post office. Again, I was discouraged from using the second-class rate.

"Large non-refundable application fee . . . too much paperwork . . . complicated form . . ." the clerk stated.

As I later found out, both of these clerks worked at the front counter in the post office. Neither one was qualified to explain the details of second- and third-class mail permits.

Any questions pertaining to second- and third-class mail should be directed to the bulk-mail clerks at your post office. They are specialists who can answer any questions you might have.

For second- or third-class bulk mailings:

1. You must have 200 pieces or more.
2. Pieces must be the same size and weight.
3. A deposit must be paid in advance. Checks or cash will not be accepted at the bulk mail office. You should keep a running total of your current bulk mail deposit balance, as shown in Figure 109. When you see that the balance is below a predetermined amount, mail a check, addressed to Postmaster, to your local post office. The amount should cover two or three months' mailings. Be sure to write your permit number on the lower left-hand corner of the check, with the notation, "Bulk Mail Deposit for Permit No. ____." (You should do this at least three or

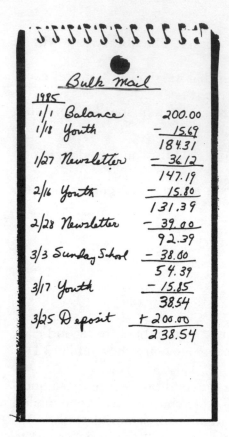

Figure 109

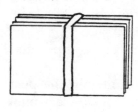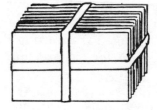

Up to 1" Thick   1" to 4" Thick

Figure 110

four days or more in advance of your next mailing, to allow sufficient time for the deposit to be processed and credited to your account.)

4. Mail must be sorted and packaged by zip code.
5. Packages must be secured with rubber bands (Figure 110). Packages up to 1 inch thick must be secured with one rubber band around the girth. Packages between 1 inch and 4 inches in thickness must be secured with two rubber bands, the first around the length and the second around the girth. Packages must not be more than 4 inches thick.
6. Pressure-sensitive identification labels, provided by the post office, must be used on packages:

(a) 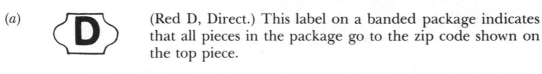 (Red D, Direct.) This label on a banded package indicates that all pieces in the package go to the zip code shown on the top piece.

(b) 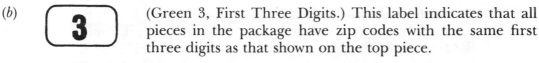 (Green 3, First Three Digits.) This label indicates that all pieces in the package have zip codes with the same first three digits as that shown on the top piece.

(c) 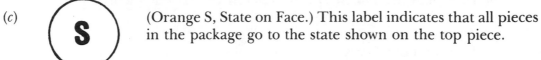 (Orange S, State on Face.) This label indicates that all pieces in the package go to the state shown on the top piece.

SECOND-CLASS MAIL

Postage rates for second-class mail are among the lowest offered. The Postal Service is able to lower processing costs because the mailer presorts the mail and meets other preparation requirements.

Basic requirements for second class postage are:

1. You must pay the $220 application fee. Yes, it is nonrefundable if the permit is denied, but bona-fide churches holding regular worship services will generally be granted a second-class permit. In addition, this is a one-time fee. There is no annual renewal.
2. Each second-class publication must be issued at a regular frequency of at least four times a year. You must determine the number of issues that will be published each year and tell the post office. Examples in Figure 114 are permissible statements of frequency.
3. If you want to change the frequency, you must file an application for second-class reentry for a fee of $35. You can get away with occasionally skipping an issue or publishing an extra issue, but if the frequency varies regularly, second-class privileges will be revoked.
4. Second-class publications must consist of printed sheets. They may not be reproduced by stencil or mimeograph.
5. All mail must be in bags provided by the post office.
6. The correct label must be in the label holder of the bag.

```
Daily
Semiweekly (twice a week)
Weekly
Biweekly (every two weeks)
Bimonthly (every two months)
Semimonthly (twice a month)
Monthly
Quarterly
Four times a year in Feb., Apr., Oct., and Dec.
```

Figure 114

7. The proper form must be filled out.
8. The church's identification statement must be included; it consists of the following items:
   (*a*) Name of publication and publication number (assigned by the post office). For example, "THE McGREGOR CHALLENGE (USPS 123–456)." The publication number may be omitted if the identification (ID) statement appears on the front cover.
   (*b*) Date of issue. This may be omitted if the ID statement appears on the front cover.
   (*c*) Statement of frequency.
   (*d*) Issue number. Every issue of each publication must be numbered consecutively. The issue number may be omitted if the ID statement appears on the front cover.
   (*e*) Church name and address, including street number, street name, and zip code.
   (*f*) Second-class imprint, which reads "Second-class postage paid at (city, state)."
   (*g*) Notice of pending application. If copies are mailed while an application is pending, a notice must be included that reads "Application to mail at second-class postage rates is pending at (your post office city, state, and zip code)."
   (*h*) Mailing address for change-of-address orders. This reads, "Postmaster: Send address changes to (your church's name and mailing address)." You must include this information, and pay the required fee for each address correction, which is 25 cents at the time of this writing.

Figure 115 is an example of an identification statement.

Processing Second-Class Mail

You have printed your newsletter and put on the address labels and sorted them by zip code. Now what?

Follow these steps for processing second-class mail:

1. When you have six pieces or more that have the same five digit zip code, package these together with rubber bands and put a red "D" at the lower left of the address on the top piece only. Set these aside.
2. For the pieces of mail left, check to see if you have six pieces or more that have identical first three digits of the zip code. Package these together with rubber bands and place a green "3" at the lower left of the address on the top piece only. Set aside.

```
"THE McGREGOR CHALLENGE (USPS 123-456) is
published  bi-weekly  at  $26  per  year  by
McGregor Baptist Church, 7224 Colonial Boul-
evard,  Fort  Myers,  FL   33912.  Second-class
postabe  paid  at  Fort  Myers,  FL.  POSTMASTER:
Send  address  changes  to  McGREGOR  BAPTIST
CHURCH, 7224 Colonial Blvd. SE, Ft. Myers FL
33912."
```

Figure 115

HANDLING THE MAIL

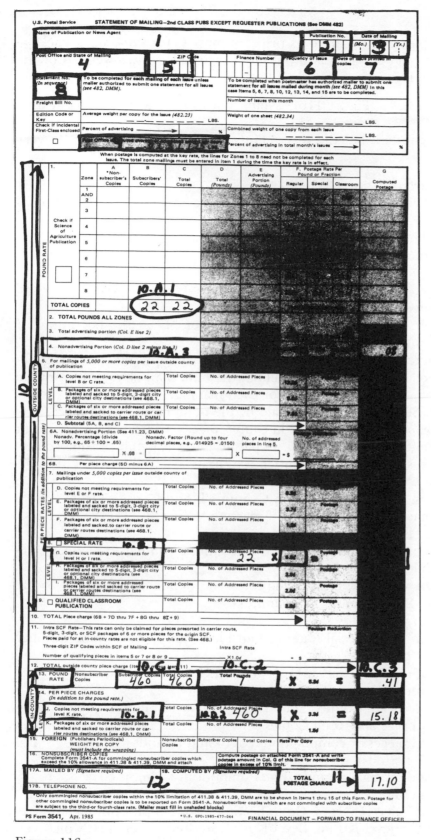

Figure 116

3. For the remaining pieces, if you have six pieces or more to the same state, package them together with rubber bands and put an orange "S" at the lower left of the address on the top piece only. Set aside.

Complete Postal Form 3541 (Figure 116). (Note: Rates shown are in effect at time of writing.)

The form looks complicated, but the instructions for filling it out are really very simple:

1. Name of your church.
2. Publication Number (assigned by the postal service when your application is approved).
3. Date of Mailing. The actual date you take the mailing to the post office.
4. Your post office and state.
5. Zip code.
6. Frequency of issue.
7. Date of issue printed on copies.
8. Statement Number (in sequence). Start with number "1" at the beginning of each year, and number consecutively.
9. Post Office-computed average or combined weight per copy. When your application is approved, before your first mailing, the bulk mail clerk will compute this weight for you. It will be the same for each mailing.
10. Figuring the cost: Second-class mail is paid by the pound and by the piece. You also pay a rate for outside-county and in-county pieces. Churches, as nonprofit organizations, qualify for Special rates. Separate in-county and outside-county pieces. Compute costs for outside-county pieces first.
    (a) Outside County, pound rate:
        (1) Count pieces. Enter total copies in Columns B and C on the form.
        (2) Multiply total copies by computed average weight. ($.0131125 \times 22 = .288475$, or less than one pound).
        (3) Enter the weight in Column D, Line 4 (assuming you have no advertising in your publication).
        (4) Compute the weight by multiplying the total pounds in Column D by the Special rate. Enter amount in Column G.
    (b) Outside County, piece rate:
        (1) Go to Section 8-G (Special Rate for Outside County). Enter total number of addressed pieces.
        (2) Compute rate for each piece. Enter total in Column G.
    (c) In County, pound rate:
        (1) Go to Section 13 (In County, Pound Rate). Enter number of copies under Subscriber Copies and Total Copies.
        (2) Multiply total pieces by computed weight to find pounds ($460 \times .0131125 = 6.03$, or 7 pounds).
        (3) Compute rate for total pounds. Enter amount in Column G.
    (d) In County, piece rate:
        (1) Compute per piece charges. Go to Section 14-J. (Copies not meeting requirements for level K rate. Level K is a rate for carrier sort, which you would only use if you were mailing many thousands of pieces.)

HANDLING THE MAIL

(2) Enter total number of addressed in-county pieces.

(3) Compute cost. Enter amount in Column G.

11. Total amounts in Column G. This is the amount of your postage.

12. Sign at 17A, complete 18 (person who computes figures), and include your telephone number at 17B.

Place the packages of mail into a mail sack, obtainable at the bulk mail office in the post office.

A label, similar to the one shown in Figure 117, must be placed in the label holder on the bag (or sack).

These labels are available from the bulk mail clerk. You can also make your own if you wish. Note that there are three lines on the label.

The first line is for the destination location:

1. When all the mail in the sack is for the same five-digit zip code, this line includes destination city, state, and zip code.

2. When all the mail in the sack is for only the first three digits, for example "339," this line shows city, state, and the first three digits only. This would include five-digit packages as well. For example, a mailing has 250 pieces. All are for the Fort Myers area, which has "339" as the first three digits. The individual packages are:

33901 – 45
33902 – 12
33903 – 51
33904 – 18
33907 – 75

This group has five-digit packages, each one with a red "D" on the top piece.

339   – 59

This group consists of pieces having less than six pieces with the same zip code. They are bundled together with a green "3" on the front.

3. When the mail in the sack has some five-digit bundles, some three-digit, or other zip codes or both, the destination on the first line will be your post office, where the sack will be opened and the pieces sorted. The designation "DIS," indicating district, must be included on the first line. For example, for a mixed sack of mail for McGregor Baptist Church, the first line reads "DIS FT MYERS FL 339."

The second line on the label indicates the contents or class (second):

1. Use NEWS if your newsletter or printed material is published weekly or more often.

Figure 117

2. Use 2C if your printed material is published biweekly or less often.

The third line on the label indicates the city, the state, and the first three digits of the zip code of the city of origin; see Figure 118.

You can save money by using second-class mail. One major disadvantage, though, is that you must specify how often you will mail a publication, which eliminates any special mailings. For example, if you say you are going to publish a newsletter monthly, or twelve times a year, you would not be able to send a special mailing second class in addition to that. If your church decided to mail postcards announcing a special event coming up, you would not be able to use your second-class permit. You can't use the permit for anything except the publication specified in your application.

THIRD-CLASS BULK MAIL

A postcard announcing a Sunday School Picnic mailed to 200 youth and children, a twice-monthly newsletter sent to 1,000 members, or a 10,000-piece mailing to the entire community announcing a special one-week revival—all can be sent under one third-class bulk mail permit.

The following guidelines and specifications apply for third-class privileges:

1. You must pay a one-time application fee of $50.00.
2. You must pay an annual calendar year fee of $50.00.

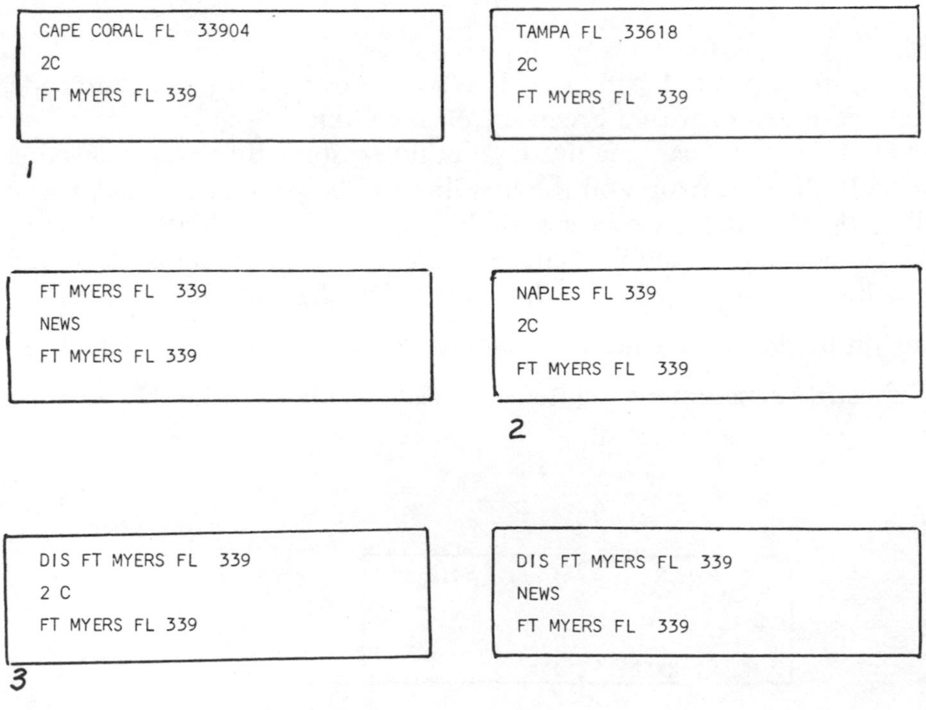

```
CAPE CORAL FL  33904

2C

FT MYERS FL  339
```

```
TAMPA FL  33618

2C

FT MYERS FL  339
```

1

```
FT MYERS FL  339

NEWS

FT MYERS FL  339
```

```
NAPLES FL  339

2C

FT MYERS FL  339
```

2

```
DIS FT MYERS FL  339

2 C

FT MYERS FL  339
```

```
DIS FT MYERS FL  339

NEWS

FT MYERS FL  339
```

3

Figure 118

HANDLING THE MAIL

3. All mail must be in bags (sacks) or trays. (The post office will provide trays as well as sacks. They are not as dirty as sacks and are less cumbersome.)
4. The correct label must be placed on the end of the tray or bag.
5. P. O. Form 3602 or 3602PC must be filled out.
6. The permit imprint must be in the upper right-hand corner of the address area. Figure 119 is a permit imprint. Permit imprints for third-class bulk mail must show the following:
    (a) The endorsement Nonprofit Organization or Nonprofit Org or Nonprofit, indicates that the mailing is at the special third-class rate for nonprofit organizations.
    (b) The legend, "U.S. Postage Paid."
    (c) The city and state of deposit.
    (d) The permit number.

Processing Third-Class Bulk Mail

Although third-class mail is processed similarly to second-class mail, there are some differences.

For nonprofit organizations, special rates apply. Pieces that weigh more than 3.5069 ounces and are mailed at the five-digit or basic rate are subject to the per pound rate and the applicable per piece rate.

Pieces up to 2.6029 ounces must be paid at the prescribed minimum per piece rate for each presort level.

"Presort level" refers to Basic, Five-Digit, or Carrier Route Sorting. A small church would use the basic and 5-digit route sorting only. The carrier route sorting is used for very large mailings of thousands of pieces.

At the time of this writing, the per-pound rate is $.253 for all sorts. The piece rates are $.085, Basic presort and $.071, five-digit presort.

As most mailings for small churches are sent at the per-piece rate, I will discuss this type of mailing here.

To qualify for the five-digit presort:

1. There must be 125 pieces of mail or more with the same five-digit zip code. There must also be a total of 200 pieces that qualify for the five-digit rate.
2. If some pieces in your mailing do not qualify for the five-digit presort rate, they count in the total pieces of the mailing but will be charged at the basic rate.
3. Each five-digit zip code that qualifies for the five-digit presort rate must be put into a separate sack or tray, with a correct label. For example, if you have five zip codes of 125 or more each, you would use five separate containers, one for each

```
Non-Profit Organization
    U. S. Postage
       PAID
    Fort Myers, FL
    Permit #311
```

Figure 119

zip code. Even if you have one small package of 125 newsletters, it still has to be in a separate sack or tray to qualify for the lower rate.

4. A list, by zip code and quantity, as shown in Figure 120, is required.

After you have labeled your mailing, and the pieces have been sorted by zip code and counted, follow this procedure to process it:

1. 125 pieces or more that have the same zip code are packaged together as previously shown, with a red "D" on the top piece.
2. Put each zip code into a separate sack or tray and place a label in the label holder. (See the following section on labels.)
3. Using the remaining pieces after Step 1 has been completed, see if you have 50 to 124 pieces (and at least 125 or more to a 3-digit sack or tray) to the same 5-digit zip code. Package these together and put into 3-digit sack or tray and label as follows:

   Line 1: City, state and 3-digit prefix
   Line 2: Contents
   Line 3: Office of mailing

   The pieces you have sorted in Steps 1 and 2 are eligible for 5-digit rate if you have at least 200 or more pieces that qualify for the 5-digit rate.
4. If you have 10 to 49 pieces which have the same five-digit zip code, package these together and put a red "D" at the lower left of the address on the top piece only.

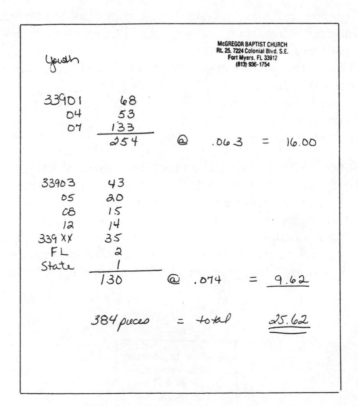

Figure 120

HANDLING THE MAIL

5. If you have ten pieces or more of mail left over that have only the first three digits of the zip code, package them together and put a green "3" at the lower left of the address on the top piece.

FOR ZONE RATED MAIL USE FORM 3605

U.S. Postal Service
STATEMENT OF MAILING WITH PERMIT IMPRINTS

MAILER: Complete all items by typewriter, pen or indelible pencil. Prepare in duplicate if receipt is desired. Check for instructions from your postmaster regarding box labeled "RCA Offices."

Permit No. 311

Post Office of Mailing	Date	Receipt No.	Mailing Statement Sequence No.
Ft Myers, FL 33907	2/6/86		31

Check applicable box

- ☐ *International*
- ☐ *Other (Specify)*

1st Class
- ☐ *ZIP + 4 Nonpresort*
- ☐ *ZIP + 4 Presort*
- ☐ *Carrier Route*
- ☐ *Presort First-Class*
- ☐ *Single Piece*

2nd Class
- ☐ *Newspapers and magazines entered at the applicable third-class rate*

3rd Class
- ☐ *Carrier Route*
- ☑ *5-digit*
- ☑ *Basic*
- ☐ *Single Piece*

4th Class
- ☐ *Library Rate*
- ☐ *Special 4th Class Single Piece*
- ☐ *Presort Special 4th Class*

Processing Category *(See DMM 128)*
- ☑ *Letters*
- ☐ *Flats*
- ☐ *Machinable (Regular Parcels*
- ☐ *Irregular Parcels*
- ☐ *Outside Parcels*

Weight of a single piece . — — — lbs.

RCA Offices:

TOTAL IN MAILING		NUMBER OF			
Pieces	Pound	Sacks	Trays	Pallets	Other Containers
384			1		

Name and Address of Permit Holder *(Include ZIP Code)*
McGREGOR BAPTIST CHURCH
Rt. 25, 7224 Colonial Blvd. S.E.
Fort Myers, FL 33912
(813) 936-1754

Telephone No. 936-1754

☐ Check if non-profit under 623. DMM*

Name and Address of Individual or Organization for which mailing is prepared *(If other than permit holder)*

☐ Check if non-profit under 623. DMM*

Name and Address of Mailing Agent *(If other than permit holder)*

POSTAGE COMPUTATION

Pound Rate	1. Pound Rate Postage Charge	No. Pounds	Rate/Pound $	Postage
Piece Rates	2. ZIP + 4 Presort	No. Qual. Pieces	Rate Per Piece $	Postage
	3. Presort First Class	No. Qual. Pieces	Rate Per Piece $	Postage
	4. ZIP + 4 Nonpresort	No. Qual. Pieces	Rate Per Piece $	Postage
	5. Carrier Route	No. Qual. Pieces	Rate Per Piece $	Postage
	6. 5-digit	No. Qual. Pieces 254	Rate Per Piece $ 063	Postage 16.00
	7. Basic	No. Qual. Pieces 130	Rate Per Piece $ 0.74	Postage 962
	8. Rate Category	No. of Pieces	Rate Per Piece $	Postage
	9. SUBTOTAL (1 through 8) ▶			Postage 25.62

10. Additional Postage Payment *(State reasons for additional postage payments)*

No. Pieces	Rate/Piece	Postage
	$	

11. ☐ Check if applicable third class bulk piece rate is paid by meter. *(Form 3602-PC required)*

12. TOTAL POSTAGE *(9 plus 10)* where applicable) ▶ Total Postage $25.62

*The signature of a nonprofit mailer certifies that: (1) The mailing does not violate section 623.5 DMM and (2) Only the mailer's matter is being mailed; and (3) This is not a cooperative mailing with other persons or organizations that are not entitled to special bulk mailing privileges; and (4) This mailing has not been undertaken by the mailer on behalf of or produced for another person or organization that is not entitled to special bulk mailing privileges.

Signature of Permit Holder or Agent *(Both principal and agent are liable for any postage deficiency incurred)*
Jennifer Horton

Telephone No. 936-1754

PS Form 3602, Dec. 1984

Willful Entry of false, fictitious or fraudulent statements or representations hereon punishable by fine up to $10,000 or imprisonment up to 5 years, or both (18 USC 1001).

Figure 121

6. For any leftover mail, see if you have ten pieces or more for the same state. If you have, package them together and put an orange "S" on the top piece.
7. Put any further pieces that are left over in a package and slip a sheet of paper marked MIXED·STATES on the top, under the rubber bands.
8. The pieces of mail described in steps 4 to 7 should be put in one sack or tray, with the correct label attached (Note: If none of the pieces of mail qualifies for the five-digit presort rate, then all pieces can be put in one sack or tray.)
9. Complete the required form (Figure 121).

Labels for Third-Class Bulk Mail

Labels are available from your bulk mail clerk or you may make your own. The three lines on the label must be completed as follows (see Figure 122):

1. The first line indicates the destination:
   (*a*) When all the mail in the sack or tray is for the same five-digit zip code, the first line will include the city, the state, and the five-digit zip code.
   (*b*) When all the mail in the sack or tray is for the first three digits of the zip code, the label will indicate the city, the state, and the first three digits of the zip code.
   (*c*) When the mail in the sack or tray has the first three digits, the mixed states, or other zip codes or both, the city, the state, and the first three digits are on the first line, prefixed by the notation DIS. For example, a mixed sack for Ft. Myers would read "DIS FT MYERS FL 339."
2. The second line on the label indicates the contents, either *letters* or *flats*, meaning that the pieces being mailed are either letter sized or flat sized, as described at the beginning of this chapter.
   (*a*) Use "3 CL LTRS" if the pieces are letter sized.

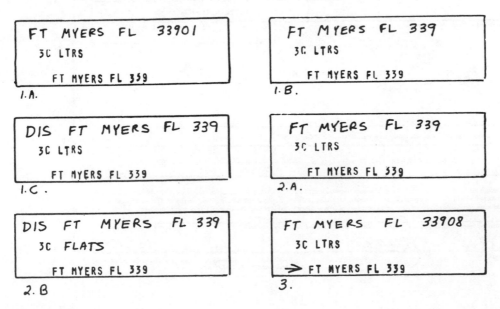

Figure 122

```
           TWO-LETTER STATE AND TERRITORY ABBREVIATIONS


Alabama...............AL    Kentucky..............KY    Ohio..................OH
Alaska................AK    Louisiana.............LA    Oklahoma..............OK
Arizona...............AZ    Maine.................ME    Oregon................OR
Arkansas..............AR    Maryland..............MD    Pennsylvania..........PA
American Samoa........AS    Massachusetts.........MA    Puerto Rico...........PR
California............CA    Michigan..............MI    Rhode Island..........RI
Colorado..............CO    Minnesota.............MN    South Carolina........SC
Connecticut...........CT    Mississippi...........MS    South Dakota..........SD
Delaware..............DE    Missouri..............MO    Tennessee.............TN
District of Columbia..DC    Montana...............MT    Trust Territory.......TT
Florida...............FL    Nebraska..............NE    Texas.................TX
Georgia...............GA    Nevada................NV    Utah..................UT
Guam..................GU    New Hampshire.........NH    Vermont...............VT
Hawaii................HI    New Jersey............NJ    Virginia..............VA
Idaho.................ID    New Mexico............NM    Virgin Islands........VI
Illinois..............IL    New York..............NY    Washington............WA
Indiana...............IN    North Carolina........NC    West Virginia.........WV
Iowa..................IA    North Dakota..........ND    Wisconsin.............WI
Kansas................KS    N. Mariana Islands....CM    Wyoming...............WY
```

Figure 123

(*b*) Use "3 CL FLATS" if the pieces are larger than the letter size.

3. Line three on the label indicates the origin. It includes the city, the state, and the first three digits of the zip code.

The following restrictions apply to third-class bulk mail:

1. Matter handwritten or typewritten, including identical copies prepared by an automatic typewriter or carbon copies of such matter is not third-class bulk mail. Material produced by computers, unless it has the character of actual and personal correspondence.
2. Printed material cannot contain personal notes. For example, if you are mailing a newsletter, you cannot write any personal messages on individual copies.
3. Blank printed forms, filled out in writing, for example, notices of meetings, certificates, or contribution records, are not in this category.
4. Printed cards or letters bearing a written date when the date is not the date of the letter or card but rather is a date when something is to occur or has already occurred are not in this category.
5. Matter containing the endorsement "Postcard" or "Double Postcard" is not in this category.
6. Material having the character of actual and personal correspondence is not in this category.

ZIP CODES AND STATE ABBREVIATIONS

All outgoing first-class mail should include the zip code in the address. The post office will deliver first-class mail that does not have the zip code indicated, but delivery is often slower.

All other classes of mail must have the zip code clearly indicated. If you don't know a zip code for a particular address, call the post office and ask. Office supply stores carry zip code books. For a complete, nationwide list of zip codes, you can order Publication 65 from the *Superintendent of Documents, U.S. Government Printing Office, Washington, DC 20402-1575* for under ten dollars. Most main post offices also carry the directories, and smaller post offices can order you a copy.

The U.S. Postal Service has established abbreviations for the states and U.S. territories, which should be used on all outgoing mail (Figure 123). The two-letter abbreviations should be in capital letters, with no punctuation, followed by two spaces and then the zip code. Properly addressed mail reaches its destination quicker.

PART SIX

USING COMPUTERS IN THE CHURCH OFFICE

With all the computer talk these days, it seems that everyone is, or should be, knowledgeable about what a computer is, what it does, and what it can accomplish in the church office. In fact, however, the majority of church office workers have no idea how a computer can help them. They have had their work experience in the ministry and not in computer technology.

Recently I called on a pastor who was busily typing on a Canon electronic typewriter. "We're just trying this out," he said. "We're in the market for a new typewriter."

Noticing a Texas Instruments computer and a TV monitor on a table in the corner of the office, I asked, "Why don't you get word processing for your computer?"

He gave me a blank stare, and said, "I don't know what you're talking about."

"You know," I emphasized, "Word processing."

"You have to explain what you mean," he replied. He went on to say that the computer, which had been donated by a member of the church, wasn't really used very much, and even then it was the donor who spent the time trying to enter budget information for the finance committee. The tone of his voice indicated that, to him, it was a toy that wasted time and took up space.

Several years ago, two very generous church members donated a complete computer system to McGregor, which included a Radio Shack TRS 80 Model III, a Daisy Wheel II printer, and a half-dozen software packages.

The problem was that, at the time, there was no church software written for that particular computer, at least none the office workers were aware of. The Radio Shack technicians tried to work with the financial secretary to set up a system for entering tithes and offerings and quickly discovered that the computer was just too small for the membership of the church.

Because no one in the office knew anything about computers, or how to use the word processing or other software, the computer was placed in storage. When I joined the staff as office manager, I asked where the computer was, because I knew I had seen it in the office one time when I visited.

"Oh, that's no good, it doesn't work," one of the staff members told me.

I dragged the computer out of storage and set up the word processing software, which came complete with training tapes. After learning how to use the Superscripsit word processing program, I was able to show the ministers its great capabilities of letter-writing, bulletin preparation, sermon preparation, to name just a few benefits. They were impressed.

Although many church workers are talking about computers, saying, "Yes, someday we want a computer," in actuality, a surprisingly small number of churches have actually made the move to computerization. In fact, of all the churches surveyed for this book, only 10 percent had computers.

I believe that the hesitancy in moving into computerization is because basic information is lacking in the following three areas:

1. What a computer is;
2. What the computer does and can do for the church;
3. How and where to buy a computer.

The next three chapters offer this basic information.

18

What Is a Computer?

You are slightly bewildered . . . panic-stricken . . . at the thought of having a computer in the church office. You've read books and articles about computers, and they don't make any sense. You're a fairly intelligent person, yet you don't understand the technical jargon. You say you never will, and don't even want to. Yet . . . what if? What if it could help you deal with the workload? What is a computer, anyway? What is it for?

First of all, understand that operating a computer is like driving a car. You don't have to understand the technology to go somewhere. Once you understand the basics, you can go full speed ahead.

WHAT IS A COMPUTER?

A *Computer* refers to the computer itself, all support equipment, the machine-readable instructions, and the facts it processes. The actual computer is a processing unit, which, by itself, can do nothing. In order to process information, the computer needs additional *hardware*, plus *software*.

You've heard these two terms, but what exactly do they mean?

Hardware is the machinery, all the physical parts that make up the computer system, including:

1. Computer
2. Keyboard
3. Disk drives and disks
4. Video monitor
5. Printer

The hardware parts may be separate or they may be combined in one or two pieces of equipment. For example, the Radio Shack Model III and its newest version, the Model 4D, have the keyboard, disk drives, video monitor, and computer combined; only the printer is separate (see Figure 124).

Software is the term used to refer to the planned, step-by-step instructional programs that tell the machine what to do. Purchased software programs come on 5¼- or 8-inch disks (also called floppy disks). Many types of software programs are available, and your biggest challenge is to find the ones that best suit the needs of your church.

Let's look at each piece of equipment separately.

The *computer* is the central processing unit (CPU) that houses the computer's memory, or *workspace,* which it needs to work on the data entered by you, the user, either by way of software or the keyboard. The computer has room in its memory to work on material before it sends it out as output. A computer is able to sort through piles of data and produce information quickly. The larger the computer, the greater its processing capacity.

How much room is there in the computer's memory? That depends. There are three sizes of computers: *mainframes* (large), *minicomputers* (medium-sized), and *microcomputers* (personal computers, or "PC"s). The distinction between these sizes is not always clear. The terms *micro* and *personal* are almost interchangeable. References here and in the following two chapters will be to personal computers, the ones most often used in churches.

The memory in personal computers, measured in *kilobytes* (K), varies from 16 to

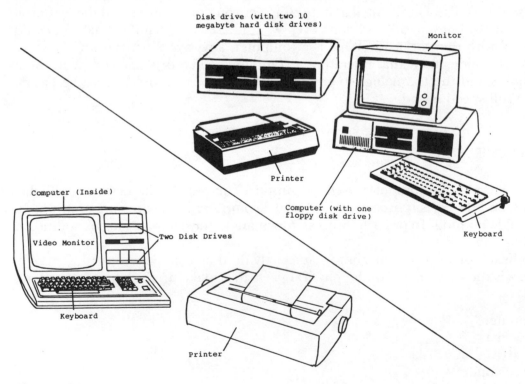

Figure 124

USING COMPUTERS IN THE CHURCH OFFICE

256 K and upward, as technology improves. A computer with only 16 K has approximately 16,000 *bytes,* or single storage locations (one for each character).

This seems like a lot. Suppose, however, that you have a small computer on which you want to type a sermon. If the pages are 8½ × 11, single-spaced, with a half-inch margin at the top and bottom, the 16 K memory would be filled up after four pages.

When you buy a computer, consider the memory capacity carefully. Be sure it will be large enough to meet your needs.

There are two types of memory in the central processing unit. These are:

1. Random-Access Memory (RAM). This is the "working space" of the computer, where it does its figuring, maneuvering, and calculating. Data can be written in and read from any storage location. The size of the RAM limits the size and complexity of your software. For example, as I mentioned before, the Radio Shack TRS 80 Model III at McGregor has a RAM that is too small to accommodate the membership and contribution records of 2,500 church members. There just isn't enough working space.
2. Read-Only Memory (ROM). The ROM refers to those programs permanently recorded in the hardware by the manufacturer, that the CPU always has to have access to. The ROM cannot be changed by the user.

The *keyboard* is similar to the typewriter keyboard, but has some extra special keys. The keyboard is used to communicate with the computer. You tell the computer what to do by typing data or pressing certain keys that give specific instructions to the computer.

The *disk drives,* or *readers,* are slotted boxes where you put the program *disks.* The disk drives are "record players" for the disks on which information is stored.

A *floppy disk* is exactly that, a thin, tough, flexible round plastic disk that looks like a 45 rpm record, encased in a 5¼- or 8-inch square jacket. The disk is coated with a substance that can be magnetized, and data are recorded on the disks as magnetized spots on concentric tracks.

When a particular program on a floppy disk is used, the disk must be put into the disk drive. The computer pulls information off the disk, works with it in its random access memory, and puts the added or revised information back on the disk for storage. The disk is removed when the program is finished.

A *hard disk* can also be used with personal computers. Hard disks are faster and can hold many times the data of a floppy disk. Hard disks can be permanent, located inside the computer's housing, or in removable cartridges stored outside the computer housing.

The *monitor* is a cathode-ray tube (CRT), just like the tube of a television set. (Television screens can actually be used as computer monitors.) The computer communicates with you by way of the monitor. You can see what is happening to your text. A *cursor,* a blinking light or a light the reverse color of the screen, lets you know where you are on the screen or "page" at all times.

The *printer* puts the information on paper. It actually produces the "hard copy," or the typed copy on the page. The printer receives its instructions from electronically coded commands from both the computer and itself.

The printer is connected to the computer by a cable, the *interface cable.* There are two types of interface cables:

1. *Serial.* This type of cable sends information to the printer one bit at a time, one

right after the other. (A *bit* is the smallest measurable unit; eight bits equal one *byte,* the amount of space required in memory for one character.) Serial transmission is slow, printing in a single direction like a typewriter, typically 10 to 300 characters a second.

2. *Parallel.* With the parallel interface cable, information moves to the printer from the computer seven or eight bits at a time. Parallel transmission is much faster and is usually bi-directional. It is also more expensive.

Most new computers on the market today will accept either a parallel or serial interface. Others accept only one or the other. The printer manual of instructions tells you which type of printer you have.

Two major types of commands tell the printer what to do:

1. Functional commands. These commands tell the printer to perform such functions as to print a different character, return the carriage, double space, turn the platen to advance the paper, double underscore a word or phrase, or print characters in bold face.
2. Print commands. These instruct the printer to print a character on the page.

A printer has two basic types of print:

1. *Dot matrix printers* print a series of tiny dots for each character (Figure 125). The quality of dot matrix print cannot compare with that of the daisy wheel printer (Figure 126).
2. *Daisy wheel printers* have petal-like print wheels with characters at the tip of each spoke; they produce type identical to that of a typewriter. A number of styles of type are available, and interchangeable, for any type of daisy wheel printer. Computer-generated pages of type from the daisy wheel printer are indistinguishable from those done on a typewriter (Figure 126). As characters are printed with the daisy wheel, it rotates, and a hammer strikes the "petal" of the character being printed. The impression is then transferred to the paper.

SOFTWARE

Software tells the computer what to do. There are two types of software programs:

1. *Operating systems* (disk operating systems or DOS) are programs that control the functions of the computer. Most computers use either MS DOS or PC DOS, de-

```
THE DOT MATRIX PRINTER produces print that
looks similar to this.  Some dot matrix
printers are better, and a few are much, much
better.  But, unless the printer costs
thousands of dollars, you will always be able
to tell that work has been printed on a
computer.  This simply is not desirable in
the church office.
```

Figure 125

USING COMPUTERS IN THE CHURCH OFFICE

```
THE DAISY WHEEL PRINTER produces letter
quality print that looks exactly like
this. The cost of a daisy wheel printer
is higher than that of a dot matrix
printer, but it's well worth the dif-
ference in price.  Church offices need
to have work going out of the office
that looks individually-prepared.
```

Figure 126

termined by what language a particular computer understands. The TRS-80 Models III and 4D use TRSDOS. There are also other machine languages. Two computers that are both written in the same "language" are said to be "compatible." Computers that are *not* written in the same language cannot communicate with each other. When the computer is turned on, and the DOS disk is put in the disk drive, the program communicates with the computer. The computer must have the operating system (DOS) loaded into its memory before it can function. The DOS tells the computer where information is stored on disks and what to do so the applications programs will work. The operating system runs the whole time the application program is operating. You must purchase a disk operating system when you purchase a computer.

2. Application programs tell the computer to do certain tasks. One example of an application program is word processing. Other examples for churches are data bases for membership records management and for financial management, including the maintenance of contributions, the General Ledger, and accounts payable. You don't have to buy application programs when you buy a computer. You could write your own programs, although this would be a very large undertaking, which is not recommended for church software applications.

Technology is changing rapidly, and hundreds of computers, and as many brands of accompanying hardware, are on the market today. All the computer systems, though, contain the above basic components, which remain the same.

19

Computers in the Church Office

"Choose your software first, then buy your hardware," is the number one rule when you are buying a computer. The software you buy will determine the efficiency, effectiveness, and usability of your computer to do the work you want it to do.

If you look forward to having your computer doing certain things, you can end up being extremely disappointed if you haven't thoroughly checked out the capabilities of the software. You may find, if you buy the hardware first, that there are no church programs available for the computer you have purchased.

"First determine your needs, decide what you want, and then find the software," is another rule of computerization.

"Okay," says one pastor. "But how can I know what I want it to do if I have absolutely no idea what it can do?"

Word processing, data bases—these are vague, meaningless "computereze" terms to the novice. What are the possibilities of these software generalities? How can they help in the church office?

WORD PROCESSING

Word processing is a very sophisticated form of electronic typewriting. You write and edit on the computer without pencil, paper, or typewriter. Then you print out error-free pages. Information is stored on disks, and retrieval and editing are speedy and efficient.

To explain the functions of word processing, I am going to give a demonstration of work actually done at McGregor on the TRS 80 Model III, using Superscripsit Word Processing. (Since the church got this computer, the Model III has been superseded by a new version, and Superscripsit software has since been upgraded to Model 4 by the manufacturer.) Other word processing software programs will vary in operation specifics. The principles are the same, however.

1. Preparing the Sunday bulletin. Our bulletin has the same format every week. This example of the Order of Service will show the ease in typing the weekly format:

(*a*) I turn the computer and printer on.

(*b*) I insert the disks in the disk drives. In this case, "TRSDOS," the *operations* program, and "Superscripsit," the *applications* program, are on one disk, and the file for the bulletin is on another disk (Figure 127). Although there is room on the applications disk to include the bulletin, we prefer to keep all files or *data* separate from the Superscripsit.

(*c*) I tell the computer I want "Superscripsit" by typing "Scripsit" on the keyboard, and pressing the "Enter" key.

(*d*) The computer asks me what I want to do, by listing a number of options on the monitor screen. One of the options is

"<O> Open a document"

(*e*) I tell the computer I want to "Open a document" by pressing the letter *O,* as indicated on the screen.

(*f*) The computer asks me, by way of the screen, what file I want. I tell the computer I want the Order of Service for the Bulletin, by typing in the previously determined name of the file.

(*g*) The file, or page, appears on the screen, exactly as I left it the previous week. (The width of any page can be up to 16½ inches wide, and the length can be up to ninety-nine lines. The length of any document, though, can expand to fill the entire disk space, if needed. This is approximately 160,000 characters for a single-sided or 320,000 characters for a double-sided disk.) Because only fourteen *lines* are visible on the screen, I cannot see the entire Order of Service. By "scrolling" with the up and down arrow keys (↑ ↓), I can see the entire page (Figure 128). The "left" and "right" arrow keys permit movement from the left edge to the right edge of a document.

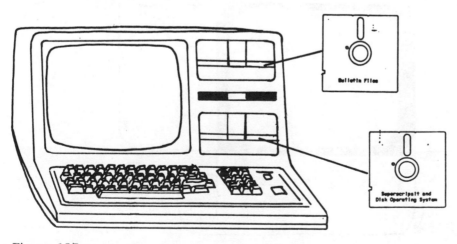

Figure 127

(*h*) I type new hymn numbers and names, sermon titles, special music, and other information directly over what is on the screen. I tell the computer to center the hymn and sermon titles.

(*i*) I proof the changes I have made, using the arrow keys to scroll the length of the document. (It isn't necessary to take the time to proof the entire document, only the changes. This saves time.)

(*j*) I tell the computer to print the finished document by pressing two keys.

(*k*) The computer instructs the printer to print the error-free page. The whole process has taken less than five minutes!

2. Another example of the tremendous amount of time saved with word processing is in the preparation of our newsletter:

(*a*) I "open a document" to enter information for the newsletter layout. Because this is a new file, I tell the computer the specifications for the pages, such as the number of lines on a page, desired linespacing (single, double, space-and-a-half, etc.), and the size of type I want to use (10- or 12-pitch, proportional).

(*b*) The screen is blank, except for a "tab line" at the bottom. I use this line to set my margins and tabs by pressing a few keys.

(*c*) I type and print articles for the newsletter that are 5 inches wide, and give them to David, the newsletter editor.

(*d*) "This is too wide. I'd like this article to be only 3½ inches wide. It has to fit in this space," he says, showing me the available space on his layout sheet. I go back to the computer, press a few keys, and change the margin. Immediately, the entire article is the desired width (Figure 129), without my having to do any more typing.

3. The preparation of long documents on the computer saves time because words,

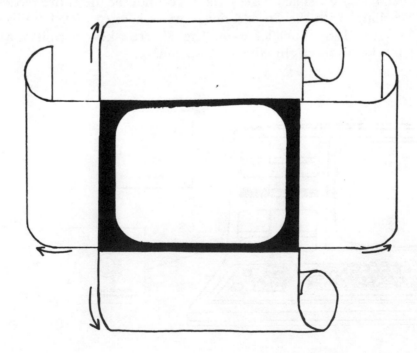

Figure 128

USING COMPUTERS IN THE CHURCH OFFICE

Understanding Our Long-Range Strategy

In our present stature as a leadership church in our community, we are often being asked to help financially in various worthy causes and mission-type projects. We are all certainly "for" anything that is done for Christ, and none of us ever likes to say "no" to a brother in obvious need. However, the volume of requests becomes overwhelming, just like the requests in your personal mail. We have to say "no" at times.

How can we sort out our responses with an open mind and a clear conscience? One way that will help us is to understand our long-range strategy, and to be consistent with it, rather than to frustrate it.

With ... anned to cut

Understanding Our Long-Range Strategy

In our present stature as a leadership church in our community, we are often being asked to help financially in various worthy causes and mission-type projects. We are all certainly "for" anything that is done for Christ, and none of us ever likes to say "no" to a brother in obvious need. However, the volume of requests becomes overwhelming, just like the requests in your personal mail. We have to say "no" at times.

How can we sort out our responses with an open mind and a clear conscience? One way that will help us is to understand our long-range strategy, and to be consistent with it, rather than to frustrate it.

With our eyes wide open, we planned to cut all spending to the ... order to pay off our ...

Figure 129

sentences, paragraphs, and even larger blocks of text can be changed by giving the computer a few instructions. (McGregor is in the process of revising its Constitution and By-Laws. Thirty-one pages of single-spaced text have been entered onto a disk and printed, and 300 copies were made and distributed to church members for examination, corrections, and approval.) Some special features of word processing allow the speedy entry of data:

(*a*) Automatic carriage return;

(*b*) Automatic word-wrap (if a word doesn't fit on a line, it moves to the next);

(*c*) Automatic underscore and double-underscore;

(*d*) Special "Recall Tab Line" keys, to tell the computer what margins and tabs I want for a particular paragraph. (I don't have to reset margins if they change within a document. The computer remembers up to fifty different margins for any one document.)

(*e*) Special "User Keys" that are programmed to tell the computer to remember and copy words and phrases that occur frequently;

(*f*) Automatic page numbering;

(*g*) Automatic hyphenation. When the document is typed, I tell the computer to go back through and hyphenate all the words that were too long for lines. (I can say "Yes" or "No" before the word is actually hyphenated.)

4. Already many changes have been suggested by the members. To make additions, I will insert text, to remove information, I will delete text, and changes in words or sentences will be made by typing over the previous information . . . and all by using a few keys to command the computer to make the changes. *No retyping.*

I hope these examples give a clear picture of how word processing can help in the church office. Almost everything that can be typed can be done with word processing software, quickly, easily, and without error. (The only exception I have found is in filling out forms that have predetermined lines and spaces.) The benefit of word processing alone makes the use of a computer worthwhile.

MEMBERSHIP DATA BASE

Data bases are software programs that allow you to enter large amounts of data into the computer and then, through instructions to the computer by way of the keyboard, to obtain the desired information on either the video monitor or on printed reports. The most common data base used in churches is the Membership program. The following examples illustrate its use. (At McGregor, we use an IBM PC-XT, with a 10-megabyte external drive, to hold all our membership and financial records. We use software from Shelby Systems, Memphis, Tennessee.)

1. The computer asks me what I want to do with the membership file, by way of this "menu" on the monitor (Figure 130).
2. Since I want to update an existing record, or add new members, I select option "1." The desired screen appears on the monitor. Each individual has a family number. I request an individual by that number. (New members are assigned the next available consecutive number.)
3. I have keyed in number 00791-01, for Alyce Morgan. Her "screen" (Figure 131) appears on the monitor. I change her address by moving to that field and typing new information directly over the old.
4. On this screen, I can enter a lot of information about an individual, such as sex, marital status, member or nonmember, how received, date received, and Sunday School information. Other information is the birthdate, age (automatically computed and updated monthly by the computer), as well as fields for several other codes. The "Special Profile" field allows me to give a three-digit special code that will allow me to pull special records from the membership file.
5. Another example of the type of screen used for membership records is this "Members Profile Update" screen (Figure 132). There is room for eighty three-digit codes, determined by the church, that can be assigned for each individual. These codes are used for talents, interests, organizations, or whatever else we want to

```
                              MENU: MEMBER      OPTION:
  →    1. MEMBERS MASTER UPDATE             13. FULL MEMBERSHIP LIST
       2. MEMBERS PROFILE UPDATE            14.
       3. MEMBERS PASTORAL CARE UPDATE      15. SELECTION ROUTINE
       4. MEMBERS VISITS UPDATE             16.
       5.                                   17. CREATE MAILING DISKETTE
       6.                                   18. ENVELOPE MASTER LIST
       7. MEMBERS INQUIRY                   19. PROFILE MAINTENANCE
       8.                                   20. PROFILE LIST
       9. INCREASE AGE(RUN MONTHLY)         21. CONTROL FILE MAINTENANCE
      10. PROMOTION MENU                    22.
      11. MEMBERSHIP TRANSFER               23.
      12. REMOVE DELETED RECORDS            24. SIGN OFF
```

Figure 130

USING COMPUTERS IN THE CHURCH OFFICE

```
CMD 1 - RETURN              MEMBERS MASTER UPDATE          CMD 7 - EOJ
                         CMD 3 - SEARCH  CMD 4 - DELETE   CMD 5 - UPDATE
FAMILY # 00791 - 02      CMD 6 - PROFIL  CMD 8 - PASTORL  CMD 9 - ALT ADR

TITLE Mrs NAME Morgan, Alyce           ADR 476 Keenan Ct
                                       CTY Ft Myers      ST FL ZIP 33907
                                       PH#    4894146           ALL

 BUSINESS NAME                         POS
                                       PH#    9391000
HH (H,I,C,A)              SEX (M,F)         F    MARITAL STS (S,M,D,W) M

MEMBER (M     )   M      HOW RECVD (LSB  ) L   DATE RCV          010181

SUNDAY SCHOOL (Y,N)  Y   S.S. DEPT.     A02A   S.S. CLASS          MF2

AUXILIARY GROUP (Y,N)    AUX. DEPT.            AUX. CLASS

BIRTH DATE     113046    AGE              39   SPECIAL PROFILE

VISIT AREA               MAILING CODE      C   ENVELOP #        00000

PLEDGE/SPOUSE (Y,N)      COMMENT                012586
```

Figure 131

```
CMD 1 - RETURN              MEMBERS PROFILE UPDATE          CMD 7 - EOJ
             CMD 6 - MEMBERS  CMD 8 - PASTRL   CMD 9 - ALT ADR

FAMILY # 00013 - 01 Anglemyer, Bob

 1 JEX   2 YSG   3 TYO   4       5       6       7       8       9       10

11      12      13      14      15      16      17      18      19      20

21      22      23      24      25      26      27      20      29      30

31      32      33      34      35      36      37      38      39      40

41      42      43      44      45      46      47      48      49      50

51      52      53      54      55      56      57      58      59      60

61      62      63      64      65      66      67      68      69      70

71      72      73      74      75      76      77      78      79      80
```

Figure 132

specify. On the screen for Bob Anglemeyer (Figure 132), three codes are entered. These codes tell me that Bob is a Joy Explosion Leader (JEX), a Young Singles leader (YSG), and a teacher in the youth department (TYO).

6. To use the information in the membership data base, I tell the computer to go back to the menu by pressing a key. I can select any option shown. The one we use most frequently is Option 15, which allows us to specify how we want a particular report to print out. For example, we can print a directory, labels for a

mailing, prospect and visitation reports, lists of teachers, Sunday School rolls, or attendance cards, just to name a few of the types of reports possible. We can specify particular information to be printed with this selection routine.

7. Suppose I want to print a list of the youth Sunday School teachers. I tell the computer to print a list containing all the names of every person who has a "TYO" profile code. Or, the minister of music wants to send a letter to his one hundred choir members. I tell the computer to select the names of all persons coded with "CHR."

8. Every field on the two screens can be used as criteria to select specific individuals for a report. Any combination of fields can be used as well. For example, I want to send a letter to all of the *women*, who are *members, married* and *between the ages of 20 and 45*. It is possible to select just these persons by telling the computer what I want (Figure 133).

HOW ELSE CAN A COMPUTER HELP?

In addition to word processing and membership programs, several other programs will help ease the workload in the church office and thus allow church workers to spend more time on people work and less time on paper work.

1. *Contributions.* Enter weekly contribution records of every member, for a number of different funds. Print summary totals. Print statements as often as you wish. Print annual mailing-ready individual record statements for each member.

2. *General Accounting.* Set up a chart of accounts. Divide accounts into subgroups so you can track individual departments or accounts. Post checks to the General Ledger, enter bank deposits. Print such reports as the chart of accounts, Dis-

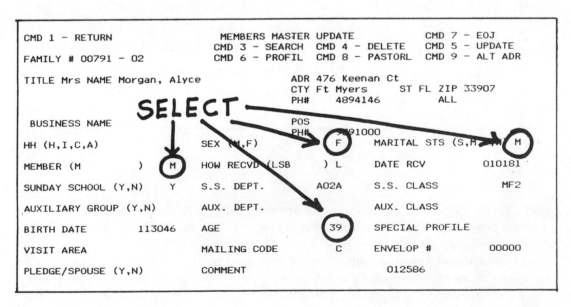

Figure 133

USING COMPUTERS IN THE CHURCH OFFICE

bursements Journal, or financial statement. Reconcile the bank statement. Prepare the proposed budget for the new year. Adjust figures, and let the computer compute the new totals for the entire budget. Write checks, maintain payroll records. Prepare an income statement (profit and loss) or a balance sheet.

3. *Sacramental Records.* Keep information on marriages, confirmations, baptisms, ordinations, or other significant religious data. Print out lists of each category.

4. *Attendance.* Keep records of attendance for worship services or Sunday School. Generate reports of persons who miss church for two or three weeks, for pastoral follow-up.

5. *Graphics.* Design illustrations, flyers, banners, and other graphics work. Print pictures, graphs.

6. *The Bible.* There is software that has the complete Bible on one disk. You can tell the computer to search for any word or phrase or to compare scripture references. Build a library of topical scripture references.

This partial list gives you an idea of the tremendous possibilities of a computer in the church office.

"Our church can't afford a computer," says one pastor. "We only have 200 members."

As technology improves, computer prices are dropping rapidly. For example, when the TRS-80 was donated to McGregor, the hardware cost over $6,000. Today similar equipment is available for under $3,000. In fact, the same equipment was advertised in the for sale ads recently for $1,200. The person selling the computer was "moving up" to a bigger system.

Shop around for the software that will do what you want it to do. Then shop around for a computer that it will run on. You may be able to find perfectly good used equipment for a fraction of the cost of new equipment. Someone else's old technology may be perfect for you.

20

How to Buy Software and Hardware

McGregor Baptist Church is a large, multistaff church, with seven ministers, four secretaries, and me, the office manager. We have two computer systems: the Radio Shack TRS-80 Model III and the IBM PC-XT. Both these systems were donated by generous church members, without prior determination of needs or investigation of available software, before I joined the office team.

SOFTWARE

Although the TRS-80's memory is too small to maintain membership and financial records, the Superscripsit software is wonderful for word processing. I have no typewriter, and I use the computer exclusively for all my typing needs. The keyboard is almost identical to that of a typewriter. The one-piece design of the computer-keyboard-monitor gives a solid "feel" to the keyboard touch and the way it handles, similar to an IBM Selectric typewriter. I like it. I also like the Superscripsit, although I know it isn't necessarily the best word processing software on the market, nor is the technology the latest. There are other programs with more advanced features, such as automatic word count, automatic proofread, and complete dictionaries. One word processing package, Word Perfect 4.1, even offers a complete Thesaurus.

A year ago, Radio Shack closed out a portable Model 4 and I bought one, along with a daisy wheel printer, for one of the secretaries. She, too, uses it for all her typing. The information on all the floppy disks can be used in either machine, so we can interchange work and disks. The cost of her computer and printer (on sale) was under $1,100, which is approximately the cost of a top-of-the-line typewriter.

Now there is church software available for the TRS-80 and all other Radio Shack computers. One company selling this software is Custom Data (P.O. Box 1869, Alamogordo, NM 88310). Radio Shack has evaluated this software and has given Custom Data's software a five-star (excellent) rating.

Last year our financial secretary was seeking a contributions software program, and we ordered a "demo" disk from Custom Data. It was very clear and easy to use and produced the reports we wanted to have available. The problem, though, was the size of the computer's memory. We couldn't use the software we wanted. A small church, however, having far fewer members, would be able to use the software package with no problem.

What are we using for membership, contributions, and financial data? And how did we happen to select Shelby Systems software?

The software we are now using is our third software package. Here is the story of our movement into computerization.

For a number of years McGregor used a service bureau to maintain membership records, Membership Services, Inc., in Irving, Texas. Additions, deletions, and changes to the records were sent by mail. And if we wanted a set of labels or printouts of the membership, we had only to dial a toll-free number and make our request. Monthly offering envelopes were mailed from the service bureau from our master list. In lieu of no computer, the service bureau did an excellent job of maintaining our records.

There is a time lag in using a service bureau, however. Allowance has to be made for mailing time, as well as the bureau's processing time. For example, Joe and Mary Jones join the church on April 7th, but our cut-off date for processing information for May's envelopes was April 3rd. This meant that Joe and Mary were not on the church's master printout, nor did they receive offering envelopes until June—almost a two-month delay.

The financial and contribution records were still being done completely by hand—a big job for the financial secretary. So our present IBM computer, with its accompanying hardware (peripheral equipment), was donated.

"We want this computer to be right," the donors told the computer salesman. "It has to be large enough for all the church records."

"This computer will handle five churches your size," the salesman responded, as he picked out the system that he felt the church needed.

We have an IBM PC, with an IOMEGA dual 10-megabyte (meg) disk drive, and an Epson LQ-1500 dot matrix printer. The combined system operates like the IBM PC-XT. Is it right for our church? "No."

For now, the 10-meg disk is adequate. We only use it for membership and financial records. Because we use the TRS-80s for word processing, and because the Epson printer is dot matrix, we have not purchased word processing for the IBM. (We plan to add a letter quality printer and the word-processing package in the near future.) Also we are not using the Shelby Systems software to the fullest extent yet. If we were, and when we do, and when we add word processing, we will more than likely fill up the disk. That time will come. For now, though, we are making the best of our hardware situation.

Finding software has been a challenge. When the hardware was purchased, the computer salesman also sold the donors a software package that he said would be perfect for our needs. Supposedly it was a proven, integrated church software package. Not knowing any better, they proudly delivered the whole package to the church office.

Integrated means that different programs share the same information. For example, data entered on the membership program for members' names, addresses, and offering envelope numbers are also shared by the contributions software. Or the financial program shares the information that has been entered in the contributions software. Data do not have to be entered more than once into an integrated software package.

Attempts to use the software were futile. The training manuals were poorly written. It was impossible to enter certain fields of information we felt were important. The financial package was a business, not a church package. "Error" warnings kept appearing on the screen, indicating "bugs" in software. It was terrible. And we couldn't return it for a refund. (There is no need here to mention the name of the software company because they have since gone out of business.)

So there we were, with a computer, but no suitable software.

Sheila, the financial secretary, had half a year's worth of contribution records that she had saved to put on the computer. "We have to hurry and get *something*. I have to get these offerings done," she said frantically.

Membership records were piling up, because they had also been saved for our own computer. The pressure to "hurry up and get something" was overwhelming.

Membership Services also sells complete church software systems. As they already had our membership records on their computer system, they advised us that, if we purchased their software, they could then put all the data from their system onto disks for our computer, and we would not have to enter any membership data on our computer.

This is a process that, for the size of our church and the availability of time and personnel, could take two or three months. Because of our urgent need to have an in-house computer system, we decided to go ahead with the purchase of the Membership Services (MSI) software, sight unseen.

We found the membership package to be quite workable and fairly easy to use. It was "user-friendly." (*User-friendly* means that the software communicates with the user in commonsense English, not in Computereze.) But it was written in a programming language that made the use of the software very sl-o-o-o-w for the size of our data files. We have approximately fifty membership changes a week—new members, address updates, Sunday School class changes, phone number changes, people getting married, etc. Each member's screen took too long to change after the information was entered. Sometimes we would have to wait up to a full minute just to change from one record to another. This doesn't seem like much time, but multiply that by the number of changes, plus the time of actual input, and we were spending 2½ or 3 hours on a task that should have taken no more than 30 minutes.

The slowness of the program made it undesirable, although we did use it for many months. We didn't use any capabilities of the membership package other than printing mailing labels and master membership lists. Since we couldn't return it, we had to make the best of it.

We were able to return the contributions package, after negotiations with the company. Sheila was terribly unhappy with the program and refused to use it from the start.

(Note: Membership Services, Inc., has upgraded this software package, so that it now runs much faster. The upgrade came too late for us, though, as we had already examined and bought the Shelby package. I loaded the upgraded version into our computer, just to see if it really was any better, and the change was dramatic. Many

USING COMPUTERS IN THE CHURCH OFFICE

churches do use MSI software and are very happy with it. In fact, had the update come sooner, we probably would not have been prompted to change from the MSI software.)

Back to being stuck with a drawer full of offering envelopes to be posted, Sheila was desperate. "What will I do?"

"We aren't going to buy another software package without knowing what we're buying," I told her. And she agreed.

A computer programmer volunteered to write a very basic contributions program that would suffice for the year. Relieved, we were able to take the time to figure out what software would be best for us.

A committee was formed to find the best solution to our computer problems. (Good idea, but a year and a half too late.) Phone calls were made to other large churches with computer systems, and visits were made to several of them. (Good idea, too.)

I wrote to all the church software companies I could find advertised in the publications that came into the church office, as well as those advertised in postcard packages of advertisements (reader service cards mailed to pastors). I read all the literature sent by these companies, and I also read every computer article I could get my hands on. The committee met a number of times to discuss our findings. Several of us attended computer demonstrations, just to see how different systems operated.

Several facts became very clear:

1. Our computer system was (and is) too small to meet the growing needs of our church. An office our size should have a multi-user system, so each person can have a terminal, and at least a 30-meg disk drive.
2. The re-entry of all membership data was going to be very time-consuming, and we would have to allow for it in scheduling our time.
3. Several "computer consultants" were no more than computer salesmen, and each one selected the hardware that would be "right" for us.
4. Although many companies had "demo" disks available, these demos had only fifty or one hundred names in them. It was impossible to determine the speed at which the programs would run for 3,000 or more names. A number of programs looked good.
5. Software packages were fairly expensive. The possibility of another wrong purchase scared all of us. We didn't want to waste the church's money.

Our frustrations were compounded with the realization that, if we were to spend $3,000 to $4,000 on software now for our present system, we would find it unusuable when the system became totally inadequate.

Then one day a computer salesman from IBM stopped by the church office and invited me to a demonstration of a church software package from Shelby Systems, which I had never heard of. By that time, my head was spinning with software and hardware information. What's one more demonstration, I thought. I had promised myself that I would keep an open mind in this search for the perfect software, so I agreed to attend.

Several committee members, the pastor, and I went to the demonstration. The screen formats looked similar to a half-dozen other software packages. The promises were the same, the information being maintained on the files was the same.

What made the big difference, and why did we decide on the Shelby Systems software? (Note: This is not necessarily an endorsement for you to buy Shelby Systems software. Rather, I want to explain why we chose this company, and what you should look for in selecting your software package.)

1. The demonstration file contained 6,400 names and addresses. It was an actual, working church membership list, not a partial demo. I could see the speed of the actual, working program.
2. Shelby would convert our existing data to Shelby software. We would not have to re-enter membership data.
3. Shelby promised a 100 percent money-back guarantee within thirty days after the date of installation if we were not completely satisfied.
4. They provided references of satisfied churches who were presently using Shelby software. (And, yes, I did call several of these churches.)
5. Shelby Systems had been in business for many years. I knew they were not likely to go out of business, and thus would continue to be available for customer support.
6. At some point in the future, after we get our brand-new buildings paid off, we will be "moving up" to larger computers, eventually ending up with a multi-user system and the IBM 60-meg central processing unit. Shelby Systems provides:
   (a) Conversion of software to upgraded versions;
   (b) Application of 80 percent of the purchase price of the present software to the cost of upgraded software;
   (c) No relearning of how to use converted software, since it will be very similar to the version we would presently be buying.

For further study, I requested copies of all reports the software would generate and copies of every screen used for input. I and the committee compared the benefits of Shelby Systems software with two other software packages. The others looked good, and we were impressed with them. However, the possibilities Shelby Systems offered gave them the edge. We were sold.

Shelby offers in-house training, training at their center in Memphis, and video training tapes. Because we already had some computer experience, we opted for the training tapes, which are very thorough.

We have been using the membership package for about six months and have been pleased with it from the start. Customer support is very good. If we have a problem, we can call and have an immediate solution. (They do not have a toll-free number, which may be an important consideration for many churches. We feel that the excellent customer support and the quality of the software package outweigh the long-distance charges.)

Sheila, our financial secretary, finished out the year with the handwritten contributions package and is just getting started with Shelby's offerings program. A company representative came to the church before the start of the new year and helped her enter the chart of accounts in the General Ledger program. Sheila thinks the financial software is great and is happy we have chosen Shelby Systems.

You may not be fortunate enough to have a full demonstration of a software program. You may be bewildered by the large selection of church software. And for smaller churches, the speed of the software would not be nearly as important because the computer would not have to look through so many records. The more records there are, the longer the computer takes to search through them.

So how can you decide? Take the following steps to assure that your software purchase will be all that you want it to be:

1. Have the software company send you a demo disk (if you already have a computer) or go to a computer store and request that they order the demo disk to be tried on the store's equipment. (If the store won't order the disk for you, find a store that will.)
2. At the computer store, work with the demo yourself. Take your time to examine everything the package offers carefully. Don't take the word of the salesperson that the software will do everything you want. (I don't have anything against salespersons, but remember, they are trying to sell you the hardware. Most computer salespersons really don't know much, if anything, about church software.)
3. Be sure that the church software program will work with (interface with) one of the major, proven word processing programs available today.
4. Find out if the software program is new and if all the bugs have been worked out. (No new program is ever bug-free.)
5. If it's a toss-up between several software companies, call the companies and talk to the marketing representatives (a fancy name for salespersons). Find out what each will do for you. Will they:
   (a) Provide references?
   (b) Give you a money-back guarantee?
   (c) Apply the cost of the demo disk to the purchase price?
   (d) Upgrade your software if you move up to a bigger system?
   (e) Apply any of the purchase price to an upgraded system?
   (f) Provide customer support?
   (g) Reduce the price?
   (h) Sell only those portions of the total package that your church wants and needs?
   (i) Provide adequate training, either in your church or at their location or by video training tapes?
   (j) Provide updates as they become available? At what cost?
   (k) Put all their promises *in writing*?

HARDWARE

What things have to be considered when you buy the hardware? After you've made the software decision, you have many options for purchasing the hardware. What size memory do you need? Hard disk? Floppy disk? How much should you expect to pay? What other considerations are there?

The random access memory (RAM) size is crucial. It must be large enough to hold both the disk operating system and the software and have space left over in which to work. The 256 K RAM (approximately 256,000 bytes) size is becoming commonplace as the personal computer technology advances. A very small church, one that does not expect to increase its membership greatly, might not need to have that much computer memory. Talk with your local dealers for specific information about memory requirements.

The keyboard is the most frequently used point of contact the user has with the machine. Be sure that you "try out" the keyboard and that it is comfortable for you and for whoever else will be using the computer. The arrangement of extra keys on some keyboards makes data entry difficult. Feel the keys. Make sure the touch, sound, and action are right for you. Some keyboards have a solid typewriter-like feel to them, others have light-plastic, clackety-clack keys that feel like those on cheap toy typewriters.

Disk storage can be either on hard or floppy disks. The disadvantage of floppies is that, to use each program, the disk has to be put in and out of the drive each time. With a hard disk, data are always ready. A 10-meg hard disk will store about the same amount of data as thirty floppy disks. A hard disk drive costs more, but you save on the cost of disks. If your church is small, though, you may only need to use floppies.

Printers vary in speed and quality. A dot matrix printer is much faster than letter quality, but for most jobs in the church office, speed is not all that important. If your budget allows it, choose a good letter-quality printer. For certain applications, such as graphics, when you want to print charts, graphs, pictures, and various sizes of fancy type, you would definitely have to have a dot matrix printer. But your first consideration should be the quality of your correspondence. Some churches have one of each kind of printer. Be sure that your printer is compatible with the computer you want to buy, and be sure that it will produce the results you expect.

It is a good idea to buy all hardware from one source, and it should be a local distributor. Even though you can buy hardware inexpensively through the mail, it is very important to have a local source for service. If you buy one piece here and one piece there, you will have a problem when it comes to having the hardware serviced. If something goes wrong, no one wants to take responsibility. Vendors have a tendency to point their finger, saying that it is someone else's responsibility to fix the equipment.

Consider the technical support you will receive from your hardware source. What kind of training will the dealer provide? Is there a charge? What kinds of warranties come with each piece of equipment? Will a repair person make "house calls" or will you have to take the hardware to the store to be serviced? Will they give you advice over the phone? Will they allow you to return or exchange a piece of equipment if it isn't right for your needs, for example, within thirty days?

Compare the price of different brands of equipment. Although IBM is the industry leader, is there another brand, for less money, that works just as well? Or do you want the assurance of quality the IBM name gives you? Be sure that all the equipment you buy is compatible. The salesperson will be able to advise you about what works well together. Stick with the well-known brands, so you know that you will have parts, service, and additional new programs available.

Don't expect the computer to be in operation the day you bring it into the church office. The initial installation takes some time. If you have to do it yourself, you must take the time to read the instructions before hooking up the wires and the cables.

You have to take the time to learn how to use the software. Even if someone will be training you, it is still necessary to read through the manuals so you will have an overall view of the programs and what they will do for you. All data must be entered. This process takes time.

It is a good idea to get intensive training after membership data have been entered. For one Presbyterian church in Pensacola, Florida, the money and time spent on immediate training proved to be wasted. The software representative gave an intense, three-day session, covering the full expanse of the software's capabilities. But by the time the secretaries had put in all the data, several months later, they no longer remembered what to do with the data. It is suggested that you get just enough help to put in the data and then have the company representative come and train personnel.

A computer is a valuable tool. It has certainly changed the way we live and the way we do business. Whatever the size of your church, you can find a system that will fit your needs for whatever price you want to pay. Let it help you in your ministry of church record keeping.

PART SEVEN

OFF THE RECORD: USING SPECIAL HELPS

The purpose of this book is to serve and assist the church office worker. The practical application of procedures throughout the book will help you with record keeping and save you time.

There are other areas besides record keeping when having the right information or equipment at your fingertips will help you carry out the work in the church office, and other times when you have to find information and answers. A knowledge of the resources available and the kind of information they provide will make your search much easier.

This section lists resourses and "tricks of the trade."

Chapter 21 lists reference resources: books you should have in the church office, available resources, and supply sources.

Chapter 22 is a potpourri of helpful hints and ideas for handling situations and tasks in the office.

21

Where to Find Information: References

Many reference materials are available to help make your work easier. The following resources, kept close at hand for ready reference, will provide answers and give guidance in many areas. Save time, improve your skills, and prevent frustration by using the materials available to help you.

BIBLES, BIBLE COMMENTARIES, BIBLE DICTIONARIES

These are helpful in preparing and typing sermons. They are also helpful in that you will be able to hand one to the church members who come to the church office looking for the pastor to help explain a Bible passage, only to find the pastor isn't in. Church members appreciate being able to find the answers to their questions through your provision of these books.

CATALOGS

Vendor catalogs provide a wealth of information. Take the time to browse through them, so you're aware of new products on the market not only for the office, but for all areas of the church. You will be able to tell people in the church where they can find supplies, equipment, or program materials. Provide one drawer for catalog storage.

DICTIONARIES

A dictionary is an absolute necessity. It will tell you many things about a word, such as its meaning, spelling, pronunciation, and origins. Even if you are a good speller, others in the office may need help. And there are times when you need to know more than just the spelling. A complete, comprehensive volume is a valuable resource.

Examine different dictionaries at the bookstore, such as Random House, Merriam-Webster, Oxford, and American Heritage, to see which one best suits your needs. A desk-sized (Collegiate) one should provide all the information you need.

LIBRARIES

Many local public libraries provide an information service and will give information over the telephone. "Ask us anything," they say. Take advantage of this service if you need an answer to a problem or question and don't know where to look. They will also give out information on rules of grammar, spelling, foreign phrases, geographical locations, and much more.

MAPS

Local street maps help visitation teams who may not know where to go or how to get there when making calls.

In addition, they will help you. Mark maps by zip code areas, by taking a map to the post office and asking one of the clerks to mark off the different areas, using a highlighter marker. Write the zip codes on the map with a highlighter.

Then when you are preparing records, and individuals have written down their address, but not their zip code, you can look on the map and immediately determine the zip code.

Get a map for any area where you have members or prospective members. If possible, mount the maps on boards and hang them on a wall.

SECRETARIAL HANDBOOKS

Every office should have a secretarial handbook, and the church office is no exception. These handbooks provide information on how to be a secretary, which will help anyone who works in your office.

Two excellent handbooks are *Webster's New World Secretarial Handbook, New Revised Edition* (Simon & Schuster) and *The Professional Secretary's Handbook* (Houghton Mifflin Co.).

TELEPHONE BOOK

Keep the telephone book close at hand, so you don't have to waste time getting up when you, or someone else, wants to look up a number.

Find out what useful information is provided in the front and back sections of the book. Every publication will provide different information, but as an example, the Fort Myers phone book provides, besides telephone numbers, the following information:

1. Emergency telephone numbers on the inside front cover;
2. Instructions for requesting service from the phone company;
3. Instructions for obtaining service, telephone credit cards, vacation service, handicapped services, and cable information;
4. An area map;
5. Listings of toll-free calling areas;
6. Instructions for direct distance dialing;
7. Long-distance rates and instructions;
8. International direct distance dialing instructions;
9. National area codes;
10. A time-zone map;
11. Billing information;
12. Legal information pertaining to telephones;
13. State legislator listings;
14. Local zip codes;
15. A hurricane-tracking map (a local sport in the summertime);
16. Information about local community life;
17. A human services guide, listing agencies, organizations, libraries, etc.
18. Tips on crime prevention;
19. An emergency medical guide, listing specific situations and treatments.

Look over your new directory when it arrives. You'll be surprised what helpful information you'll find.

Sometimes a number listed in the phone book will have been changed. If you don't need to put the new number on your Rolodex because you feel you won't need it again, save yourself some time. When the information operator gives you the new number, write that number in the book on the page where the old number is listed, even if you think you won't use it again. A few seconds now saves minutes later.

If your church is in an area served by several telephone companies, be sure to get a copy of each telephone book.

THESAURUS

A *thesaurus,* a book of synonyms (words and phrases of the same meaning) and antonyms (words and phrases of opposite meaning), is a tool for transforming ideas into words. When you want to express an idea, but can't quite find the right words, the thesaurus will help you.

Roget's International Thesaurus (Harper & Row) includes about 250,000 words and phrases, arranged in categories by their meanings, with an index.

By following the format of the book, you can track down words, and come up with the exact words and phrases that will help you express your ideas clearly and concisely. Use the thesaurus to compose letters, write sermons, and to increase your vocabulary in any area of writing.

WORD FINDERS

Word finders are small books showing words, spelled and divided, without meanings. These books allow you to look up a word quickly, to check on how to spell it or hyphenate it, without having to look through many pages of a dictionary.

Two word finder books are *Webster's Instant Word Guide* (Merriam-Webster) (35,000 words) and *20,000 Words* (McGraw-Hill).

There is even a word finder for people who don't spell well—*The Spelling Helper Dictionary* by Dennis A. Oliver (Hialeah, FL: Denco International Publishing Co., 1980). Hard-to-find words are also "spelled" phonetically, the way they sound. You can look up a word even if you don't know how to spell it.

ZIP CODE DIRECTORIES

Obtain a local zip code book from an office supply store or get the national zip code book from the U.S. Postal Service. Keep it on your bookshelf for immediate reference.

SOURCES OF SUPPLIES

Send to these companies for catalogs and information about products that are needed in the church office and for the work of the church:

Christian Mail Order Book Stores

Baptist Book Store (Broadman Forms)
P.O. Box 24420
Nashville, TN 37202

Cokesbury
201 Eighth Avenue, South
P.O. Box 801
Nashville, TN 37202

Gospel Publishing House
1445 Boonville Avenue
Springfield, MO 65602

Morehouse-Barlow Co.
78 Danbury Road
Wilton, CT 06897

Envelope Service Companies

Each of the following companies will supply one or more of the following types of envelopes:

Yearly boxes for fifty-two (or fifty-three) weeks, for individuals
Printed-to-order sets, according to customer specifications
Monthly sets of envelopes

Semi-monthly sets of envelopes
Bi-weekly sets of envelopes
Single styles, with one pocket
Duplex styles, with two pockets

Contact individual companies for specifications and prices:

McDaniel Envelope Co., Inc.
P.O. Box 5272
Richmond, VA 23220

Duplex Envelope Co.
P.O. Box 5445
Richmond, VA 23220

Membership Services, Inc.
P.O. Box 225450
Dallas, TX 75265

Morehouse-Barlow Envelope Service
P.O. Box 269
Chester, WV 26034

Graphics Supplies

Make your printed materials come alive. Order mimeo and offset art sheets, calendars, Gospel illustrations, bulletin cover illustrations, clip art, and more for newsletters. Write for catalogs to:

Hartco Products Co., Inc.
170 West Pearl Street
West Jefferson, OH 43162

Knight Media
60 Benzing Road
Antioch, TN 37013

Logos Art Productions, Inc.
346 Chester Street
St. Paul, MN 55107

Artmaster
500 N. Claremont Boulevard
Claremont, CA 91711

Cello-Tak (gives up to 50 percent quantity discount)
35 Alabama Avenue
Island Park, NY 11558

Newsletter Helps

The "how-to" of planning and producing a church newsletter is contained in an excellent publication by George Knight, of Knight Media. The book shows how to create attractive, readable newsletters; how to write and lay out copy, edit, and use photographs and artwork; and how to accomplish all the tasks necessary to produce a quality publication.

The Newsletter Newsletter (Communication Resources, Inc., Box 2625, North Canton, OH 44720), provides monthly issues containing clip-art, fillers, and instructions on writing the church newsletter.

Office Supplies

I believe it is a good idea to purchase supplies locally to support the local economy, if you receive a substantial discount for your supplies. It does pay to shop by mail, but be very careful. Know who you are ordering from.

Two very reputable mail-order office suppliers are:

The Drawing Board
256 Regal Row
P.O. Box 505
Dallas, TX 75221

Quill Corporation
100 S. Schelter Road
P.O. Box 4700
Lincolnshire, IL 60197.

22

Helpful Hints

This chapter offers capsules of information for many situations that arise in the church office. Here is an alphabetical listing of how-to's to help make your work easier.

BENEVOLENT ASSISTANCE

What can you do to help people who come into the office for a handout?

The Fort Myers area is a high-transient area. Churches on the main travel path often have two or three occasions a week when someone comes into the office and says, "I'm hungry" or "I'm out of gas" or "I have no place to sleep tonight."

Here are some guidelines for handling persons seeking assistance from your church:

1. Understand that the person definitely has a problem, and needs help. Says one pastor, "Yes, I know that a lot of these people are just looking for a free ride. But even these people have a problem. Anyone who goes to a church office for help definitely has a problem. And maybe the little bit of help we can give them will lift them up, and make a change in their life."

2. Be sure you have a clear understanding about the church's policy in handling benevolent cases. For example:
   (a) Does the pastor want to talk with each person?
   (b) Will a member of a "Benevolent Committee" talk with them? Or call them?
   (c) What type of information should you obtain from the person before giving assistance?

3. Never, under any circumstances, give money; instead, give something:
   (a) For food, there are two things your church might do:

(1) Set up a "food pantry," by requesting nonperishable food items from the members of the congregation. When someone asks for food, you or a member of the committee can give out some of the goods.

(2) Establish an account at a local restaurant. Elizabeth, secretary at a local Baptist church, says, "We send them over to McDonalds, and tell them to order what they want. Once a month, we pay the bill."

(b) For gas, establish a credit account with the closest service station. This account is used only in benevolent cases, as follows:

(1) At Cypress Lake, we phone the gas station, inform the manager that someone is coming, and give him the make of the car and its license number. Also, we tell how much gas to give.

(2) In another church, the secretary is authorized to issue a form to the person for ten gallons of gas at the station down the street.

(c) For lodging, refer to your local community agencies. Some agencies have overnight lodging accommodations for those in need. Call your local government offices for information about available community agencies in your area. Under certain rare circumstances, several churches put people up in motels.

(1) For example, the van of a family traveling through the area broke down. The man used every available cent to repair the van, and it was late at night. It happened to be a Wednesday, and the pastor was working at the church after the evening service. The man explained that he had no more cash, and the pastor met with the family and determined that it was bona-fide situation of a family in desperate need.

(2) Never let someone you don't know stay in your home. It is not safe, and it could cause you problems. Recently a church member saw five people walking along the highway. They were dirty and looked very tired. Because it was a cold night, she picked them up and took them home, where she fed them and gave them a place to sleep. A week later, the five unemployed adults were still there because they had no place to go, and she didn't have the heart to put them out.

CALENDAR

The official church calendar should be posted on a wall where everyone can see it. It is very important to keep information up-to-date. The calendar should be large and preferably lined.

If you have the room, it is helpful to spread the pages of the calendar out on the wall (Figure 134). Cypress Lake's official calendar pages are put on poster board (because the walls are not smooth) and attached to the wall. Four months are visible at a glance, with the pages being rotated as each month is completed. Completed months are saved for reference for two years.

For ease in maintaining the official church calendar, you should instruct all who make entries on the calendar to:

1. Use a pencil, so canceled events can be erased.
2. Include the name and telephone number of someone who can be contacted for information regarding a scheduled activity.

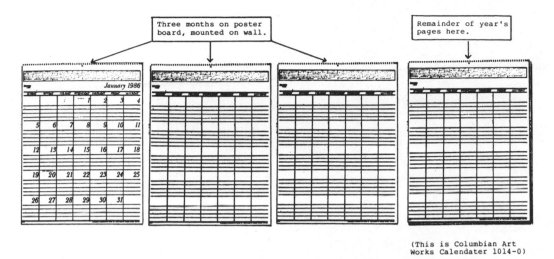

(This is Columbian Art
Works Calendater 1014-0)

Figure 134

EASY COLUMNS

You want to make a graph with five equally spaced columns. The width of the graph is 3¾ inches. Here is an easy way to make the columns without having to figure out fractions of an inch.

1. Use a ruler that is larger than the width you want to cover.
2. Pick a number divisible by the number of columns you want, but larger than the area you want to cover. In this example, 5 is larger than 3¾, and it is divisible by the number of wanted columns. $5 \div 5 = 1$. You are going to use 1-inch intervals on the ruler to make the columns.
3. Place the ruler at an angle on the paper, so the "5" is at the top right edge of the right side of the graph, and the left edge of the ruler, the "0," is touching the left side of the intended graph.
4. Place dots (in pencil, so you can erase them later) at 1-inch intervals.
5. Move the ruler partway down the graph, keeping the "5" and the "0" on the lines. Place dots again.
6. Move the ruler all the way down so that the "0" is touching the lower left-hand corner of the intended graph, and the "5" is still on the right line. Place dots (Figure 135).
7. Connect the dots vertically and you have five equally spaced columns (Figure 136).

This technique will work with any size of paper or any number of columns. Follow the same procedure. For example, suppose you want to make ten columns on a 24-inch wide piece of poster board. You would need a yardstick, rather than a ruler, because 30 is the first number larger than the width of the paper that is divisible by ten. Thus, you would have $30 \div 10 = 3$. Columns would be marked off in 3-inch intervals.

Sometimes it is necessary to extend the left line downward to make the third set of dots. If it is, place a piece of paper at the bottom of the page, and in pencil, lightly

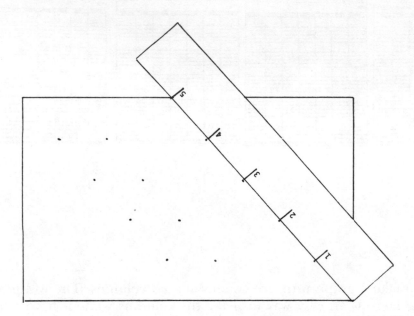

Figure 135

extend the line. Also, you should always make three sets of dots because your lines will be straighter.

CORRECTION FLUIDS

Fluids for making corrections are available from your office supply store. But are you aware that there are a number of different types?

Do you get frustrated because the correction fluid smears when you attempt to cover up a word on a page that has been photocopied? Or because you can't cover up hand-written errors?

There are different types of correction fluid for various uses. They are:

1. Regular. This fluid is for original typewritten work.
2. Copies only. This fluid does not smear when applied to photocopied material.
3. Pen and ink. This correction fluid will cover handwritten pen and ink drawing or writing.
4. Colors. Several colors, buff, yellow, blue, and pink, are available so that you can cover up typing errors on colored paper.

Using the right correction fluid will help you produce better-looking work. Use the correct fluid for the job.

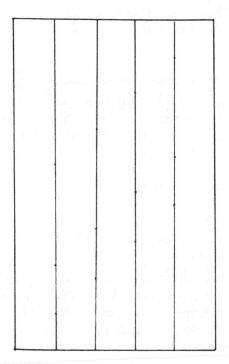

Figure 136

CORRECTION TAPE

Correction tape, a self-adhesive white paper, is available in various widths to cover one, two, or more lines of type. The tape comes in two forms:

1. Rolls. To use the tape from a roll, it is necessary to first cover up the line to be corrected. Then the paper is put back in the typewriter, and the correction is typed directly on the tape.
2. Sheets. These 4 × 6-inch sheets of paper, manufactured by Avery, have lines of tape, double-spaced, on which your corrections are typed. Then you place the typed strip over the lines to be corrected. The page is not put back in the typewriter.

OPERATING A FOLDING MACHINE

When freshly printed material is folded, ink can build up on the rollers of the folding machine. This buildup frequently causes the papers to jam and rip. Don't call the repairman; clean the rollers yourself.

Ask your equipment repairman for a small bottle of "blanket wash," if you do not already have some for use with an offset press. You should also buy a package of cotton squares.

Wet a cotton square with blanket wash and wipe the rollers thoroughly, turning them by hand as you work. After the rollers are clean, run some scrap paper through the machine to absorb any remaining blanket wash or loosened ink.

KEYS

Beth and Joe, a young engaged couple, want to get into the church early Friday evening to decorate for their wedding the next day, but they need a key.

Alyce, the missions leader, wants to set up tables for her girls' day camp in the fellowship hall. She will need the master key, because it will be after 5:00 P.M. before she can get to the church office, and no one will be there to let her in.

Security poses a problem in many churches. We don't want to hinder the activities of persons or groups who have to get into buildings, but we don't want many sets of keys floating around either. What can be done about it?

How can you get keys back that are lent to church members? And how do you keep members from having extra keys made?

1. Keep a limited number of loan-out keys. At one church, only two are lent to members. Each key has a number, "1" or "2." The keys are kept in individual envelopes, with a "Sign-Out, Sign-In" sheet attached (Figure 137). The individual must personally sign the key out and is personally responsible for either signing the key back in or delegating the task to another responsible person. If the key is not returned when the individual said it would be, the individual is reminded by phone to return it.
2. Be sure that DO NOT DUPLICATE is etched on each loan-out key. Reputable keymakers will not make a copy of a key with this imprint.

LABELS FOR MAILINGS

Keeping the mailing list up-to-date is a never-ending task.

Avery manufactures labels on 8½ × 11-inch sheets, and they are wonderful. Simply type a master sheet and copy it for each mailing.

| | | Key # _____ |
Signature Out	Date	Signature In	Date

Figure 137

The problem, though, is that people are moving all the time. It is impossible to keep up with them and to keep the address list organized.

Grace, a secretary in a 1,500-member church, says, "We try to keep the names in zip code order, so it makes the mailing easier. But then, when changes come in, we have to move names or add or delete them. It's hard to find the names on the list because they're not in alphabetical order. It's a mess!"

Here are two ideas for organizing your mailing list:

1. The CopyMaster System for Master Lists. This product is available from your local office supply company. With the use of your copier, the system lets you keep your master mailing list updated and organized without retyping. The starter set consists of a special binder and five clear plastic $9\frac{1}{2} \times$ 12-inch pages, with thirty-three pockets a page. Insert cards, containing names and addresses, are put in the pockets. As you add or delete names, you simply rearrange the cards in any order you choose, which makes it easy to maintain alphabetical or zip code order without retyping. Then you make copies of the pages, using Avery, Quill, or another brand of self-adhesive mailing labels that your copier will accommodate.

2. A Member's Home Computer. When I served at Cypress Lake, one of the members offered to put our church membership on her computer so she could help keep the mailing list up-to-date. I gave Marge our unorganized list, and she entered all the names and addresses in one evening. The following day, she brought me an alphabetical printout of the mailing list. "When you want to do your mailing, I'll bring you a set of labels, in zip code order," she said. Once a month, a few days before the monthly mailing, I gave her our list of changes. A day or two later, she provided the labels, ready for the bulk mailing.

Keeping the membership list on the computer is a simple task, involving very little time once the master list is entered. Then it is possible to obtain a list in alphabetical or zipcode order, which makes your work much easier.

MEETING REMINDERS

Note all meetings on the official calendar. Although committee members at some churches want telephone calls as reminders of meetings, most feel that a notice in the mail serves the purpose better.

If you want to make telephone calls, be sure to write out the information and have it in front of you as you are speaking to individuals on the telephone. You will not leave out any details if you do this.

NEWSPAPERS

A subscription to the local newspaper provides help in these areas:

1. Information about births, deaths, marriages, and divorces helps you keep up with membership data. Check each section against your roll, especially the inactive members.

2. Visitors who are waiting to see someone will have something to do, besides talking

to you. You can say, "Please have a seat, here's the newspaper for you to read." Then you can get back to your work.

NOMINATING COMMITTEE WORKSHEET

In most churches, committees are selected annually to fill the many volunteer positions necessary for the survival of church programs and church activities. A task of the church office worker is to prepare the list(s) of names for the nominating committee.

The process of selecting the committee members evolves over a period of numerous meetings of the nominating committee, when new names are added or deleted each time. This means that a new list is typed each time, so the committee will have up-to-date information for each meeting.

The format shown in Figure 138, typed on 8½ × 14-inch paper, eliminates repetitive list-typing and allows the committee to follow the progress of the selection of new committee members.

PROCEDURE MANUAL

The *Procedure Manual,* or the *Desk Book,* is a set of instructions for all the work you do. It is a permanent set of instructions that serves as a reference manual for persons

WORKSHEET FOR NOMINATIONS FOR 1985-1986				PAGE 1 of 7
1984-85	#1	#2	#3	Confirmed 1985-1986
GENERAL OFFICERS				
Clerk, Joyce Huntley				
Asst. Clerk, L. Wilbourne				
Treasurer, Fred Bunnell				
Asst. Treasurer, H. Donati				
AUDIO VISUAL				
Dave Linebaugh, Chairman				
Rick Carpenter				
Hal Colby				
Rick Diehl				
Randy Honeycutt				
Ed Perry				
Dan Ringdahl				
BENEVOLENT				
Jim Davidson				
Joe McLarry				
BUILDING AND GROUNDS				
Midge Holbert, Chairman				
Charles Eland, Deacon				
Frank Adkins				
Joe Cherry				
Cliff Clay				
Vera Dial				
Frank Gardner				
Johan Otterlei				
David Steinmetz				
BAPTISM COMMITTEE				
R. & M. Dodd, Co-Chairmen				
Barney & Mina Creech				
Tom & Betty Garito				
John & Irvine Ruhe				
Ray & Flora Turkoski				
EDUCATION ASSISTANCE				
Earl Kidder, Chairman				
Dolores Adkins				
Faye Erickson				

Figure 138

working in the church office. The book must be clear. In addition, you must explain the system both to its users and to those who will help you implement it.

You will need a looseleaf three-ring binder and dividers. While preparing the manual keep in mind that you want to answer questions and provide information for all tasks, so that someone new coming into the office would be able to look up a task in the manual and know how to carry it out.

What types of information should be in the manual? And how should it be arranged?

1. Information about daily work is the top priority—how to do specific tasks.
2. Indicate the days the work is to be done. This daily schedule should be in one section. Simply a list, it tells a person what to do, on what day. For example:
   (a) Monday
   > Type dinner list
   > Make tape labels
   > Type visitors' letters
   > Type new members' letters
   > Process new members
   > Mail Sunday School postcards
   (b) Tuesday
   > Label and mail tapes
   > Staff meeting
   > Gather material for newsletter
   > Send notices for baptism
   (c) Wednesday
   > Type newsletter
   > Make labels for mailout
   (d) etc.
3. Prepare an alphabetical section of each task, explaining how to do specific tasks (if not already included in *The Church Office Handbook*). Include the little details that will help a person know exactly how the task should be done in your office.
4. Have a section for Emergency Information. This should include the following:
   (a) The location of fire exits, alarms, and extinguishers.
   (b) The location of the first aid box.
   (c) Emergency telephone numbers or a guide to how to find them on the Rolodex.
   (d) Equipment repair telephone numbers.
   (e) Instructions about church policy in cases of various emergencies.
6. Instructions for maintaining the official church calendar.
6. Also include the following information:
   (a) Purchasing information—suppliers, supplies generally used, discounts to be expected from suppliers.
   (b) Anniversaries and birthdays of staff and office workers.
   (c) Special meeting dates of various committees.
   (d) Mail pick up times and instructions for mailing.
   (e) How, what, and when to handle outgoing mail, bulk mailings.
   (f) How to handle Petty Cash.
   (g) The daily personal routine, such as lunch periods, coffee breaks, office hours.
   (h) How the telephone is to be answered.

(*i*) The church policy for visitors, transients, benevolent cases.
(*j*) A floor plan of the building(s).
(*k*) A list of volunteers willing to help in the office.
(*l*) Samples of forms used in the office.
(*m*) The personal preferences of the staff for correspondence.
7. "Who's Who," to orient the new worker to her coworkers, the staff, and lay leaders. Provide an organizational chart and include home telephone numbers.
8. Include the policies of the church regarding vacations, sick time, and holidays.
9. An index, so that a person can quickly look up information in the manual.

Keep in mind that you are preparing this manual for someone who knows nothing about your work. Put in as much detail as possible. Keep the information current by making timely changes, as needed. This manual is not your personal property. If you leave the church for any reason, the manual stays on the job, ready to help the person who will follow in your footsteps.

SCRAP PAPER

Save paper costs by accumulating a supply of "start-up paper" for your duplicating machine. Instruct people not to throw away leftover flyers and other printed material. Use the paper to start up your machine. Keep the supply of used paper by your mimeograph machine or press, and use it to run through the machine while you are setting and testing paper alignments and machine settings. Also use this paper instead of good paper when you are setting and testing the folding machine.

You will save a large amount of money over the course of a year if you reuse this scrap. (Throw away any dog-eared paper; it could jam the machines.)

SUPPLY ROOM

Keep your supply room organized and maintain an adequate stock of regularly used items. Don't overstock.

In one church, the secretary got a great price on one hundred cases of paper, plus a "free" tape recorder for placing the order. The problem was, there was no place to put the one hundred cases. They were all over the office, in the supply and workroom, making it almost impossible to move around or to get other supplies.

If you don't have room to keep large amounts of supplies, don't order large amounts. A "good price" for an item isn't good if you are going to trip over piles of that item.

It helps to keep a list of supplies that are regularly used in the office, especially if you are going to be on vacation, or leaving the church, and someone else will be coming into the office. If some item is out of stock, it is hard to know that it's missing, unless it is very commonplace, like paperclips or mending tape.

Set aside a day or two a month to check your supplies. Note the date in your 3 × 5 box, and when the day next comes up, you can inventory your stock.

Let the staff know where supplies are kept, so they will not be bothering you for these things.

Have a definite place for all your supplies. Keep small items in boxes, with or without lids. Be sure to label all boxes, so you know what is in them.

Don't be a packrat. Get rid of those fifty bulletins left over from Christmas, Easter, Mother's Day, and the 4th of July celebration. Use them as "start-up" paper for your duplicating equipment.

TELEPHONE LOG

Long-distance calls are an added expense for the church. Frequently the calls last much longer than they need to. One minister states, "When I call my friend [another pastor] for information or advice, we end up talking for an hour. The bill is terrible! I don't know what to do about it."

What can be done to limit the length of long-distance telephone calls? The first thing is to be aware of the passage of time while you are on the telephone. Know what you are going to say ahead of time, and stick to the subject.

One church staff uses three-minute egg timers (each member of the staff has one). When the person on the other end of the line answers the phone, the caller flips the timer over, and the sand starts running through.

Each staff member has learned to accomplish the purpose of the call within three minutes, by watching the sand flow through the timer, and the church's phone bill has dropped considerably.

All long-distance calls should be accounted for, with personal calls being paid by the individuals making the calls. A pad of telephone log sheets (Figure 139) by each telephone will allow the caller to record calls immediately. Filled-out sheets are turned in to the person paying the bills. When the telephone bill comes in, each person is assessed for his or her personal calls.

With the help of this book, and your well-written procedure manual, you and the workers in your church office should have no trouble carrying out the necessary record-keeping tasks.

TELEPHONE LOG

DATE	PLACE CALLED	NO. CALLED	CALL PLACED BY

Figure 139

BIBLIOGRAPHY

ADMINISTRATION

Ditzen, Lowell R. *Handbook of Church Administration.* New York: Macmillan, 1962.
Myers, Marvin. *Managing the Business Affairs of the Church.* Nashville, TN: Convention Press, 1981.
Rutherford, Robert D. *Administrative Time Power.* Austin, TX: Learning Concepts, 1978.

COMMUNICATION

Anderson, Richard C. *Communication: The Vital Artery.* Los Gatos, CA: Correlan Publications, 1973.
Percy, Ethel. *Releasing the Potential of the Older Volunteer.* Los Angeles: University of Southern California Press, 1976.

COMPUTERS

Capron, H.L., and Brian K. Williams. *Computers and Data Processing.* Menlo Park, CA: Benjamin/ Cummings Publishing Co., 1982.
Parker, Charles S. *Understanding Computers and Data Processing.* New York: CBC College Publishing, 1984.
Spangenburg, Raymond, and Diane Moser. *Personal Word Processing.* Belmont, CA: Wadsworth Electronic Publishing Co., 1984.

FINANCE

Crowe, J.M., and Merrill D. Moore. *Church Finance Record System Manual.* Nashville, TN: Broadman Press, 1959.
Dyer, Mary Lee. *Practical Bookkeeping for the Small Business.* Chicago: Contemporary Books, Inc., 1976.
Espie, John C. *Handbook for Local Church Financial Record System.* Nashville, TN: United Methodist Publishing House, 1976.
McLeod, Thomas E. *The Work of the Church Treasurer.* Valley Forge, PA: Judson Press, 1981.

MAILINGS

U.S. Postal Service. *Second-Class Mailings,* Publication 114. Washington, DC: U.S. Postal Service, August 1984.
————. *First-Class, Third-Class, and Fourth-Class Bulk Mailings,* Publication 113. Washington, DC: U.S. Postal Service, October 1984.

PASTOR

Holck, Jr., Manfred. *Clergy Desk Book.* Nashville, TN: Abingdon Press, 1985.
Worth, B.J. *Income Tax Law for Ministers and Religious Workers.* Winona Lake, IN: Worth Tax Service, 1984.

CHURCH SECRETARY

Diamond, Susan Z. *Records Management . . . A Practical Guide*. New York: Amacom, 1983.
Hoskins, Lucy Renfro. *The Work of the Church Secretary*. Nashville, TN: Convention Press, 1981.
Soukhanov, Anne, ed. *The Professional Secretary's Handbook*. Boston: Houghton Mifflin, 1984.

Index

TWENTY USEFUL FORMS TO COPY

DAILY TIME STUDY

Day_____ Date_____

Time		
From	To	Tasks/Phones/Interruptions, etc.
_____	_____	_____
_____	_____	_____
_____	_____	_____
_____	_____	_____
_____	_____	_____
_____	_____	_____
_____	_____	_____
_____	_____	_____
_____	_____	_____
_____	_____	_____
_____	_____	_____
_____	_____	_____
_____	_____	_____
_____	_____	_____
_____	_____	_____
_____	_____	_____
_____	_____	_____
_____	_____	_____
_____	_____	_____
_____	_____	_____
_____	_____	_____
_____	_____	_____
_____	_____	_____
_____	_____	_____
_____	_____	_____
_____	_____	_____

Mr
Mrs
Miss _____

Date
Joined _____

Address _____ Birthdate _____

_____ Zip _____

Other Family Members   Relationship   Birthdate   Church Member

_____   _____   _____   _____

_____   _____   _____   _____

_____   _____   _____   _____

_____   _____   _____   _____

Special Information _____

Employment: Husband _____ Wife _____

PERSONS IN FAMILY
(Church Members)

	Date Received	Separate Card	Entered on Perm. Rec.	Pastor

PERSONS IN FAMILY
(Not Church Members)

	RELATIONSHIP	BIRTH DATE

CHRONOLOGICAL MEMBERSHIP RECORD

Membership Number	How Received	Prior Church or Date of Baptism	Date Received or Dismissed	Name	Birthdate	Current Status	How Dismissed	New Church or Comments	Dismissal Number

A = ___   I = ___   N = ___

PRESS FIRMLY WITH BALLPOINT PEN - YOU ARE MAKING 4 COPIES

DECISION CARD

MR/MRS/MISS _____   DATE _____

Address _____

                                    Birthdate(s)

Phone: Home _____ Work _____

                                    Zip Code _____

MARITAL STATUS: ( )Married ( )Widowed ( )Divorced ( )Single

OTHER FAMILY MEMBERS: NAME _____   DATE OF BIRTH

                        _____   _____

                        _____   _____

DECISION:
( ) Accepts Christ as Personal Saviour and Lord
( ) Desires Membership in this Church:
    By Baptism _____ By Statement _____
( ) Desires Membership in this Church by Letter from:
    Name and Address of Church _____

( ) Other Decision _____

NEW MEMBERS' CHECKLIST

NAME & ADDRESS	PHONE	DATE JOINED	BIRTHDAY								

Name	Date Deleted														Comments

DELETIONS

Date	Name & Address	Information To Be Changed	Comments

MEMBERSHIP UPDATES

CHECKING ACCOUNT BALANCE RECORD

Date	Description	Misc.	Disbursements and Debits	Deposits and Credits	Balance

LOOSE CHECKS

Date_____

Name	Amounts					

Date_____

DESIGNATED RECEIPTS

Amount	Name	Cash	Check

```
Checking Balance        _____

Designated:
Building Fund           _____
Missions                _____
Children's Home         _____
Memorial                _____
Benevolence             _____
Taxes                   _____

_____  _____
_____  _____
_____  _____
_____  _____

Total Designated        _____
  (Subtract from
   checking balance)

= Money Available       _____


To Pay This Week        _____




Date_____
Initials_____
```

Paid To: Account Charged_____

                                  Account Number_____

-----Date Due-----	-----Amount-----	-------Date Paid-------	---Check Number---

Paid To_____ Account Charged_____

Account Number_____

Date Due	Gross Pay	--WH--	--SS--	* -C-SS-	-Net Pay-	------Date Paid------	Check -Number-

* Church's Portion; Not deducted from Gross Pay.

EXPENSE VOUCHER REQUEST

DATE _____

NO. _____

PAY TO: _____

(NAME)

_____

_____

(ADDRESS)

AMOUNT: _____

FOR: _____

_____

(DEPARTMENT)

SIGNED - (DEPT. HEAD)

_____

OFFICE USE ONLY

PAID

DATE _____

CK. # _____

NAME _____

CONTRIBUTIONS RECORD FOR JAN. 1 TO DEC. 31, YEAR: 198 __

	BUDGET	BUILDING FUND	SPECIAL GIFTS		BUDGET	BUILDING FUND	SPECIAL GIFTS		BUDGET	BUILDING FUND	SPECIAL GIFTS		BUDGET	BUILDING FUND	SPECIAL GIFTS
JAN				APR				JUL				OCT			
2				2				2				2			
3				3				3				3			
4				4				4				4			
5				5				5				5			
FEB				MAY				AUG				NOV			
2				2				2				2			
3				3				3				3			
4				4				4				4			
5				5				5				5			
MAR				JUN				SEP				DEC			
2				2				2				2			
3				3				3				3			
4				4				4				4			
5				5				5				5			
QTR				QTR				QTR				QTR			
+				+				+				+			
=				=				=				=			

GRAND TOTAL _____

STATIONARY
EQUIPMENT INVENTORY

Description	Location	Date of Purchase	Purchase Price	Comments	Replace-ment Cost

MOVEABLE
EQUIPMENT INVENTORY

Description	General Use	Special-ized Use	Trained Persons Only	Person in Charge of Equipment	Location of Equipment	Date of Purchase	Purchase Price	Replace-ment Cost

REQUISITION FORM

Date _____

Please order:

Quantity	Item & Description	Price	Amount	Charge To

Requested by _____ Phone _____

Order from _____ Need by _____

Special Instructions:

TELEPHONE LOG

DATE	PLACE CALLED	NO. CALLED	CALL PLACED BY